Cave Mountain

ALSO BY BENJAMIN HALE

The Evolution of Bruno Littlemore
The Fat Artist and Other Stories

Cave Mountain

A Disappearance and a Reckoning in the Ozarks

BENJAMIN HALE

HARPER

An Imprint of HarperCollins*Publishers*

HarperCollins books may be purchased for educational, business, or sales promotional use. For information, please email the Special Markets Department at SPsales@harpercollins.com.

hc.com

FIRST EDITION

Designed by Elina Cohen
Photograph © Gunnar Rathbun / Shutterstock

Library of Congress Cataloging-in-Publication Data has been applied for.

ISBN 978-0-06-339812-2

$PrintCode

For my parents, Charley and Leigh
and
in loving memory of my uncle,
Jay Hale
1939–2024

CONTENTS

Cave Mountain

Sunday, April 29, 2001

On SUNDAY, APRIL 29, 2001, MY FATHER'S OLDER BROTHER AND his wife, Jay and Joyce Hale, took their granddaughter, Haley Zega—the only child of their only child—on a day trip to the Buffalo National River Wilderness in Newton County, Arkansas, in the heart of the Ozark Mountains. Jay was sixty-two years old at the time, Joyce was fifty-nine, and Haley was six. That morning Jay and Joyce drove their powder blue 1984 Ford F-150 truck from their home in Pea Ridge, Arkansas, to the home of their daughter, Kelly, and her husband, Steve Zega, in Fayetteville, picked up Haley, and drove about an hour and a half to the Hawkbill Crag Trailhead on Cave Mountain, where they met up with their friends and fellow Sierra Club members Claibourne Bass and Dennis and Michelle Boles.

My uncle Jay and aunt Joyce had been friends with the Boleses—both public schoolteachers—for nearly thirty years, and Jay had been friends with Clay Bass since the two had met in the Cub Scouts when they were in the first grade. Jay and Clay, both engineers, had formed their boyhood bond taking machines apart and putting them back together, building things, destroying things—"Something got blowed up every day," said Jay. Jay and Joyce owned a mechanical engineering business they ran from their home in Pea Ridge, and Clay Bass owned Highroller

Cyclery, a bicycle shop in Fayetteville.

Jay and Joyce had been married for forty years. They met in 1960: Joyce, an undergraduate studying marketing at the University of Arkansas, bought with money she had made herself, a tiny plot of land in Fayetteville, and built, with a combination of that same money and her own sweat equity, a tiny two-story house on it; she lived on the first floor and rented the separate-entrance apartment on the second to a graduate student in engineering a few years older than her, who had seen an ad for it in the classified section of the *Northwest Arkansas Times*—her future husband, Jay.

The visuals of these characters: Jay is a short, stocky man with elfin eyes, silver hair, and a lifelong beard (nearly all Hale men are scientists or engineers with requisite beards; I always feel a little like a soft urban dandy when I am clean shaven); Joyce is tall and willowy, with silver hair that she has kept short since before I started forming memories sometime in the mid-1980s. Whenever I picture them in my mind's eye, they are both wearing jeans, hiking boots, and plaid flannel shirts, and I'm sure you can with reasonable accuracy imagine the other adults they were with similarly attired. My cousin Haley was a perfectly ordinary—physically, anyway—six-year-old girl with long sandy-blond hair and the very round head and squinty elf eyes that mark our clan, wearing shorts, sneakers, little pink socks, and a baggy gray Cape Canaveral T-shirt. Her mother, Kelly, sent her off that morning with her grandparents with her security blanket and a big red sweatshirt.

Dennis and Michelle Boles had suggested the day trip. Each year in the last weekend of April, the Newton County Wildlife Association would host an easy, guided group hike to see the mountain wildflowers then in full springtime bloom. It was around the last frost, and the Buffalo River valley would be stippled with birdsfoot violets, wild sweet williams, pink azaleas, and early buttercups, the mountain meadow boiling with honeybees and little blue butterflies. Dennis and Michelle joined this hike every year, and that year they invited along Jay and Joyce, who thought it a perfect opportunity for a day trip with their granddaughter. Their daughter, Kelly, had grown up in the woods, on Jay and Joyce's twenty-five-acre property in Pea Ridge that the family nicknamed Hale Holler, but grown-up Kelly—she was thirty-two that year—worked as an administrator for the North Arkansas Symphony Orchestra, her husband, Steve, was a criminal defense lawyer and a National Guardsman (he was away on duty at the time), and they lived in the relative comfort and convenience of modern civilization in Fayetteville. Haley had thus far grown up in suburbia, with mown lawn or flat concrete under her feet most of the time she'd spent outdoors in the Natural State.

Jay and Joyce had always been passionate naturalists, conservationists, environmentalists, and outdoorspeople. Some of my fondest memories of my childhood are of walking in the woods with them in Hale Holler, and one couldn't have better tutors in all things sylvan. Some people's souls form beside the ocean, and they don't feel fully alive unless water comprises at least half the horizon; of the primeval places that haunt and enchant humans, that beckon with beauty and danger, Odysseus and Ishmael head out to sea. But I go with Hansel and Gretel and the rude mechanicals and Dante Alighieri into the woods. In the temperate forests of the Arkansas Ozarks my aunt and uncle had taught me about the plants, the trees, the animals, the weather, the lore, the signs, and the patterns of nature, and they wanted to do the same for Haley. When I was sixteen, I think, Jay gave me a copy of one of the top ten books that changed my life, Edward Abbey's memoir *Desert Solitaire: A Season in the Wilderness*, which has made many people, including me, think seriously about becoming a US park ranger.

There was also, as there always is for Jay and Joyce, a motive of principle: They wanted their daughter to raise an environmentalist. (That was in the same spirit with which Jay had given me that copy of *Desert Solitaire*.)

"We were always looking for an opportunity to take Haley out of her urban life," Joyce told me. "And since we lived in Pea Ridge in a rural setting, her visits there were always a nice contrast to the life she lived in Fayetteville. There she had all of the wildlife that Kelly had found fun when she was growing up. So having that natural setting was very important to us. We, of course, were active in the environmental movements, and it's always hard to protect something in the environment if you've not had personal experience with it."

Dennis and Michelle Boles's good friend Doc Chester, a retired anesthesiologist, owned about seven acres of land on top of Cave Mountain with a couple of cabins on it; one was a house with all the modern amenities, which Doc lived in, and the other was a more primitive little building called Faddis Cabin that had no door or glass in the windows but that oddly—and as it would turn out, luckily—had a working landline telephone in it. Doc often let his friends use the cabin as a starting point for exploring the Buffalo National River Wilderness. Although they had lived nearby for most of their lives and had hiked other trails on Cave Mountain, Jay and Joyce had never hiked the Hawksbill Crag Trail before, but the Boleses had visited Doc Chester's property on Cave Mountain many times, and knew the area well.

The three parties—the Boleses; Clay Bass; Jay, Joyce, and Haley—drove separately up the steep, narrow, rocky dirt road and met up around midmorning at the Hawksbill Crag Trailhead, where the Boleses guided the three-car caravan up the road about seven hundred feet and turned onto the small private road that leads a little over a mile to Doc Chester's property. As it happened, Doc was home that morning, working in his yard with a chain saw, dismembering a dead tree he had just cut down, and the group chatted with him for a little while before setting off on their hike.

The plan for the day was to take a short hike from the cabin down to Hawksbill Crag, a famous Arkansas landmark, continue hiking to another vista at the top of a small waterfall, head back to the cabin, eat lunch, then drive not quite thirty minutes down the mountain to meet up with a larger group at the Upper Buffalo Wilderness Trailhead for the Newton County Wildlife Association's annual wildflower hike. The trek from Doc Chester's cabin to the waterfall is about nine-tenths of a mile. It was about a quarter after ten when they parked their vehicles at Doc Chester's cabin. The wildflower hike was set to begin at one in the afternoon.

I should emphasize the extreme rusticity of the area where Jay and Joyce went hiking with their friends and granddaughter that day. The entire population of Newton County, Arkansas, is only about 7,000. The county is mountainous, mostly wilderness, all of it within the highest elevations of the Ozarks. Its county seat and biggest town is Jasper, which has a population, as of the 2020 census, of 547. There used to be more people living in the Buffalo River valley. The 150-mile-long Buffalo River, one of the few remaining free-flowing rivers in the lower forty-eight United States, originates in the Boston Mountains of the Ozark Plateau and flows more or less from west to east through Newton, Searcy, and Marion counties before flowing into the White River in Baxter County, which eventually flows into the Mississippi River, which eventually flows into the Gulf of Mexico. From the *Encyclopedia of Arkansas*: "With the passage of the Flood Control Act of 1938, the U.S. Army Corps of Engineers included the Buffalo River in its planning for a system of dams on the White River. Two potential dam sites eventually were selected on the Buffalo, one on the lower portion of the river near its mouth and one at its middle just upstream from the town of Gilbert (Searcy County)." The hydroelectric potential of the Buffalo River valley had been a distant item of interest on the US Army Corps of Engineers' to-maybe-one-day-do list for more than twenty years, and the Corps started moving on it in the early 1960s, surveying and drawing up plans. Two opposing organizations formed, one for the proposed dams—the Buffalo River Improvement Association, headed by James Tudor, the owner of a local newspaper, the *Marshall Mountain Wave*, who had a close working relationship with Third District Congressman James Trimble, who also supported the dams, arguing that the reservoir and hydroelectric plant would bring a lot of new economic activity to the area, which it undoubtedly would have—and another against the dams, the Ozark Society, headed by environmentalist Neil Compton. Several years of political maneuvering and legal fighting ensued, with the anti-dam Compton in one corner and pro-dam Tudor and Trimble in the other, ending with Governor Orval Faubus withdrawing his support for the dams in 1965 and Trimble losing his seat to his anti-dam opponent, John Paul Hammerschmidt, in 1966. The USACE withdrew the dam proposals, and at Compton's urging, Hammerschmidt, along with Senators William Fulbright and John McClellan, introduced legislation to create the Buffalo National River, which would protect most of the river and about 94,000 acres of land around it under the National Park Service. The legislation passed in 1971, and Nixon signed it into law in 1972.

It does not appear that the fate of the local residents who lived in the area the proposed reservoir would flood figured much into the considerations of either the pro-dam developers or the anti-dam conservationists. Basically, at first the people who lived in the valley were informed that the government would be building a lake on top of them and they would be forced out of their homes and compelled via eminent domain to sell their properties at probably below-market rates—and then, after years of legal and political squabbling, the great solution the conservationists came up with was to make it all government land, which meant that they had to move, anyway. The prevailing attitude of the people who lived in the valley at the time was: How about the third option, *Just leave us the fuck alone?* Most of the people who were forced to move did not move very far away; they held on to their resentments and passed them along to their friends, family, and neighbors and down to their children. So there are deep-rooted and long-standing tensions between local residents of the area and the government, which they see as meddlesome, untrustworthy, and incompetent: keep that in mind for later.

This story begins on top of Cave Mountain, which is traversable by one very narrow dirt road: Cave Mountain Road, which turns off of Arkansas State Highway 21 just north of a bridge over the Buffalo River, then winds southwest up the mountain and back down the other side to Arkansas State Highway 16. The Hawksbill Crag Trailhead sits at about the highest point on the road. The trail leads from the road into the woods down the mountain a little ways and forks: If you're coming from the trailhead, the right tine of the fork leads a short distance down to a creek and a small waterfall, where the creek you just hopscotched across spills over the shelf of the bluff and you can stand at the top of the waterfall and take in a magnificent view of the Buffalo River valley; the tine on the left leads along the bluff that peers out over the valley, and from there it's about half a mile's hike to Hawksbill Crag, a dramatic arrow of rock jutting into the air two hundred feet above the forest below. This is the thing you have probably come to see, or rather to stand on its vertiginous perch with the majestic view of the valley behind you while your friend takes a picture of you. The view from the top of Hawksbill Crag truly romances the heart with natural beauty, a sight Thomas Cole or Albert Bierstadt would have liked to paint—or Caspar David Friedrich, who would have put a brave little human figure in the corner of it, gazing into the sublime. I saw it for the first time late in an afternoon in December, when the weather had cleared up a little and let the sunshine in after raining all day, turning the milky mist steaming up from the river valley below a brassy amber, the peaks of the mountains on the other side of the valley islands in the clouds, everything glowing gold.

If you look it up on AllTrails, the trail officially ends at Hawkbill Crag, AKA Whitaker Point, but it actually continues on from there, hugging the crest of the bluff, getting narrower, rockier, and scarier. When I first hiked it in mid-December of 2022, there were points along the trail north of Hawksbill Crag that looked so precarious—in a few places you have to walk through small streams over loose, jagged, slippery rocks at the razor's edge of the cliff—that I thought it safer to bushwhack it off the trail through deep damp leaf mulch a little farther up the mountain, cross the stream at a less deathly place, and bushwhack back down to the trail. I was glad that none of the friends I had grown up hiking Colorado's mountains with were there to see me, but I felt like less of a coward for detouring around its diciest-looking spots when I later learned of the local notoriety of this trail's treacherousness—Google "Hawksbill Crag + fall + death," and you get a sense of its death toll: one every few years, most recently in 2019 and 2016. As it winds north and east along the bluff line, the trail gets thinner and thinner, less and less there, until it peters out beside a tree stump with a metal Private Property/No Trespassing sign nailed to it, and a muddy sheet of laminated paper I found lying facedown in the leaf litter beside it that reads

NOTICE TO HIKERS

This trail <u>DEAD ENDS</u>

at Private Property ahead.

It <u>DOES NOT</u> loop back to the trailhead!

In order to return to the trailhead you need to

turn around and hike back out the same way

that you came in.

If you proceed in this direction you will get

lost, and hike farther than you need to.

Thanks!

It's understandable that someone arriving at that notice might believe the trail loops back to the trailhead, because the map on the trailhead marker indicates that it does. Perhaps it used to. (Note to National Park Service: I understand this probably isn't high on your priority list, but that map at the Hawksbill Crag Trailhead needs updating.) I picked up the laminated paper sign, wiped some mud off it, pinned it behind the metal sign nailed to the tree stump, and that was as far as I went.

On that late April Sunday midmorning in 2001, the group of Sierra Club friends did not arrive at Hawksbill Crag as most hikers do, from the direction of the trailhead; they came a back way that the Boleses knew from Doc Chester's land, which is the private property that sign is warning you not to trespass on. The way from the cabin to the waterfall is only a little less than a mile, which would take an able-bodied adult not stopping perhaps about fifteen to twenty minutes there and fifteen to twenty back, but considering the rocky terrain and the fact that they had a little kid with them—plus they would want to stop and gaze at the beauty at the two vista points—the party reserved about an hour and a half for the day's first adventure, which they reckoned more than enough time to make the short hike there and back without feeling rushed. Kelly had sent her daughter off that morning with a big red sweatshirt and her security blanket, but as the day had warmed—it was in fact a beautiful spring morning in the Ozarks, sunny and about 70 degrees Fahrenheit with nothing but occasional light cloud cover in the forecast—and they would not be long, they left with light clothing and carrying one bottle of water. They left Haley's blanket and sweatshirt in the truck. They set out from the cabin at about ten thirty in the morning.

With the Boleses guiding, they hiked south through a flat open field behind the cabin and found the narrow social trail that leads to the Hawksbill Crag Trail. The place where they stepped onto the trail lies within sight of the cabin, about 150 feet from it. This unofficial trail winds around a small pond on Doc Chester's property and then leads steeply downhill into the woods. "The walk in," Joyce wrote in her account of the day, "was short and easy to navigate with an interesting variety of things to point out to a child. Shooting stars and pink azaleas were at their height. Tree leaves had not gained their full summer size and allowed the mottled light to filter semi-brightness. Pale spring greens were transitioning into deeper summer hues."

In a short time, perhaps about ten minutes, they came to Hawksbill Crag, oohed and aahed atop it, then continued hiking on the trail, which gets much wider and easier going on the south side of the lookout point at Hawksbill Crag, along the top of the bluff to the fork where, from the direction they were coming, the path on the right leads up the mountain to the trailhead on Cave Mountain Road and the one on the left leads a short way down to the small waterfall.

Now, a waterfall is a picturesque sight, but only when you're standing at the bottom of it. This one is certainly no Niagara Falls; for most of the year Whitaker Creek is just a trickling stream that high up on the mountain, falling about thirty feet from a ledge. There are two flat shelves of rock on that side of the mountain: the higher one, from which the water falls, and a lower one maybe fifteen feet below it, too far a fall to safely jump. There is just no place to get a good look at the waterfall from the higher shelf. The first time I was there, I held on to a young tree, slender but strong enough to hold my weight, and bending it leaned over the edge of the cliff as far as I could, trying to get a look at the waterfall, until I started thinking what I was doing wasn't a good idea. Apparently there is a way of scrambling down the rocks on the other side of the creek in order to see the waterfall and another way that involves climbing down a certain tree on the lower shelf that you can hop into from the upper one (and that's the way Jay and Clay got down that day); either of these ways is only for the more advanced-level hiker, which Jay certainly was and six-year-old Haley was not. Jay and his old Boy Scouts comrade Clay Bass climbed down to the lower shelf from which you can see the waterfall, saw it, and climbed back up, while everyone else, including Joyce and Haley, stayed on top, resting and soaking up the view of the mountains. It was about a quarter to noon. Hiking to the crag and the waterfall had taken a bit more time than they'd thought it would, and if they wanted to get back to the cabin, eat lunch, and make it to the organized group hike to see the wildflowers that would begin at one, they would have to head back ASAP and make a little hay on the way back, too. By the time they began to hike back up the trail that passes Hawkbill Crag and leads back to the cabins, Haley was steaming with waterfall jealousy.

Child and grownups were at an impasse: Haley wanted to see the waterfall, but it was time to go. She sat down on a rock at the top of the waterfall and refused to move. She said she wanted to be carried. She was being difficult. She was being childish. She was a child.

Joyce told the others to go on ahead back to the cabin and fix lunch—she would stay behind and deal with the kid problem. The others headed back up the trail, though Clay stayed behind to keep Joyce company. Now it was three: Joyce, Clay, and Haley on the rock, unbudging. After many minutes of Joyce's exhortations had failed to move her, Joyce and Clay resorted to the nuclear option of getting a kid to do something she doesn't want to do: Play upon the fear of abandonment. "She was sitting there and pouting," Joyce said, "and I said, you sit right there so I can tell your mother where you are when she comes to get you. We're going.' Huff, huff."

Then: Walk out of sight around the bend and wait. You have to wait kind of a while, because if this trick is going to work, it has to work the first time. If you come back too soon, she'll know you're bluffing. And eventually, Haley came—begrudgingly, defeated by the grownups, dragging her heels, saddest, angriest little girl in the world—her mood probably spoiled for the rest of the day, lunch and beautiful meadow full of wildflowers probably tainted with a petulant drop of poison. But she came.

Good, then—we have movement. Clay and Joyce started walking forward again. They continued up the trail until they were again just out of Haley's sight. They stopped and waited again. Haley, again, pouting, dawdling, eyes downcast, face leaden with despair, emerged. Clay and Joyce continued up the trail around the next bend, stopped, and waited. And waited.

A long time passed.

Joyce told Clay to go ahead and join the others. She was going to have to go down there and drag Haley back by a rope or something. Clay left. Joyce went the other way.

Haley was gone.

I myself, having seen the place, am still a bit baffled as to how Haley got so lost so fast. At the fork in the trail, one way goes to the waterfall, one leads along the top of the bluff to Hawksbill Crag, and one leads across the creek and up the mountain to the trailhead on Cave Mountain Road. Granted, I saw it in the winter, when the nakedness of the trees affords much more visibility. They were there at the height of spring, when the leaf cover makes dark, narrow corridors of the trails, and a shout only carries perhaps ten or fifteen feet.

Joyce went back down the trail all the way to the waterfall: no Haley. She did not even begin to tingle with panic until she hiked back up from the waterfall, and saw the fork. Was this fork in the trail in-between the last place Haley had shown herself and the last place where they had stopped to wait for her? She had thought they'd gone past it, but now she wasn't sure. She went up the trail that leads up to the trailhead aways, shouting her granddaughter's name. From this moment on, Haley's name was being shouted in the woods by ever more and more mouths, round the clock. Haley did not appear to be on that part of the trail. Eventually Joyce ran into two hikers who were coming down from the trailhead. They had not seen a little girl on the trail.

Soon Joyce and those two hikers and then in a short while Jay, Clay, and the Boleses had spread out up and down the trail looking for Haley, wildflower-viewing plans now definitely scrapped, shouting her name into the thick muffling foliage. What began with their frantic shouting eventually became the largest search-and-rescue mission in Arkansas history.

2

Hale Holler

I SHOULD TELL YOU A FEW THINGS ABOUT THESE PEOPLE AND A few things about Arkansas. I grew up in Colorado, but both sides of my family are from Arkansas. My parents met when they were students at the University of Arkansas in Fayetteville in the 1970s. My father grew up in a tiny town in the north-central Arkansas Ozarks called Horseshoe Bend, and my grandparents on my mother's side are from Paris, Arkansas; my grandfather was a coal miner for a time; my roots there reach down deep and far back. When I was growing up, we would usually drive across the icy brown flatlands between the Rockies and the Ozarks—eastern Colorado, Kansas, Oklahoma—in December for the Christmas holidays, and we would often visit in the summer, too. My mother's parents lived in Rogers, just north of Fayetteville, and Jay and Joyce lived about twenty minutes away on twenty-five acres of hilly, mostly wooded land near Pea Ridge: Hale Holler. That was where they had the office and machine shop they ran their mechanical engineering business out of—Jay was the head engineer and Joyce did the accounting, and they had a handful of employees: their own house, which had been on the property when they had bought it in 1970 and another house they built for Jay and my father's mother. Usually when people say they "built a house" they mean "had it built," but the verb is literal in Jay and

Joyce's case. The house they built for my grandmother had a pneumatic mechanical elevator in it, which would grunt and hiss in punctuated lurching harrumphs of energy on the way up and breathe a long smooth sigh on the way down. Almost immediately upon entering our grandmother's house after that usually two-day drive across the barren winter prairie my brother and I usually managed to get two or three rides out of it before the grown-ups made us stop. The elevator—its floor was just a flat, treacherous wooden platform, no gate or rail or anything—was in fact the only way of getting between the first and second floors of the house, and I was a little heartbroken when, after my grandmother died, Jay and Joyce had to replace it with stairs in order to get the building up to code to rent it.

Most of my favorite childhood memories of Arkansas happened in Hale Holler: my grandmother, the elevator, the long spiral staircase on the outside of the house that Jay also wrought out of iron, catching crawdads in the creek that ran through the property with my little brother, James, and our cousin Ike, walking in the woods with Jay and Joyce, walking in the woods by myself.

Jay built that elevator, and he also built motorcycles, guns, and even the airplane he sometimes flew out to Colorado to visit my parents (I loved driving out to Boulder Municipal Airport with my dad to pick him up). Jay often visited Colorado, where he and Joyce had lived for a few years in the 1960s before moving back to Arkansas in 1970, shortly after Kelly was born, and up until a few years ago they still owned the land they used to live on, a beautiful spot on a secluded road up in the mountains west of Boulder in Fourmile Canyon. They had lived a very off-the-grid existence in Colorado, sleeping in a camper-trailer for a time, bathing and washing their laundry in Fourmile Creek. Their first child, a son, was born when they were living in Colorado, died as a baby, and he is buried on their land there. The weight of that tragedy, and its association with the place was one of the reasons they moved back to Arkansas. Jay also had a few other good friends in Colorado, most notably Judd Johnson—

another scientist/machinist/motorcyclist/mountain-man, who looks like Willie Nelson with coke-bottle-lens glasses, another favorite character of mine when I was a kid. He still lives up there. Sometimes when Jay was visiting, he and my dad and I—sometimes with my younger brother James, and sometimes with Judd if he was free—would drive up to their land in Fourmile Canyon to shoot Coke cans off a log: there was a .22 rifle my dad had, Jay often brought a classic Colt .45—"the gun that won the west," the same model six-shooter that Wyatt Earp and Doc Holliday would have brought to the OK Corral—and one year in particular (we shot it in subsequent years, too), I remember Jay presenting my father with the gift of an antique Spanish Mauser that he had machined new parts for and reconditioned himself. Developed by the German weapon designer Paul Mauser for the Spanish Army, the Mauser Model 1893 is a wonder of artillery engineering, a five-round bolt-action 7×57mm rifle that saw its most extensive combat action during the Spanish Civil War; it's the gun the dying man in Robert Capa's famous photograph *Loyalist Militiaman at the Moment of Death, Cerro Muriano, September 5, 1936* (better known as *The Falling Soldier*) is frozen forever losing his grip on and the same gun with which Ernest Hemingway shot elephants in the Serengeti—and regardless of my personal opinions on killing fascinating and endangered animals for fun, the thing fires with such thunderous powerful that one can easily imagine it stopping an elephant.

About twenty years ago, Jay started building another airplane, a Kitfox Classic IV, but the work was slow going as it was a purely extracurricular activity; old age caught up with him before he could finish it, and its half-fleshed-out chassis still sits in the machine shop in the basement of the house in Fayetteville they moved into in 2005, four years after Haley went missing.

One interesting complication of writing nonfiction is that reality is a moving target. Jay was alive for most of the time it took me to write this book, though he was sick with prostate cancer and dementia, and he died at the age of eighty-five on Thursday, May 30, 2024—five days ago as of this writing.

Jay was a mechanical engineer, my father is a laser physicist, and both of them were and are machinists. My dad uses his machine shop mostly to make very small metal parts for lasers, wherein precision is incredibly important; a mistake on the micrometer level could be the difference between the laser working or not. Though Jay usually worked on scales at least a decimal place to the left of that, my dad always had a reverence for his big brother's wisdom on all things machining related. Until he retired, Jay's machine shop was a professional endeavor, much bigger and better equipped than my dad's home shop, and my dad often bought machines from him, including its *pièce de résistance*, a 1964 Bridgeport J-head mill that he outfitted with a digital readout that uses superfine graduated glass scales to get sub-thousandth-inch resolution/accuracy, which might sound a bit like installing a GPS system in a Studebaker, but: Jay and my father would adamantly insist that the Bridgeport models from fifty-sixty years ago and even further back, as long as they've been well-maintained, are still superior to most of the metal-working machines manufactured now. That was the machine our dad taught James and me how to use when we, at different points, worked for his micro–side business, Pathfinder Laser Products, which manufactured a device he invented for measuring the beamwidth of infrared lasers.

Anyway—Jay's dementia steadily worsened over the year before he died, the fog around his mind thickening by the day, but one trick that could reliably bring him back to clarity for a moment almost until the end was to ask him about some sort of machining or engineering problem. The Proustian madeleine that takes me back to my childhood is the smell of machine oil. The machine shop: lots of tiny, spiky corkscrew slags of metal on the concrete floor if my father was working and had not yet swept them up (wear shoes); a framed print of Picasso's *Guernica* on the wall; if it's wintertime the Sauron-like great red eye of the kerosene space heater roaring on the floor; if it's summertime the windows open and NPR on the radio; if morning or late afternoon, marbles-in-his-jowls Carl Kasell reading the news (blessedly boring 1990s news!); otherwise, classical music, the whirring of fan belts or shriek of mill bit biting metal, and the smell of machine oil.

———

If I have nostalgia for the world I grew up in—and I do—part of it is a forlorn pining for the way things were in that brief period of time bookended by the end of the Cold War (post-1990, a crumbly chunk of the Berlin Wall also sat on a shelf in that machine shop) and the constitutional crisis of the 2000 presidential election. Most would probably name 9/11 as the moment that ended that never-such-innocence-again era, but to me that election was the first event of bizarre, world-reordering chaos. I was born in 1983; I graduated from high school in 2001. I remember that time—about 1989 to 2000, my ages six to seventeen—as a time of boundless optimism, of genuine hope and excitement for the future. Much of that optimism was, in hindsight, illusory; from 1994 on, Newt Gingrich was already sowing the seeds that would bear poison fruit in the coming decades, and so, for that matter, was Bill Clinton, with some help from Joe Biden, too: for one thing, the North American Free Trade Agreement (NAFTA) would not, with time, prove the splendid idea it seemed in 1992. But I remember it as the time Francis Fukuyama described in his 1992 book of now-famously-wrong projections, *The End of History and the Last Man*. The West had won the Cold War; liberalism, capitalism, and democracy had won; people lined up for blocks to eat at the McDonald's that had just opened in Red Square in Moscow; apartheid had ended in South Africa; a peaceful compromise looked to be on the brink of possibility in Israel/Palestine. Borders were opening, trade walls—and concrete walls—were coming down; an exciting new thing called the Internet was somehow going to flatten the earth and launch us into a brave new world; and Tommy LeSavage and I huddled over his family's Macintosh Centris playing *Myst* and marveling at the unprecedented quality of its graphics. Everywhere the twentieth century's bad old demons were dying, and in 1992 and 1996, comfortably over half the country didn't give a shit who was president. (My middle school teachers shook their heads at the shame of it back then, but I have since come to consider low voter turnout a perverse measure of a democratic nation's good civil health.) The image I regard as the emblem of the era I saw on the front page of *The Denver Post* in 1993 the day after my tenth birthday (yes, I was a daily newspaper reader at the age of ten, and drinking black coffee, too—I couldn't wait to grow up), of Yitzhak Rabin shaking hands with Yasser Arafat with the young Bill Clinton standing a head taller than both old men between them with his hands patting their backs, bringing them together. That was the way things were going to be now. In the beginning of the covid pandemic, during the long early months of lockdown, my wife, Caitlin, and I somehow got into a jag of rewatching 1990s action movies we'd seen in the theater as teenagers: *True Lies, Face/Off, Con Air, Broken Arrow, The Rock* (the IMDb.com descriptions of so many of the films begin with "Terrorists have stolen/hijacked a . . ."), and we spoke often about the general backdrop of peace, prosperity, economic and political stability against which these utterly absurd plots were set and that in a way made them possible. It saddens me to have watched that relatively stable, comfortable, and mostly functional world be destroyed by one thing after another over the last twenty-five years.

Soon after I began writing this book, Joyce had to place Jay in a palliative care facility in Fayetteville. It was a painful but necessary thing she had to do; his dementia and other comorbidities had gotten too difficult for her to handle, and he needed 24/7 access to professional medical care. She visited him there every day. On one of my visits to Fayetteville, in October 2023, she told me that some old friends of theirs, the brothers Bill and Cleve Cox, had come out to visit a few days before, and unexpectedly seeing old friends had brightened Jay's mood and brought his mind into the light for an afternoon. That occasioned Joyce telling me about one of the many fascinating engineering projects Jay had been involved with. Bill and Cleve are the CEO and president/chief pilot of Aerial Solutions, a company that specializes in aerial tree trimming by helicopter. Jay designed the Air Saw, a stack of radial saw blades that dangles from a helicopter. If you are driving through a densely forested area and pass a row of power lines marching through the middle of a neatly cut corridor that looks as if a giant out of a Goya painting buzzed through the forest with a brobdingnagian lawn mower, there's a good chance those flat walls of vegetation were cut with an Air Saw. The invention was the brainchild of Jay's good friend Randall Rogers, a helicopter pilot. Jay developed a hydraulic saw with Rogers, who tragically died in an accident while demonstrating the prototype in 1984. Jay was devastated by his friend's death; he arranged for Rogers's widow to have sole ownership of the patent, and then swore off working on the project any further. But the following year, two other helicopter pilots, Joe Harting and Bill Cox, formed the company Aerial Solutions, bought the rights to use the patent from Rogers's widow for a significant sum, and coaxed Hale Engineering back on board, resulting in four more patents. This is from an article about the company in the *Chicago Tribune*, October 15, 1990:

> Today's saw is lighter, safer and easier to use, says James Hale, Hale Engineering president. The thrust of the redesign was to abandon the hydraulic concept and change to a gasoline-powered unit. It now uses ten 24-inch, carbon-tipped blades, driven by a 40-horsepower engine. Total weight of the saw and 90-foot-long extension is about 650 pounds.
>
> Hale and Aerial Solutions partner Cox also developed a special sling for the attachment point underneath the helicopter. The sling combined two concepts critical to the company's success: the ability to stabilize the saw at higher flight speeds and, at the same time, not interfere with the mechanism that drops the saw in an emergency.

The last attribute mentioned—the sling—prevents the kind of accident that killed Randall Rogers: the saw got snagged on something, and he wasn't able to drop it, which caused the helicopter to crash.

And I can't not tell the story of Jay inventing the paintball gun.

Jay worked on a lot of interesting engineering projects: He worked for Beechfield Aircraft developing cryogenic tanks for the Apollo missions; he worked in ultrasonics for a time; more recently he and Joyce were part of a team led by the Syrian American solar physicist Shadia Habbal that would travel to literally random spots on Earth to take high-resolution photographs of solar eclipses, work that took them to Syria, China, Australia, and most recently Idaho in 2017. In the early 1970s, shortly before leaving to start his own engineering company with Joyce, he worked for the Rogers-based Daisy Manufacturing Company, the maker of the Red Ryder BB gun immortalized in *A Christmas Story* ("You'll shoot your eye out!").

In 1971, Charles Nelson, who owned the Michigan-based Nelson Paint Company, had come up with an idea. Forestry workers and cattle ranchers have to mark trees and cattle: ranchers with a paint marker or something like that, and foresters usually with a can of spray paint. This chore is particularly laborious and time consuming for foresters, as it often involves climbing over fences, crossing creeks, and hiking up and down bluffs to mark trees. Nelson envisioned the paintball gun as a time-saving device. He had the paintball figured out—he filled veterinary pill gel capsules with paint—and he figured that a BB gun manufacturer would be the one to ask about the gun. Daisy Manufacturing assigned the job to Jay. The delicate puzzle of engineering was to design a mechanism that would shoot the ball hard enough it would explode on impact with tree or cow, but not so hard that it would blow up inside the gun.

The way Jay told the story, it happened on Christmas Eve 1971. Daisy had shut down early for the day and held a company Christmas party and dinner. When everyone had cleared out after the party, with the bullpen engineering office quiet and empty for once, giving him space to think, he sat down and sketched the first blueprint for the design in about an hour. The pistol he designed uses compressed carbon dioxide gas to propel the paintballs; cocking the gun simultaneously readies the hammer and loads a ball into the barrel; when you pull the trigger, the hammer knocks open a valve that lets the gas into a chamber, which fires the ball. Jay built a prototype that he would shoot against the wall of an abandoned building, fine-tuning the exact amount of compressed carbon dioxide the gun needed to work properly. James C. Hale is the only name on the patent, but of course Daisy owned the rights to use it. For many years, Daisy manufactured the Nelspot 007, which the Nelson Paint Company advertised in catalogs for forestry and agricultural equipment, making a modest profit selling it to cattle ranchers and foresters. Not long after, Jay left Daisy, and considered trying to buy the rights to the patent from them in order to switch the contract with Nelson to his own company, but he ultimately decided not to bother with it.

The earliest proto-paintball games were probably played by ranchers or loggers fucking around on break or something, but in 1981, the godfather of paintball the game, a sporting equipment retailer named Bob Gurnsey, happened across an ad for the Nelspot 007 in an Agway catalog. He ordered a bunch of them, devised a list of rules with his friends, stock trader Hayes Noel and writer Charles Gaines (who wrote, among other things, *Pumping Iron: The Art and Sport of Bodybuilding*)—those three giants among manboys form the holy trinity of paintball's foundational mythology*—and they invited nine other friends to participate in the first official paintball game on a 125-acre plot of rugged, wooded land near Gaines's home in the White Mountains of New Hampshire: The great teenage war game was born.

Sometime in the early 1980s, Charlie Nelson was in northwest Arkansas for a meeting with Daisy and stopped by Hale Holler to visit Jay and Joyce, bringing with him some catalogs: an ad for the Nelspot 007, reworked for the new target clientele of *recreational* users, had spread from the agricultural to the sporting goods catalogs. "Have you seen what they're doing with our gun?" Jay remembered him saying.

Paintball exploded—ha—in the 1980s and became a multimilliondollar industry, of which revenue Jay never received a nickel, though he felt no resentment; he had been a salaried employee of Daisy when he

---

* And as in most mythologies, the gospels are not synoptic: According to the latter two, the whole thing sprang from a boozy late-night argument in Martha's Vineyard about which of them was better equipped to survive in the wilderness. It's also unclear whether it was Gurnsey or Gaines who first happened across the ad for the Nelspot.

had designed the gun, the company owned the intellectual property, that's the way it works. Neither he nor Charlie Nelson had ever once had the thought that humans might want to shoot *each other* with it for fun. In order to make the horse pills full of paint explode against the wall he was shooting them at, Jay'd had to make the impact velocity pretty high—much greater than that of a BB gun—and with a much bigger projectile—i.e., getting shot with one certainly wouldn't kill you, but it would hurt like holy hell. "Shooting 'em against that wall," Jay said, "always made me feel bad for the cows."

Another story: One time, when Kelly was a kid sitting in her father's lap as they rode his Triumph 650 Bonneville, buttoned into the oversize leather motorcycle jacket he wore so he could zip her inside it to transport her—this would have been in the mid-1970s—they were riding behind a poultry truck (along with Walmart, Tyson is one of northwest Arkansas's biggest employers; poultry is big business there), and a chicken fell off the back of the truck and landed in the road. Jay stopped the motorcycle, walked over and picked up the chicken, and they rode, all three of them zipped into the big motorcycle jacket with Kelly on Jay's lap and the chicken on Kelly's, back to Hale Holler, where Jay built a coop for her and she became Kelly's pet chicken.

Anything else it might be helpful to know? That Jay and Clay Bass were students at Little Rock Central High School (the family hadn't yet moved to Horseshoe Bend) in 1957, when Eisenhower invoked the Insurrection Act to override Governor Orval Faubus's attempt to use the Arkansas National Guard to forcibly prevent the school's integration and its first nine black students walked in under the protection of federal troops from the 101st Airborne Division. That Joyce baked the cake for the wedding (well, one of them) of the princess of Northwest Arkansas's local royal family, Alice Walton. I should probably also mention that my father was born when my grandmother was in her forties, by far the baby of the family; Jay was nearly twenty years his elder. The family was very civic minded and active in politics. Jay served as the chief of Pea Ridge's Volunteer Fire Department for many years. He even ran for office a few times. (I remember the slogan of one of his failed political campaigns—the pun works best when said with an Arkie accent: "Vote Democrat? Hale, yes!")

Catching crawdads in the creek at Hale Holler? My cousin Ike and I had developed a foolproof crawdad-catching technique: They have a fight-or-flight-type response to a sudden sign of danger, jetting backward, fast, maybe six or seven inches. So: Carefully place your net or bucket directly behind a crawdad, then jump into the creek right in front of it, and it'll jet back directly into your net or bucket. There was one time when we caught a really impressive bucketful of them and took them back to the house to show the grown-ups. We were going to throw them back into the creek; we just wanted to boast about our haul. But our grandmother took the bucket, thanked us for them, and boiled them up for dinner that night. We intrepid hunters had caught the family dinner.

That grandmother, Mary, was one of my favorite human beings to have walked the Earth, someone I loved deeply. She taught me to play poker (and bridge, backgammon, cribbage, and dominoes—less important but still significant games in my life). After her husband—my father's father—died of a heart attack in his midfifties when my dad was fifteen, long before I was born (there is a story my father sometimes tells about having to attend a "Fathers and Sons" Boy Scouts dinner alone a week after his father died), she and a close friend, also recently widowed, traveled down to New Orleans and hopped aboard a banana boat for a tour of the Caribbean and South America and back: remarkably adventurous for two single middle-aged Southern women and illustrative of Mary's character.

Christmases in Hale Holler from about 1987 to 1998 were some of the happiest times of my life. My father's family was big and happy, and Mary was the axle around which the wheel turned. It was a great contrast to my mother's parents, twenty minutes away in Rogers: bitterly unhappy people who hated each other so much that I am amazed they did not part unto death (his).

As a child I had a stuffed rabbit that I took everywhere and left everywhere, which more than once an obliging employee of some motel somewhere in Kansas or Oklahoma mailed back to our house. One time I left the rabbit at Mary's house in Hale Holler, and Mary, an avid knitter (one of her shawls, a wedding gift from Jay and Joyce, is draped across the back of our living room couch), mailed him back—it was winter, shortly after Christmas—wearing a little blue sweater with white trim she'd knitted to keep him warm on his journey through the US Postal Service. He wears it still, on a shelf in my parents' basement.

I remember Mary sitting in her armchair, knitting, and me on the floor: watching *Murder, She Wrote* through the snowy reception that was the best that TV could pick up in the boonies, watching *Jeopardy!* Mary's crush on Alex Trebek was a frequent subject of teasing within the family; she saw in Alex Trebek a last bastion of a certain kind of genteel midcentury manhood: his polished poise, his gray suits, his exquisite manners, and especially his dapper Clark-Gablean mustache—he was just about the last man on network TV to dare a mustache. Trebek shaved it off in 2001: the year Haley disappeared, the year I graduated from high school, the year of 9/11, the year Mary died. (Coincidences? Yes.)

When I was a teenager, in imitation of Hunter S. Thompson (as a teenager I did a lot of things in imitation of Hunter S. Thompson, including a lot of acid), I started wearing Hawaiian shirts. Mary had dementia, which got really bad in her last few years. For a while the four siblings took turns taking care of her for several months at a stretch—the duty passing, in birth order, from Jay to their sisters Nancy and then Ellen, then to us—before her condition worsened to the point that she needed daily full-time medical attention and she had to go to a nursing home. But before that, she spent four or five months living with us in Colorado. There is a place near Denver called the Butterfly Pavilion, a lofty, light-infused glass cathedral of an indoor greenhouse, full of tropical butterflies. My mother, my grandmother, my brothers James and John (John was a toddler then) went to the Butterfly Pavilion that summer: 1999, maybe? It was a difficult summer; Mary's mind was half gone, and her life was mostly confusion and terror in between increasingly rare moments of clarity. The look of childlike joy on her face when the dozens of bright, brilliant tropical butterflies with metallic flashing wings flocked around me as though I were St. Francis of the Butterflies, fooled by the bright brilliant tropical flowers printed on my Hawaiian shirt, is one of my last and my best memories of her.

I think it was the next summer that my mother and I drove to Arkansas to pick up Mary's old car—a tiny tan 1982 Toyota Tercel, which became my first car, with which I would deliver a lot of newspapers and pizzas in Colorado—from Ellen and her husband, Sammy, who lived in a house they were building in a part of the Ozarks even more backwoods than Hale Holler, who sold it to me for one symbolic dollar. While we were there, my mother and I visited Mary in her nursing home. Three factors—(1) it was unusual for Mary to see my mother without her son being with her; (2) her dementia had become very bad by then; (3) I look a lot like my father—combined to cause her to think that I was my father. (My mother taught history at public high schools for most of her career and had the summers free, as did I, at least for long enough for that trip to and from Arkansas; I think my father was away that summer, testing weapon-targeting systems in a secret location somewhere in the desert in New Mexico that he was not allowed to reveal even to his family.) Mary talked about the time "I" had made a tiny cage out of toothpicks and glue, complete with a hinge and a working door to hold captive the housefly I had caught. I realized that I was representing my father in her mind, and I had no idea what to do. We sat in the windowless, low-ceilinged, fake wood–paneled, oppressively bleak cafeteria of the nursing home, and as it was midafternoon, we were almost the only people in it, except for a fat, well-dressed, clean-shaven guy in a wheelchair who wasn't old, maybe in his fifties, who wheeled himself over to our table and starting talking to me. He had a deep concave dent in one of his temples—his head misshapen into an asymmetrical peanut—and one of his eyes lolled off in the wrong direction. The guy seemed starved for a very specific kind of conversation: the friendly but guarded shallow manly small talk between two straight middle-class men who have just met.

"So, what kinda work d'you do?" he kept asking me. At the time, I worked part-time after school at an Einstein Bros. Bagels in Boulder, Colorado. However, my grandmother was right there, thinking I was my father.

"I'm a laser physicist," I said.

Afterward, I asked one of the nurses what that guy's story was, and he told me that he'd lost everything, shot himself in the head and lived.

That was the last time I saw Mary. She died the next year, as it happened, on September 11, 2001. It was my second day of classes as a freshman at Sarah Lawrence College, which is close to New York City—that was one of the reasons I'd wanted to go there—and a lot of kids from New York attend it. Some of my classmates knew people who worked at the World Trade Center who were missing and presumed dead, and I felt a little foolish telling people that my grandmother had died of old age that morning. I wasn't able to attend her funeral because all the planes were still grounded.

Mary was near the end and would have been in a very bad way four months earlier when her great-granddaughter Haley disappeared in the wilderness. She was by then always in a state of confusion and terror, and there's no way she would have understood any of it. I hope no one told her.

Mary had been the glue that kept the family together; those big happy Christmases at Hale Holler had been for her, and after she died, they quit happening. A few years later, Jay and Joyce sold their business, retired, moved to Fayetteville, and rented the houses on the big wooded property in Pea Ridge for a while before they eventually tired of landlording headaches and sold it. Mary is gone, the elevator is gone, Alex

Trebek's mustache is gone, Alex Trebek is gone, Hale Holler is gone, and the world around it is gone.

Throughout the time I spent writing this book—I began in December 2022—Jay was suffering from cancer and a half-dozen other medical problems and the same dementia his mother had suffered. Back in the fall of 2022, he had been disturbed to find himself unable to do basic math: The engineering genius could not calculate the tip on a restaurant check; it felt to him as if he had forgotten his native language. Not long afterward, he plowed into a row of traffic cones on an interstate, and then the man who had built and ridden his own motorcycles and built and flown his own airplanes had to give up his driver's license. His condition deteriorated rapidly in the last few months of his life, and he died on May 30, 2024. "He was just snowed under and asleep, so it was totally peaceful," my father said to me that day. "He's hopefully riding one of his 650 Triumphs as we speak."

3

Cave Mountain

AT ABOUT A QUARTER TO NOON ON A TEMPERATE, SUNNY SUN-
day in April 2001, Joyce, panicked now after losing about fifteen minutes of time searching for her granddaughter in what she now believed
was the wrong direction, ran ahead back along the bluff and found Clay
Bass on the trail. Heaving breath from the uphill run, she told him that
Haley had disappeared. Together they continued running up the trail,
where they found Jay, Dennis, and Michelle not far ahead of them. Once
everyone understood the situation, Dennis and Michelle went back to
the cabins to see if Haley had somehow made it there, and the others
spread out up and down the trail, scanning the dense, dark springtime
woods and calling her name. When Dennis and Michelle made it back
to the cabins, they found Doc Chester still working in his yard, sawing
up that dead tree. No, he had not seen the little girl they had come in
with, but then again, he hadn't been paying attention; he'd been con-
centrating on the work in front of him and had industrial earmuffs on
to dampen the noise of the chain saw. Michelle remained at the Faddis
Cabin, to be there in case Haley found it, and Dennis got into their car
and started searching along County Road 406, the narrow private road
that leads down from Cave Mountain Road; he also wanted to look at
the small dirt parking lot at the trailhead to see if there were any fewer

cars parked there than he remembered seeing earlier that morning, and write down their license plate numbers. Doc Chester went inside his house and called Tim Ernst, a close friend and neighbor down the road.

Tim Ernst, a photographer, nature writer, blogger, dedicated conservationist, and chamberlain and historian of the lower Ozarks, —would become a pivotal character in this story. He lived in a cabin he called Cloudland on the very edge of the bluff on the south face of Cave Mountain at one of its highest points. The view of the valley from the back decks of his cabin is as sublime as the view from Hawksbill Crag. A tall, thin, soft-spoken man with a gray beard and kind eyes with a rustic Mr. Rogers sort of serenity about him, Tim is a gentle soul if ever there were one, and every time I've seen him he's been wearing a dun-colored slouch hat, ready for a walk in the woods.

After Doc Chester called and told him that a little girl had gone missing somewhere on the Hawksbill Crag Trail, Tim gave his fiancée, Pam, a two-way radio and posted her as lookout from one of the back decks of the cabin, which hangs directly above the last thin remnant of the Hawksbill Crag Trail. (Back then, at the point directly below the cabin's back decks, the trail was so faint that most people probably wouldn't have seen it; since then, it's grown over and is gone now.) Tim stuffed a bottle of water and the other radio into a fanny pack and took off with his two dogs to help search along the bluff line. From his house Tim headed west along the bluff until he came to Hawksbill Crag.

"When I arrived at the Crag just past noon," Tim wrote, "I found a lady standing there with a couple of other hikers. She had borrowed the hiker's cell phone and was trying to talk to someone about the little girl, but she was not having much luck due to the poor cell reception."

That lady standing at the crag was Joyce. She had found another couple of hikers—not the same people as the first two she had run into on the trail earlier—doing the ooh-and-awe at the crag; one of them had leant her a cell phone, and she had used it to call 911. (Joyce did not then, and does not now, own a cell phone.) She was trying to talk to the person who had answered the call at the Dispatch Center in the Newton County Sheriff's Office in Jasper. "I could hear the sheriff's voice," Joyce wrote, "but he couldn't hear me."*

That moment—standing at the trail's most picturesque vista point at Hawksbill Crag, desperately trying to call 911 from a borrowed cell phone that wasn't working—was the first time Joyce met Tim Ernst, but she and Jay already knew who he was, because they were admirers of his work: They had bought several of his hiking guidebooks and nature photography calendars, which are display table staples of the Local Interest sections in the bookstores of northern Arkansas, and had also seen him talk at Sierra Club events. I don't think the fact that they happened to be fans of his came up at that particularly high-stress moment.

Joyce's nerves were so flooded with anxiety during this first stretch of minutes after Haley's disappearance, her memories of exactly who was where and what happened in what order are jumbled, but she is pretty sure that after that failed call from the stranger's cell phone at the crag and the brief encounter with Tim and his dogs, she went back to the Faddis Cabin, met Michelle Boles there, and called 911 from the landline. The call went through. Joyce remembers asking the dispatcher if they could bring search dogs, and being told none were readily available at the moment but they would start working on it. Official help was now on the way. It was a little over an hour after Haley had last been seen.

"Time continued to slip away," Joyce wrote. "I had to admit that we were really in trouble. Now it was unavoidable to let Haley's parents know what was going on."

Kelly did have a cell phone, and so did her husband, Steve. But they had just gotten their first cell phones, and Joyce didn't have their numbers memorized yet. Luckily, however, Joyce knew where Kelly was; they had chatted a bit when she and Jay had picked up Haley earlier that morning, and Kelly had mentioned that she planned to attend the Fay-

---

* I am a little amazed there was enough cell reception at Hawkbill Crag for even half the connection to go through. Twenty-two years later, there have appeared no more than zero bars of cell service on my phone at any point when I've been anywhere on Cave Mountain.

etteville Film Fest later that afternoon. "While the realization that Haley was really missing came on slowly for Jay and me, I knew it was going to hit Kelly and Steve right between the eyes," Joyce wrote. "I wanted someone to be there with her so that she wouldn't have to drive."

First Joyce tried one of Kelly's best friends, but, Joyce wrote, "she wasn't at home." (In the years that followed, the phrase "wasn't at home" would be displaced by "didn't pick up.") Then she thought to ask Clay Bass's wife, Cathy, who had also been invited on the hike that day but had decided not to go. Joyce got Cathy on the phone, explained the situation, asked her to go to the Fayetteville Film Fest, find Kelly there, and take her to Cave Mountain, along with some of Haley's clothes, to give a scent to the search dogs she hoped would arrive soon. On the way, Cathy picked up another good friend of the family, Fran Alexander, and together they went to find Kelly.

Back in Fayetteville, Kelly had been having a relaxing Sunday. She then worked as an administrator for the Symphony of Northwest Arkansas, which had given a concert at the Walton Arts Center the night before; she had been surfing a crescendo of work stress in the week leading up to the performance, and now that it was over, the valve had opened, the pressure was gone, her husband, Steve, had been away for a week at his annual two weeks of National Guard training at Fort Chaffee and would be away for another week, her parents had her daughter for the day, and she had a precious rare day completely to herself, with no obligations on the horizon except putting Haley to bed when her parents brought her back after dinner later that evening; a beautiful empty spring Sunday spread out before her like a wide-open field. She had told her parents that morning that she planned to attend the Fayetteville Film Fest in the afternoon, but even that was an optional commitment, subject to change if she felt like it.

Kelly drove to the Walmart Supercenter past I-49 on the west side of Fayetteville to buy plants and seeds for her garden—April is prime seeding season, and she was about to miss it—and bumped into Ashley

Garcia, the principal of Haley's elementary school, in the greenhouse of the plant and garden section. Kelly talked with her awhile in the big blue-shadow-tinted luminous humid room, telling her that Haley was off on an adventure with her grandparents that day, hiking in the woods, seeing the Ozarks' wildflowers, how excited Kelly was for the day off, and they talked about what flowers and vegetables they planned to grow in their gardens, the best things to plant at that point in the season. Kelly bought bulbs and seed packets, drove back home, ate a quick lunch, cleaned up, dressed up a little, and drove to the Fayetteville Film Fest, which was being held in an auditorium of the University of Arkansas's continuing education building on a corner of Fayetteville's town square. About an hour into the series of short films, the film that was playing abruptly stopped and a voice came over the PA, asking Kelly Zega to come to the back of the auditorium.

With a roomful of eyes on her, Kelly's breath quickened as she apologized and pushed past people's legs until she made it out of her row and into the aisle, and as the theater darkened again and the film restarted, her nerves began to prickle with dread; for some reason Cathy Bass, the wife of her father's best friend, Clay, and Fran Alexander, another close friend of her parents, were standing by the doors at the back of the auditorium, looking very serious and worried.

In a few minutes, Cathy explained that Haley was lost in the Buffalo National River Wilderness, probably somewhere not far from Hawksbill Crag Trail, where they had been hiking. There were about fifteen people on the mountain right then looking for her, the local authorities had been engaged, and more people were on the way. Joyce had asked Cathy to inform Kelly what was happening, get some of Haley's clothes for their scent, and drive her to Cave Mountain.

Kelly first called her husband, Steve, and tried to tell him the news, but he was deep in the middle of some big metal building at Fort Chaffee; Kelly, freaking out, kept trying to tell him what was happening, and Steve kept not understanding as the series of choppy calls on his cell phone kept cutting out and dropping while he made his way out of the building. When he finally made it outside, Kelly was in the passenger seat of Cathy's car, on her way home. As soon as she had communicated the situation to Steve over clear cell reception, he asked her how to get there, and Kelly gave the phone to Cathy, who calmly gave him directions from the Fort Smith area to the Hawksbill Crag Trailhead.

Kelly, Cathy, and Fran—Kelly beside herself with terror and Cathy and Fran in clearheaded battle mode—stopped at Steve and Kelly's house. "We expect she'll be found right away," Cathy told her, "but if this goes later than we hope, you should probably grab some things in case you end up needing to stay out there for a bit. And we also need you to grab some items that have a strong scent of Haley." Kelly recalls having a sudden flash of absurd panic, remembering she had parked her car on the street in Fayetteville in a metered spot and it would get towed if it sat there too long; Cathy told her they'd make some calls in a little while and deal with it, don't worry about the car. At home Kelly grabbed a pillowcase from Haley's bed, a little purple dress Kelly had made for her that she wore all the time, and some toiletries and a change of clothes, and then they were off. Cathy knew the way: a straight shot east by southeast on AR-16 all the way to Cave Mountain Road, aka County Road 5. They made it to the top of Cave Mountain late in the afternoon.

Not far from the Hawksbill Crag Trailhead, there is a graveyard next to a tiny church—and I mean *tiny*: Cave Mountain Church is basically just a one-room box smaller in square footage than some wealthy people's bathrooms I've seen, with windows, a door, a pulpit, and two rows of five pews. The authorities—the Newton County sheriff, state troopers, park rangers, local police from several nearby jurisdictions—turned this church and its dirt parking lot into the "Command Center." On one of my recent visits the church happened to be open, and I took some pictures inside. I don't think any services have been held there in a long time, and it's halfway fallen into desuetude: sagging plywood ceiling with slanting diamonds of dishwater light falling on dust-furred pews; it's a building Walker Evans would have liked to photograph, as simple and haunted as a folk song.

Kelly, Cathy, and Fran arrived at Cave Mountain Church to find a few police cars, vehicles belonging to the Newton County Sheriff's Office and the National Park Service, a couple of officers and a handful of local residents of the area—the first of many who'd heard the news and come to volunteer to help with the search—and Kelly's mother, Joyce, waiting there to meet them. Everyone else—about twenty people, including Jay, Clay, Dennis, Michelle, Tim, Pam, and now some sheriff's officers and park rangers—was out in the woods, looking for Haley.

Kelly on encountering Joyce in the church parking lot:

And what I remember so distinctly was, she came up and she just said, "Will you ever forgive me?" And I remember very distinctly saying "There's nothing to forgive. I'm not angry at all." And I wasn't. I knew she was terrified and horrified and just frantic and my mom—she's pretty high strung anyway, so when you add that level of fear on top of that, she was just beside herself. And I felt so bad for her, even though I was scared to death myself. I was just like, I don't want you to feel like this, I just want you to know it's okay, we're gonna figure this out. But she was so scared I was going be just furious. Then pretty shortly after that, Zega got there. I do remember really worrying that he was going to be mad at my parents and that he was going to lose it on them. But that is not what happened. At no point did anybody express anger to them, and at no point did he make me feel like he was angry with them. Even in private conversations, there was never any sort of blame that was levied, and that was such a relief to me, because I could only process one thing at a time. I was so worried about everybody, not just Haley, but very, very worried about my parents and him and everything that was happening.

Time began to blur for everyone at that point, but as the day waned, more and more emergency workers, mostly law enforcement officials of various kinds, arrived at Cave Mountain, more and more red and blue lights flashing on the trees as the sun began to set. The authorities wouldn't let Kelly join the search; they wanted her to stay put so they would know where to find her. "So I was pretty much just sitting there by myself," Kelly said, "just watching everything." At that time she had been having some sort of minor medical issue with low blood pressure—if it dropped too low, she would pass out—and she had forgotten to bring her medication with her. She told this to one of the cops manning the Command Center—i.e., the little one-room church—and he made some calls—Kelly knew the name of the drug and the dosage—and got someone to fill it for her at a pharmacy somewhere nearby and drive it up the mountain for her, all without a call to a doctor or insurance company, no money changing hands or anything. Newton County is a very sparsely populated area where everyone knows everyone, including cops and pharmacists, and such a wink-and-handshake social ecosystem is useful for emergency rule breaking; it's a small place where people can overpower bureaucracy. Kelly's blood pressure remained at normal levels, and she remained conscious.

Night fell. Emergency vehicles rumbled up and down the mountain on a road so narrow that for most of it, when two cars pass each other, one driver has to stop and let the other carefully squeeze around. By about nine in the evening there were two helicopters equipped with heat sensors thudding low across the valley; they took off and landed in an open field not far from the church, adjacent to the private road that leads to the small cluster of cabins from which the hikers had set out for the bluff that morning.

The incident had been on the TV news by then, and one of the sheriff's deputies approached Kelly, who was sitting on a pew in the church in a suspended state of terror and numb shock, feeling useless, and told her that Colleen Nick had called and asked to speak with her.

Kelly was already familiar with Colleen Nick; the story of her daughter Morgan's abduction had been all over the news, especially the local news, in the summer of 1995, when Kelly had been home on maternity leave, pregnant with Haley. She had spent a lot of time sitting around watching TV that summer, and the TV was spending a lot of time on

Morgan Nick. "So I always feel like this real connection to her," Kelly said,

> because I was watching it play out in the news when I was home
> and had way more time than I normally did. So I had always paid
> very close attention to the Morgan Nick story. When they told me
> that Colleen Nick had called and asked permission to speak with
> me, it actually pissed me off a little bit. Because—of course I didn't
> know her, I had sympathy for her—but I'm like, Haley has not been
> *abducted*, so why are you calling me? It was kind of a strange reaction.
> It was just irritation, what I felt. I felt like by her calling, she was
> somehow implying that Haley was truly disappearing. And I was just
> like, "That is unacceptable, that is not the way I'm thinking and I'm
> not going to. I'm just kind of annoyed by this." But then I thought,
> "Okay, she has gone to the trouble of trying to figure out how to get in
> touch with me. And the sheriff's deputy seemed to think it was a good
> idea for me to talk to her." So I'm like, Okay, fine, fine. So they took
> me over to one of the patrol cars that was hardwired with a functional
> phone. Because she couldn't have called me on my cell phone, it didn't
> work there. The communication situation, not having cellular service,
> was very problematic on a lot of levels throughout the whole time.
> So I'm sitting in this patrol car, talking to Colleen Nick, and it was a
> phenomenal conversation. She made me feel so calm. And she offered
> to come and be on site and to assist any way she could. She basically
> said, "My job is to not get in your way, my job is not to tell you what
> to do, but I have been involved with too many things like this and I
> know how I can help you to navigate some of the things that you're
> about to be faced with."

Colleen Nick did go up to Cave Mountain the next day—along with many other people—and stayed close to Kelly throughout the ordeal.

Not long after Kelly's conversation with Colleen Nick—it was now after ten at night—the cops at the Command Center relayed to Steve and Kelly that Tim Ernst had offered to put them up for the night in his house, Cloudland, and they gratefully took him up on it. Someone—she doesn't remember who—drove them down a "crazy, bumpy, wild road" in the dark down to Tim's house. Steve and Kelly stayed with him that night and the next, along with a few other close friends who came to help the second day. Jay and Joyce, Dennis and Michelle Boles, and Clay and Cathy Bass stayed with Doc Chester, some in the house and some in the cruder cabin next door.

That first night, Tim showed Steve and Kelly to the guest bedroom on the first floor of the house and left them alone. It was the first time that day they had been alone together. "It was just Zega and me," Kelly said, "and I just lost it. That was the first time that I just sobbed. Up to that point I was really trying to keep it together. And it was just like, being alone in this cabin in a stranger's house and not knowing what was going to happen, I was just overwhelmed with grief. And it just, it felt awful."

Tim's house, Cloudland, became, along with the Command Center at Cave Mountain Church, the other main hub of the search-and-rescue mission. The next morning, Steve Zega went out early to continue helping with the search. The house had a fully equipped home office for Tim's photography and publishing ventures, a good internet connection, two phone lines, a high-end desktop PC, printer, scanner, fax machine, and so on—and he turned it over to Kelly that morning; and Kelly, whom they still wouldn't let participate in the search, became the liaison-with-the-outside-world nerve center of the search-and-rescue operation from Tim's office, which made her feel more useful in the coming days. She recalls Colleen—who was there by the second day—telling her "I think this is where you need to be. This is where you can do the most good."

The number of people involved in the search ballooned to hundreds: other emergency workers from many surrounding areas, many local residents who didn't know my family but had heard the news and shown up to volunteer, and friends and relatives who had come from all over. "Zega had gotten ahold of some of his best friends in Fayetteville," Kelly said. "A lot of those were his college fraternity brothers. And they came out in fours. And then other friends of ours were coming, too, to support, some were just coming to be there with me. I remember one of Zega's best friends, Ray Dunwoody, who spent so much of his time out there searching. All these people left work, because it was Monday by this time." The people who came to volunteer their help brought tents and camper-trailers, as accommodations in the handful of cabins on top of Cave Mountain quickly filled to capacity, and the owner of a small soybean farm a little way down the road let them park their trailers and pitch their tents in his field, which he was just then about to seed. A lot of local restaurants chipped in to the search effort, sending truckloads of food up the mountain to feed everyone, and by the end of the second day, the National Guard and the Red Cross had set up a field kitchen.

I was a seventeen-year-old senior in high school at the time, out in Lafayette, Colorado; my parents, after a sleepless Sunday night and a Monday spent uselessly dragging themselves zombielike through the workday and there was still no sign of her, told me to take care of my brothers—five and fifteen years younger than me—and that night took off in the car for Arkansas.

Pollen fogged the air at the height of spring—the time to plant seeds and, the whole reason they were there to begin with, the time when the wildflowers bloom—and the wind swirled with thick murmurations of golden dust. "I remember Ray [Dunwoody] coming up to the cabin to probably get something to drink and eat," Kelly said, "and his socks were caked with yellow from all the pollen. People were practically choking from the pollen. Everybody was sneezing and hacking. It was not an easy time in Arkansas that time of year, for sure."

The next day, night, and day passed as you can probably imagine: sleeplessly—especially for Steve, Kelly, Jay, and Joyce—sick with terror; the authorities scrambling to organize everything; logistical clusterfuck and general chaos; more and more volunteers showing up to help, and most of them getting pissed off that the authorities weren't letting them do anything. Every civilian volunteer I talked to told me a similar story: rushing up the mountain as soon as they could and then "checking in" with the authorities at the Command Center, who told them to wait. (The classic intramilitary joke, "Hurry up and wait.")

According to Arthur Evans, a friend of Jay and Joyce who helped with the search, "the official searchers had all kinds of fancy stuff to find somebody in the woods, including a helicopter with heat sensors that would, of course, mostly be useful at night." There were other "gizmos," as Art called them. The search-and-rescue experts brought into the effort some sort of computer program they plugged Haley's stats into—six-year-old, forty-nine-pound female—and a topographical map of the terrain; the program crunched the numbers and algorithmically suggested likely places to look.

The authorities—many of whom were not on the clock, and all of whom were doing their best to find and rescue my cousin, and whom I am in absolutely no way trying to cast as the inept and blindly-arrogant-in-their-trust-in-technology-and-especially-their-own-authority closest-thing-to-villains in this story (that might sound like praeteritio, but I seriously do mean it)—were pretty well convinced that Haley was either still on the bluff or somewhere above it, higher on the mountain, or else was a corpse somewhere at the bottom of the bluff. On all sides, the bluff is a steep, rocky, nearly vertical wall of boulders; they did not think she would have ever even tried getting down it, and certainly could not have gotten down it any way but falling off of it. So they decided from the beginning that looking for her below the bluff was mostly a waste of time, though there were some local volunteers they allowed to look there (Arthur Evans was one of them). Almost all the search efforts were concentrated along the bluff, inside the roughly three hundred acres of woods between it and the road, and on the mountain above it.

The dogs arrived on that second day of Haley's disappearance. They were given her scent; they smelled the pillowcase and the little purple dress Kelly had brought, they smelled the red sweatshirt and her security blanket that had been in Jay and Joyce's truck since Sunday morning. Early Monday morning, a couple of K-9 officers' German shepherds picked up the scent—maybe—and, starting from approximately the place she'd last been seen on the Hawksbill Crag Trail, led their humans on a winding, crazy path through the woods right to the edge of Cave Mountain Road, where they lost it. Throughout the second day, the same thing happened with other dogs, starting at different points along the trail on top of the bluff: They kept picking up on something, sniffing through the woods all the way up the mountain to the road, and losing the scent.

Over the course of the day, the mood amongst the authorities—and many of the volunteers who were searching and those helping with all the attendant logistics, and the news media covering the story—turned darker. Many of them now feared that the reason they had not found Haley was because she was not there. Someone driving on that road had picked her up and taken her.

On the morning of the third day, Colleen Nick—who had been staying with Kelly at Cloudland and acting as a liaison between among the law enforcement agencies, the search-and-rescue operations, the media, and the family—asked Steve and Kelly to meet with her and one of the sheriff's officers in one of the spare bedrooms on the bottom floor of the cabin. Kelly:

> They intentionally got us downstairs, where it was away from all of the hubbub of people upstairs, and said that enough time has passed and because the scent that the dogs were hitting on for Haley was ending in some odd places—it was ending at the road, and they couldn't really explain that—that they were getting to the point where the likelihood of this being a search operation or rescue operation was looking less and less. And so they were going to have to redefine how they were going to approach the search. They were so careful in how they talked to us. They were just saying, "We're not stopping looking. But we've got to dial back what we're doing, and we're actually getting in our own way at this point. And there is some likelihood that she was

taken, because no one can figure out how she just . . . her scent went cold, and we haven't found her. It just doesn't make any sense." And so they were shifting from a search-and-rescue to potentially a criminal investigation at this point.

The sheriff's officer furthermore told them that the law enforcement agencies and the media were organizing a press conference to be held later that day—hosted by another nearby Cave Mountain resident, Wesley Sparks, whose house was closer to the road and big enough to squeeze in all the members of the press and their equipment—and he recommended that Steve and Kelly speak at it. Kelly again:

> Colleen sat me down and prepped me for that. Colleen said that there is nothing stronger and more understood by people than a bond between a mother and child. And she said, You have been too tough and too strong and too stoic for too long in this situation. You have got to show people that there's some emotion associated with this. And you have got to talk about what she means to you and how you are feeling right now. I now see exactly what she was telling me, and why she was telling me to lose it and cry on camera and stop being so strong and stoic and upbeat about everything. Because if you are that, people are not going to believe you. They're gonna think you had something to do with this. And she didn't tell me that then, she just told me, "People have to understand how terrible this is for you and how you would do anything to have her back home."

The Newton County Sheriff's Office held the press conference in the early afternoon of Tuesday, May 1, 2001. Tim drove Steve and Kelly over to Wesley's house. Colleen was there waiting for them and led them into Wesley's living room, where a bunch of reflective umbrellas and flood lamps had been set up, a dozen or so reporters huddled around the room, camera operators from various media organizations had cameras on tripods aimed at the couch, and there was a rat's nest of cables and cords and microphones on the coffee table in front of the couch.

Colleen spoke briefly, introducing Steve and Kelly and saying that they wanted to make statements to the press. Steve began by reading a list of the many agencies and organizations that had been involved with the search and rescue effort and thanked them. He thanked Colleen Nick and talked about what her involvement had meant to them. He thanked Tim Ernst for all his help. And he finished by reading from the text he'd written that day with his voice cracking:

The people of Newton County have been amazing. They have broken these woods with their feet and their legs and their hands to look for our daughter. Thank you. We want to thank our family and friends who have all stopped their lives, come from all over the state and country to be here, and have left their own jobs and families, and have just been here to hold our hands. Thank you all. We love you. Haley loves you. Thank you.

Then Steve moved aside. Kelly, holding Haley's blanket, leaned toward the microphones with Steve's arm on her back, and began to speak—completely extemporaneously—choking back tears as she did:

I want to thank all of you [pointing at the media people present] because our message could not get out there like it has without your assistance, and we know that everything you are doing is in the best interest of this beautiful little girl. We know that all of you who have seen her precious face know that she is a little girl who is going places. She's smart and she's tender, and she's an angel here on this earth. We know that we are blessed to have her in our lives. This is her blankie, and I bet right now probably the best thing to make her feel better would be to suck her thumb, and I don't think she can do it without this blankie.

Kelly paused, wiped away tears, put on a new face and voice of resolve, and ended the press conference with this:

And so if anyone knows where this baby is—I don't care how you know, how you find her, why you have her, where she is—it doesn't matter to us. We just want her back. She is the most important thing to us in our entire lives, and we would give up everything that we have to have this baby back in our arms and to put this back in her hands. And I would just plead that you would put her back with us.

The press conference ended a little before two o'clock on Monday afternoon, the first day of May. At that moment, as Kelly was pleading into TV cameras with the imagined stranger who she feared had abducted her daughter, three miles away from and 830 feet below the main search area, two local men, Lytle James and William Jeff Villines, sixty-one and fifty-four years old, respectively, both of them expert hunters and trackers who had grown up in the area, often hunted in the Buffalo National River Wilderness and knew it better than anyone, were, unbeknown to anyone in the search-and-rescue operation except Lytle's son, searching for Haley on their own, riding a couple of mules in the low ground along the banks of the Buffalo River.

4

Dug Hollow

T HE US ARMY THREW CAMP CHAFFEE TOGETHER IN SIXTEEN months in preparation for our entry into World War II, and they just happened to complete it on the day that would live in infamy, Japan's attack on Pearl Harbor: December 7, 1941. During the war the military detained German POWs at the massive 66,000-acre tract of land in west-central Arkansas; Elvis Presley had his pompadour shorn into a regulation military haircut there in 1958; in 1975–1976, it served as one of the main processing centers for refugees fleeing Vietnam, and most of the people who first arrived in the country there trickled south to form the robust Vietnamese immigrant fishing community along the Gulf Coast of Texas; it held about twenty thousand Cuban refugees after the Mariel boatlift in 1980 (an ugly episode in the place's history involving President Jimmy Carter, Governor Bill Clinton, a prison riot, and the Ku Klux Klan). In 1995, it was "realigned" into Fort Chaffee Joint Maneuver Training Center, and since then the Arkansas National Guard has been using it as a training facility.

Haley's father, Steve Zega, was thirty-five years old at the time and a criminal defense lawyer when in civilian mode. Steve began serving in the National Guard in 1987 and retired as a colonel in 2023. Just a few years after these events in the spring of 2001 happened, Steve was one of many National Guardsmen who were sent into active combat duty in Iraq, where he served three tours. (Steve and Kelly were married for more than another decade after all of this happened, but they have since divorced and remarried other people. For coherence's sake—so I don't have to keep writing "then husband"—I refer to them as husband and wife throughout the parts of this book that relate the events of 2001, with my apologies to their current spouses.) But before the Iraq War, back in peacetime, unless called to a mission, part-time service in the Guard meant one weekend of duty a month plus an annual two weeks of training, and Steve was at Fort Chaffee, right in the middle of those two weeks, when his wife called him in the middle of a Sunday afternoon to tell him that their six-year-old daughter had gone missing. It took him a while to glean that Haley had been lost for three hours and Kelly was on her way to the Buffalo National River Wilderness. At that moment, Kelly was in a car climbing fast into the Ozarks, and Steve answered the call on his Nokia flip phone while he was working on an upper floor deep in the bowels of an enormous building with a metal roof, practically an unintentional Faraday cage; the call got choppier and choppier until it dropped completely. It was probably only five minutes or so, but it felt like an hour that Steve spent with pulse quickening, rushing out of the building and redialing Kelly again and again, the calls going straight to voice mail. He'd had no idea that his in-laws had taken his daughter hiking that day. As an Arkansan, he vaguely knew the general location of the Buffalo River, but he didn't really know what the Buffalo National River Wilderness was, where it was, or why the fuck his daughter had gone missing there. Kelly was apparently going there. Once outside, he managed to get through to Kelly, who filled him in on the situation. The Newton County Sheriff's Office and the National Park Service were already on the scene. Then Kelly passed the phone to Cathy Bass, who gave him directions to Cave Mountain Road: take I-40 East to Clarksville, then go north on AR-21—a trip of about 100 miles, a little over two hours.

When Steve answered the call, he had been standing within earshot of his friend and comrade in the 1st Battalion of the 142nd Field Artillery Brigade, Vixen James, an active-duty guy who lived and worked full-time at Fort Chaffee. Vixen is a native of Newton County who grew up on his family's farm in the mountains outside Jasper. Not quite ten minutes later, he passed Steve, banging down a hallway in his jump boots on his way to ask their battalion commander, Lieutenant Colonel John Payne, for emergency leave to join the search for his daughter. Steve slowed enough to hastily explain the situation to Vixen in one long breath, and Vixen told him that he was from there, that he knew that part of the Ozarks like the back of his hand, and that he'd be right behind him. Lieutenant Colonel Payne granted Steve leave on the spot, and Steve, still in his full uniform and not stopping to pack anything, ran out to his car and took off.

Vixen and his and Steve's mutual friend National Guard Chaplain Wesley Hilliard decided to request leave to help with the search. Payne gave them permission to go, but with the understanding that they were still on duty and that their mission was twofold: to help search and take care of whatever Steve and his family needed, and to liaise between the search-and-rescue Incident Command and the Guard and coordinate the Guard's involvement should it become needed. Half an hour later, Wes and Vixen were packed up with a few days' clothes, provisions and toiletries, and merging onto I-40 East with the highway screaming under the wheels of Vixen's pickup truck, headed for Cave Mountain.

Forty-year-old George Stowe-Rains, a park technician with Arkansas State Parks and seasoned search-and-rescue expert, had been working with the National Park Service that Sunday afternoon at Hobbs State Park–Conservation Area about an hour away, not too far from the Fayetteville/Rogers/Bentonville area—as it happened, he was training NPS staff in search-and-rescue tactics. When he got the call, he was there with his first boss up, one of ASP's lead rangers, Jeffrey West, and as they were driving out to the Buffalo National River Wilderness together, West named him incident commander of the search-and-rescue mission. By the middle of the afternoon, Stowe-Rains stood at the hub of the operation at the Command Center—Cave Mountain Church—with a walkie-talkie crunching and squealing in his hand, trying to conduct the chaotic orchestra quickly forming around him: Newton County sheriff's officers, park rangers, police officers, and other emergency workers who had come in from neighboring counties, the setting up of mobile cell sites to ease communication, the two Black Hawk helicopters requested of the governor's office flying in. One of George's main jobs was training emergency responders in search and rescue—he had been working in that field since 1983, twenty-seven years—and he was one of the most highly trained and experienced search-and-rescue managers in Arkansas. George Stowe-Rains and Jeff West got to Cave Mountain before Kelly and Steve, interviewed Jay and Joyce, and had already begun using CASIE III: Computer Aided Search Information Exchange. This was one of the "gizmos" that Arthur Evans mentioned.

From CASIE's website (via the University of Arizona, where the program was principally developed by mathematician David Lovelock): "The program was designed to simplify most of the calculations related to managing a search emergency using modern search theory. CASIE also introduced innovative applications, like Resource Optimization and quantification of Influence of Clues, as part of a comprehensive package of SAR analysis tools." "You put the lost person behavior in it," George explained, "and the age and their physical health and the weather and everything. And then it starts using an algorithm to help you find the highest-probability areas where you're gonna find them. And you take POD [probability of detection] with POA [probability of area], and it equals POS, probability of success. The program takes all that into account and shows you the highest-probability areas, whereas before we would've had to do a lot of formulas. It does them for you." So they plugged the information—healthy, four-foot-tall, forty-nine-pound, six-year-old female, weather sunny and 78 degrees Fahrenheit—and a map of the terrain into CASIE. CASIE crunched the data, and divided the map into a grid of segments; then George assigned teams to search the segments beginning with those with the highest probability of success; when searchers reported back, George would eliminate that segment and assign them to another. It's a science, to be done as carefully, methodically, and rigorously as possible. However, increasingly throughout these days, another factor complicated the search-and-rescue mission for George and the many teams of emergency workers he had to manage: too many people on the mountain.

As Vixen recalled, "Anytime you say anything about a child getting lost, it hits everybody's heartstrings. So I mean, there was just droves of people showing up." By the time Vixen James and Wes Hilliard made it to the top of Cave Mountain in the late afternoon, Incident Command was dealing with two problems: the search-and-rescue mission to find Haley, and the personnel management issue of dealing with all of the many people who had shown up to help with the search—and the second one was fast blooming out of control.

"We were overwhelmed with volunteers that were not contacted, which makes our job harder," George Stowe-Rains said. "It was one of the biggest searches I've ever managed, and it was probably one of the most difficult because of the resources that showed up on the scene that we had not planned on or asked for. I mean, they're good-hearted, but it really challenges us, because we're trying to plan a search mission for all the trained resources we have there, and we get all the untrained resources showing up, and we have to try to plug them in somewhere and take care of them also. It really convolutes the whole deal." The crowd of well-meaning but burdensome volunteers swelled, aggravating the authorities' headache—some people, as Vixen memorably put it, "showing up in flip-flops" in order to head out into treacherously rough and rugged terrain; "bubbas," in intra-NPS slang: arrogant, underprepared idiots who blunder into the wilderness with no idea what they're doing, liable to get hurt or lost and then themselves require rescuing, thereby sapping resources and attention away from the very mission they showed up to "help" with.

By the time Wes and Vixen got there late in the day, the staging area was a zoo, with the kind of logistical management problems reminiscent of a crowded sports event or concert; it was becoming difficult to find a place to park, and the emergency responders were beginning to have to worry about traffic jams on the rocky, narrow dirt road.

At this point there occurred one of those irreconcilable factual disagreements in which one of two people must be remembering things incorrectly. George Stowe-Rains told me that the inundation of untrained volunteers gumming things up and making the search-and-rescue operation more difficult had become such a problem that "we were getting ready to get somebody to help us—State Police, National Park Service, somebody, some law enforcement agency—to just block the road and say, 'No, if you're not trained, if you can't show us credentials, you're gonna have to just go away,'" Vixen James, however, remembers that they did in fact do exactly that: Incident Command sent a park ranger to set up a roadblock near AR-21 toward the bottom of the east side of Cave Mountain Road and stationed him there to vet the volunteers trying to drive up, controlling whom they allowed in to participate in the search.

I am going to side with Vixen's memory, because he has a good and very personal reason to remember that roadblock's place in the story: Among the local residents of Newton County who went out to Cave Mountain volunteering to help with the search and who were turned away were his father, Lytle James, and his father's neighbor, good friend, and frequent hunting buddy, William Jeff Villines. Both men had been born and raised there, and both were experienced hunters who had spent their lives bushwhacking off the trails, tracking game in the hills and thorny gullies of the Buffalo River valley. Vixen's great-great-grandfather on his father's side had settled in the Ozarks in 1901, and his mother's family, the Fowlers (a family that will become important later), had been there since the middle of the nineteenth century. Vixen's father was the youngest of twelve children and had worked as a lineman for Carroll Electric for forty years in an area that had not had much electricity when he started; he had climbed utility poles beside every tiny backroad in Newton County, and he had a map of it county engraved on his soul. After he retired from the electric company, he and his wife had focused on their small cattle farm of a hundred acres and about fifty cows. "My dad was just a simple country person," Vixen said (Lytle James died at the age of eighty in 2017). William Jeff Villines came from a sprawling family that had settled in the Ozarks before the Civil War; drive around in Newton County, and you'll see the Villines name on the side of a mailbox in just about every bank of mailboxes on the shoulder of the highway beside a turnoff down a little dirt road. William Jeff was a full-time farmer, as his father had been and on the same land. Vixen: "He was a true mountain man, William Jeff's dad was, and therefore, William Jeff, same deal, had all those skills. Both William Jeff and my dad's land butts up through National Park Service land. So they both spent their whole life in that area up of the Buffalo River, fishing, river hunting, small game, deer, turkey, and stuff like that. But William Jeff especially was truly an outdoorsman, a true mountain man."

It is also worth noting that the large and spread-out Villines clan was hit particularly hard by the eminent domain episode in the 1970s. Quite a few of William Jeff's close relations had lost houses they had lived in all their lives and that had been in the family for generations, and the National Park Service had strong-armed his own father out of hundreds of acres; thus, the farm William Jeff inherited had been substantially reduced from what it had once been.

When these two men, who knew that specific area of wilderness as intimately as anyone alive in the world, showed up to volunteer their time, sweat, and deep knowledge to help rescue the six-year-old girl they had heard was lost there, they arrived at a roadblock at the bottom of Cave Mountain, where an employee of the National Park Service—an organization to which William Jeff Villines in particular was very much not personally endeared—asked to see their "credentials," and when they could produce none, turned them away. Go home, let the professionals handle this.

"Naturally," Vixen said, "that was a frustrating thing." Although he was quick to say he didn't blame Incident Command for the decision to set up the roadblock: "A lot of people don't understand that it was kind of a needed thing. If whoever was standing at that roadblock would've known that Dad and William Jeff knew the territory like they did, I'm sure they would've let 'em through. But just because there were so many people, that's how it initially happened that they got turned away."

It was Vixen who had called his father from his cell phone while he and Wes were driving up from Fort Chaffee and told him that a little girl, his friend Steve's daughter, had gotten lost near Hawksbill Crag on Cave Mountain. It was that call that had prompted Lytle James and William Jeff Villines to drive over there, where the park ranger manning the roadblock had turned them away. That had probably already happened by the time Vixen and Wes, who would have been coming from the other direction, arrived at the staging area (apparently there wasn't a roadblock at the west end of Cave Mountain Road). When they got there, Haley had been missing for more than five hours, and the search-and-rescue operation was in full swing: helicopters thwacking overhead, Incident Command trying to manage everything amidst the increasingly frustrated crowd of well-meaning yahoos, the media there by then with cameras and microphones and satellite dishes to further fuck things up for the authorities. Vixen and Wes were in their National Guard uniforms and were quickly let into the inner circle of police, park rangers, and other emergency responders buzzing about the central hub of the church and its parking lot, and from then on they were in the thick of things, attendant at every command briefing, either out in the woods searching and reporting back, or helping coordinate logistics and supplies. Vixen recalls getting the National Guard to bring in tents, food, a few water buffaloes (big water tanks on trailers), and more personnel from Fort Chaffee. The next thirty hours or so smear together in his memory. Sometime deep in the night he caught an hour or two of sleep on a cot in one of the tents that had been brought up from Fort Chaffee; Wes Hilliard didn't get any sleep at all, and neither did George Stowe-Rains. Throughout Monday, it was more of the same: teams methodically searching the highest-probability-of-success segments of the grid, the helicopters still circling and still coming up with nothing, a lot of K-9 units searching with dogs. (George Stowe-Rains: "Every police department in Northwest Arkansas wanted to send a canine over. But if they're not trained in search and rescue, if they're just trained in law enforcement stuff, they're not really a benefit.")

At some point during the day on Monday Vixen called his father again—the mobile cell towers that had been set up at various points on Cave Mountain by then made that possible—and Lytle James told his son that he and William Jeff had gone out there offering to help with the search the day before and had been turned away. And that had pretty well pissed them off. Bear in mind the government's historical role in the lives of Buffalo River valley residents as an ignorant and impersonal juggernaut of meddlesome ineptitude most recently notable for about-facing on its plan to bury everyone under an artificial lake and instead sending guys in suits to bully little old ladies into selling houses their grandfathers had built for less than market value, all for the apparent benefit of the tubers and kayakers they had always gotten along with just fine before. Their general attitude calls to mind Reagan's famous quip about the nine most terrifying words in the English language: "I'm from the government, and I'm here to help." They had been told, thanks but no thanks, the government has got this under control, go away. Fine then, we leave you, in your infinite wisdom, to it. His father was in a sulk about it.

Meanwhile, Vixen got back to work. Throughout that day, he felt himself in an awkward place, pinched between conflicting responsibilities. He had grown up in precisely this area of the Ozarks, and he knew it far better than the people who were in charge of the mission; however, he wasn't specifically trained in search and rescue, and as a military lifer he knew his place in the chain of command and wasn't in a position to question the decisions of the people higher up in it who had more expertise in this kind of work. But his gut instinct nagged at him about the trained search-and-rescue guys' faith in the efficacy of CASIE's algorithmic data crunching: { [(six-year-old girl) + (point last seen) + (weather) + (map of terrain)] + [absence of evidence of her having fallen off the bluff] } = highest-POS areas must be somewhere on the mountain on top of the bluff or higher. No one seemed to be entertaining the possibility that Haley had somehow gotten down the mountain and into the valley. No one was searching in the low ground. "As a liaison guy, I wasn't going to point out that, Hey, I think she's gone down," Vixen told me. "And I'm not belittling anything they were doing in the patterns, but we weren't getting down deep, or very far away from the starting point. And I *know* that Dad and William Jeff hands down knew that area as well as anybody that was out there. So Monday night, I grabbed the chaplain. I said, We're going to the house, grab a quick bite to eat, take a shower. I was going to convince Dad to come back. Of course he's pretty stubborn. He got his feelings hurt 'cause he got turned away. I said, 'Dad, you gotta come back. You gotta go down deep.' And he said, 'Well, we're not goin' out there to check in.' I said, 'You ain't gotta check in.' Which was against the rules, but I told him, 'You can go up and park at the campground. That's where you need to start out anyway, and run that creek.' He got on the phone with William Jeff and said, 'We're loadin' up at daylight.' And William Jeff said the same thing, about not wanting to check in. And Dad goes, 'We ain't checkin' in.'"

Here we come across another seemingly irreconcilable factual disagreement between George Stowe-Rains and Vixen James. George said he remembers that Lytle James and William Jeff Villines arrived at the Command Post at the church on the morning of the third day—Tuesday, May 1—and told the officials there that they planned to search down by the river on mules. He remembers having a conversation with them along with Jeff West. "And we thought that was a great idea," he recalled, "and we asked them if they would take a radio in case they did make a find, they could radio us. They did not want a radio. And they left." George remembers the conversation, remembers offering to give them a radio, and very distinctly remembers their refusing to take it for mysterious unstated reasons. Vixen, on the other hand, said that his father and William Jeff set out on their own that morning without trying to check in with Incident Command or communicating with anyone. There you have it; I simply feel I have to raise this caveat before continuing to narrate Vixen's version.

Early in the morning on Tuesday, the first day of May 2001, Lytle James and William Jeff Villines packed a bunch of snacks they thought a six-year-old girl might like—little plastic tubs of chocolate pudding and, weirdly, some bottles of Diet Coke—plus a camera, loaded two mules named Copper and Big Mama into a horse trailer, and towed it with Lytle's truck to the parking lot at the trailhead just off the east end of Cave Mountain Road for the trail that leads to Bat Cave (where Confederate soldiers used to mine saltpeter-rich bat guano for gunpowder; don't look for it now—the cave is officially closed to prevent human contact from spreading white-nose syndrome, a fungal disease affecting the endangered bats, and the trail leading to it is gone). On muleback they descended from Bat Cave Trail down a steep embankment to the Buffalo River and began making their way through the valley alongside its north bank.

Some months after all this happened, *Dateline NBC* aired an episode about it, in which the tan, slim, handsome *Dateline NBC* anchor Rob Stafford interviewed them sitting on some rocks beside the Buffalo: two aging men, clean shaven and heavyset in button-down shirts, Lytle wearing an Arkansas Razorbacks cap and William Jeff in a forest green cap with mesh sides and the white lettering *Villines* Hill Farm" across the front; the interview includes this mildly hilarious exchange:

Lytle James: When the government gets involved and the news media gets involved—you know, we didn't want to go gettin' mixed up in that. We didn't know what they was plottin' out, but we knew what *we* could do.

Rob Stafford: You're saying you have more trust in yourselves than you do in the media and the government?

[Awkward pause.]

William Jeff Villines: Well, for one thing, they was tellin' you where to hunt.

Leaving aside that one hears in the sheer incredulity of Rob Stafford's question a splendidly myopic prophecy of twenty years of red/blue culture war politics to come, there is a telling difference between what the trained search-and-rescue experts were doing and what Lytle and William Jeff were doing, implicit in William Jeff's choice of verb: hunt. The skill that Lytle and William Jeff brought to the search was the one they had honed over many years tracking game in that same wilderness. They were, essentially, tracking an animal: a four-foot-tall, forty-nine-pound, six-year-old female *Homo sapiens*. You can also hear it in another comment William Jeff made during the *Dateline NBC* interview: "We got to thinkin' that, well, if anything's wounded or anything's lost, most all time they'll go down to the river." And he told Tim Ernst, "You won't find the game if you don't have any sign." Because Lytle James died in 2017 and William Jeff Villines was recently debilitated by a severe stroke, I am forced to rely on sources who interviewed them at the time, and Tim Ernst's account in his self-published book *The Search for Haley: An Insider's Account of the Largest Search Mission in Arkansas History* is the fullest. "Sign," he wrote, "can be anything from tracks to scat to pawed areas in the dirt, or even broken branches where an animal—or a little girl—has passed."

Lytle James and William Jeff Villines were at home and in their natural element on muleback in rugged and difficult terrain—in *these* woods, on the bank of *this* river, in *these* mountains, in *this* vast wilderness. The two men—both of them grandfathers by now—had been born and bred here with a century of bloodlines behind them—this wilderness was where their fathers had taught them to hunt and they had taught their children to hunt. A place where one can swivel from twelve o'clock back to twelve o'clock without seeing a single man-made object might look like chaos to most people, but to them the wilderness abounded with information; they knew every faint game trail and inlet of the river and had personal memories of specific trees, all in warm human connection to everyday life and to their childhoods. Their eyes could see subtle patterns and clues invisible to a stranger to these woods—or to helicopters with heat sensors, or the algorithms of computer programs.

The two men on mules clopped along the bottom of the bluff line above the west bank of the river through dense foliage from early in the morning until the early afternoon, passing through Dug Hollow, beneath Tim's cabin and Hawksbill Crag, and then went down to the river where Whitaker Creek feeds into it. At around one thirty they rested briefly on the bank of the Buffalo to eat lunch and let their mules drink from the river. Then they turned around and headed back in the direction they'd come, continuing to search alongside the river. They had been out all day without seeing any kind of sign, and by that point they were beginning to grow doubtful they would find Haley.

Riding along the north bank of the river, they were looking for a place where they could get back onto the mountain, but couldn't find a passable gap in the steep and rocky terrain at the bottom of the slope. "That wasn't God's plan," Lytle James said, "because we never could find a place. We had to go back to the river, and that's where we found the track."

When they returned to Dug Hollow, William Jeff saw a sign: what appeared to be a small human footprint in the riverbank mud. "We weren't certain if it was a bear track because she was such a small child it didn't make a deep imprint, but we both decided it was hers," he said. "I can't describe how rough the terrain is down there, but we had to keep getting off our mules because it was too bad to ride."

Not long after seeing what they agreed could be a little girl's footprint in the mud, William Jeff spotted a poisonous cottonmouth snake coiled on a flat river rock, sunning itself in the warm afternoon. He pointed it out to Lytle, and the two men nodded and cautiously trotted past the snake without disturbing it.

At around two in the afternoon, when they neared an alcove of the Buffalo River valley about 830 feet below and two miles north of the main search area, Lytle pointed at something he saw perhaps 200 yards away, on the other bank of the river. William Jeff said it looked like an old shirt or something that had washed up on the bank. They approached slowly splashing across that shallow stretch of the river on their mules, gradually deciphering that what they were looking at was indeed a little girl, lying on a slab of rock about the size of a coffee table beside a small inlet of eddying water, with her shoes and one wadded pink sock next to her and her bare feet in the water. Her legs were blue, and she wasn't moving. They feared she was dead. When they had closed their distance to about twenty yards, they called her name. No response.

William Jeff said, "You're the little girl that everyone's been looking for." Still no movement that they could discern.

Then, Lytle told Tim, "I said, 'Your mother, father, and grandparents are waiting up on the road to take you home.' Then she raised up her little head."

The plastic tubs of chocolate pudding and a bottle of Diet Coke were the first sustenance she had taken in since before she had gone missing. She wasn't quite fifty pounds when she got lost, and she'd lost seven of them by the time Lytle James and William Jeff Villines found her.

"I remember sitting on a ledge, by the river," Haley told me recently. "And then I see the mules, the people on the mules, William Jeff Villines and Lytle James, and they came up to me. People ask me all the time, 'How did you know that they were okay? How did you know you could go with them?' I didn't have a choice. It was people. . . . I remember he carved a spoon for me to use out of a little sapling. A little makeshift spoon. They brought me snacks, because they knew they were going to find me."

It took another nearly three hours to ride from the spot beside the river near Dug Hollow where James and Villines found Haley back to Cave Mountain Road, stopping periodically to alternate the mule they put her on so as not to overburden either animal for too long. Lytle's mule, Big Mama, was named for her size; she was so wide that Haley remembers "doing the splits" on her back. At a few points the grade was so steep and the brush so thick that they all dismounted, and William Jeff carried Haley on his back while Lytle led the mules. Haley was exhausted, and slept for much of the ride back. She was cold, and Lytle quite literally gave her the shirt off his back; in one of the photographs he took, you can see her riding on Copper in front of William Jeff, swimming in Lytle's polo shirt; Lytle went bare chested for the rest of the journey. They planned to ride back to the place where they had parked Lytle's truck and horse trailer at the Bat Cave Trailhead toward the bottom of Cave Mountain Road, and then drive Haley up to the Command Center at the top of the mountain. But just a few minutes after they finally emerged from the woods onto the road, a car came rumbling up the road; riding in it were three friends of Steve and Kelly: Mark and Dawn Gieringer and Christy Lundsford, who had been Kelly's assistant when she worked at the University of Arkansas Alumni Association. They had gone on a supply run and were bringing food and water up to the staging area. At first Lytle and William Jeff were wary about handing her off to anyone else; they had worked pretty hard to rescue her, and they wanted to be the ones to bring her back. But they could see that Haley knew Christy Lundsford, and in another moment another car drove up; in it was Roger Atkinson, an Arkansas Forestry Commission ranger, who quickly persuaded them to let him drive Haley and Christy to the church. It was 5:18. Atkinson radioed Incident Command, told them that Haley had been found, he had her, and to get an ambulance ready for her arrival. Mark and Dawn Gieringer continued up the mountain in their car, and Roger followed them with Haley and Christy in the back of his. Lytle and William Jeff rode their mules back down the road to their rig, loaded the animals into the trailer, and drove up the mountain about twenty minutes behind the others.

Back up on top of the mountain, a collective feeling of deflation had followed the press conference. Tim Ernst drove Steve and Kelly back to his house on the corner of the bluff. On the way he began with, "I don't know if this is the right time to ask you this," and told them that he had the authority, via his connections with the Arkansas Forestry Commission, which regarded him as steward of this particular area of the Ozarks, to name unnamed landmarks; that particular waterfall where Haley had last been seen had no name; what did they think of naming it after her? "And I was like immediately, 'Yes, yes, yes, please,'" Kelly told me. "I loved that so much. I wouldn't say that it made me smile, but it was just like this unbelievable kindness. And some people might say, 'What, is that like a tribute? Like you're saying she's gone?' But for me it was like, 'No, this mattered to her, and this is part of her narrative and that waterfall will be there forever. Long after Haley.'"

The atmosphere on top of the mountain had tilted, slouching and exhausted and still empty handed, into a new phase, one of steeply diminishing hope. With a missing person, the critical rescue window is the first forty-eight hours; after that, the chances of finding the person alive drop precipitously. At around five o'clock on Tuesday, May 1, 2001, they were at hour fifty-four since Haley had last been seen. Some of the friends who had come out to help with the search or to comfort the family had gone home; they couldn't take off work indefinitely, and their kids still had to go to school. Life, for many people, was beginning to return to its daily rhythms without Haley in it. People were turning their thoughts toward naming unmovable things in her memory. Colleen Nick, whose daughter had been missing for six years and who of course was painfully familiar herself with this normalization stage, was by then driving back down to her home in Fort Smith, as her own children needed her.

Kelly recalled that she was sweeping the floor of Tim's cabin because "it gave me something to do," when the phone rang. Tim answered it, and came to tell her that her friend Kelly Carter wanted to speak with her. Kelly Carter was a former coworker from the University of Arkansas administration and a close friend, and the two Kellys had been pregnant at the same time; Carter's daughter, Elizabeth, had been born three months before Haley, and their daughters had gone to preschool together. Kelly Carter and her husband, Phil, had been out there with them on Monday, but they, too, had returned home—work, school. Kelly Carter told Kelly Zega that she'd just seen on the news that Haley had been found. Was it true?

"I don't know what you're talking about," said Kelly. "This is a very close friend, so I wasn't mad at her, but I was just kind of like, 'What the fuck? No. No.' And what is going on that they're announcing this on the news? Because we did a press conference, but she's not been found. And so I was like 'Well, no. We have no information, so I don't know what you're talking about.' And she was apologizing. She was so sorry. She probably thought she'd upset me even more. I hung up the phone, and I didn't even say anything to anybody, because that just really disturbed me. Of course she hasn't been found, because we will be the first people to know."

Kelly wandered in a daze onto Tim's front porch, where her husband and a bunch of other people were sitting, people who had come back from searching the woods stopping to rest, eat, and rehydrate before heading back out again. Kelly recalled that Dennis and Michelle Boles were there, as well as Clay and Cathy Bass. It was late in the afternoon, and the shadows were lengthening toward the end of the third day with no sign of her daughter. Kelly was wondering if she should tell anyone about the disturbing phone conversation she'd just had when she heard the sound of gravel spitting under the wheels of a car coming down the rough road to Tim's cabin. It was a red Chevy Tahoe; it stopped in front of the cabin, and the Sheriff of Washington County, Steve Whitmill, who happened to be a personal friend of Steve and Kelly, stepped out of the driver's seat and walked toward the cabin with a serious look on his face. He stopped, looked up at Kelly, smiled and said—when Kelly tells the story, this line is its climactic peak—"I got a little girl who's asking for her mama." Kelly flung herself down the steps and hugged him so frantically that she hit her face on his elbow and gave herself a minor black eye.

"They've got her in an ambulance," Whitmill said. "They're checking her out. She is alive, and she seems to be okay. Come on, get in the car. I'm gonna take you to her."

Kelly opened the car door, then remembered Haley's security blanket, the one she'd held at the press conference that afternoon. She ran back inside Tim's cabin, scrambled around until she found it, and then Sheriff Whitmill drove her and Steve to Cave Mountain Church, about two miles and five rollicky minutes away, where Haley was sitting in the back of an ambulance in the parking lot. Steve and Kelly climbed into the back of the ambulance with her and found their daughter spent and dazed, not smiling, not talking. Kelly couldn't hug her as violently as she wanted to because the paramedics already had one of her arms stinted with an IV drip in it; it turned out to be the wrong arm because it was the one with the thumb she would suck.

Meanwhile, Lytle James and William Jeff Villines had made it up to Incident Command in their truck, towing the horse trailer with the mules in it. Initially a cop yelled at them about parking their trailer there, but they managed to successfully explain that they were the two guys who had just rescued Haley, and in the end they were permitted to park their rig in the church lot.*

Vixen James was at the Command Center when the news came over the radio that Haley had been located at one of the checkpoints down the road. He didn't know yet if it was his father and William Jeff who'd found her, but he had a strong hunch that it was. Forest ranger Roger Atkinson delivered her to Incident Command, and Christy Lundsford stepped out of the back of his car with Haley. There were media people everywhere, TV cameras rolling. Information trickled through the crowd, confirming that she'd been found by two old men on mules, locals—then he knew for sure. Some minutes later, his father and William Jeff pulled up in the truck with the trailer, the mules nuzzling the air at its windows. His father was shirtless, as he'd put his shirt on Haley. Vixen thought about all the cameras filming the men who'd saved the lost girl stepping out of their truck, and saw his father bare above the

---

* I feel I should reiterate that I am in no way trying to depict the authorities running the official search-and-rescue operation in a negative light. It's a testament to his dedication to the mission that George Stowe-Rains was awake for the entire fifty-four hours Haley was missing; and when it was over, George said, "I left there and went to my son's baseball game at Walker Park in Fayetteville, still wearing my uniform I'd had on for three days."

waist except for his Razorbacks cap, and "of course he didn't have no tan—so here I'm thinking, 'Oh, my gosh, all these TV cameras, and my dad with his dang white belly and white back.' That'd be some deal to be on TV, here's the rescue guy, some country hick that looks white as a sheet. So I took off my military blouse and gave it to him."

At about 5:30 on Tuesday, May 1, Haley Zega, reunited with her parents, was taken by ambulance to the North Arkansas Regional Medical Center in Harrison, where she was treated for dehydration. There was nothing else wrong with her, and the hospital released her the next morning.

Tim Ernst made good on his promise to name the waterfall where the trouble began for Haley. It's now officially called Haley Falls, and Haley has climbed down that tree to see it many times since.

5

The Buffalo National River Wilderness

Tɪᴍ Eʀɴsᴛ, ᴡʜᴏ ᴀᴛ ᴛʜᴇ ᴛɪᴍᴇ ʟɪᴠᴇᴅ ɪɴ ᴛʜᴇ ᴄᴀʙɪɴ ʜᴇ ᴄᴀʟʟᴇᴅ Cloudland at the edge of the bluff, loves the land and knows it so well, he's written a few books about it. He bought the property together with his friend Bob—i.e., "Doc"—Chester in 1990. Bob Chester died a decade ago, and a few years ago Tim sold his part of the property and said goodbye to Cloudland; very off-the-grid living doesn't mix well with aging. He lives on the other side of the mountain now, about ten minutes outside of Jasper, in a much more convenient spot that's not *quite* as beautiful or remote. Tim is as loving and knowledgeable a scholar, geographer, and historian of this particular patch of the planet as one can hope to become, and he spent much of the summer of 2001 doing a lot of sylvan detective work trying to figure out where exactly Haley had gone. He thinks he more or less figured it out, and I defer to him.

If you go up Hawksbill Crag Trail from the waterfall heading north, you will see the fork—the path on the left goes to the trailhead, and the one on the right leads along the edge of the bluff, passes the crag, and continues from there until it veers left, away from the top of the cliffs, and to the untrained eye disappears into the forest floor (Haley's eye was not trained). But right after that fork, there are several places where the trail forks briefly and then rejoins itself. This often happens to hiking trails; many hikers over much time taking a slightly alternate path around a cluster of rocks or something gradually stamp out a little side trail. I don't really consider them separate trails, and it is especially true of the Hawksbill Crag Trail, where the slight deviations run so close together that different people hiking on the two briefly parallel trails would be able to clearly see each other. But again, it was spring, the vegetation was thick and shady, and Haley was a very short person. Tim thinks that Haley took one of these little side-trails and somehow walked right past Clay Bass without either of them seeing each other. Or perhaps Joyce and Haley passed each other that way, and Clay, with his adult legs, was ahead of her and she never caught up to him. But when Joyce was searching for her on the part of the trail that leads to the trailhead, Haley kept following the other part of the trail along the bluff, passing the crag, and continued on, missing the place where the others had turned left and headed up to the cabin. She kept on going, following the trail past that NO TRESPASSING sign and onto Tim's property, and kept walking right past Tim's cabin.

Haley does not remember it ("I didn't see any houses—because if I had seen any sign of people, I would have, you know, gone to the people"), but apparently right after she was found, she told adults about seeing a house where it looked like no one was home and walking past it. Perhaps she did not yet know she was lost. Tim probably was at home then, and that house would be the place where her anguished parents would stay for the next two nights. She may have passed the cabin and at some point started following a narrow game trail that led her to a part of the bluff a good ways north of Tim's cabin where the grade of the slope becomes obtuse enough to climb down into the part of the valley called Dug Hollow. Haley is certain that she climbed down off the bluff that first day, and from then on she was just blindly pushing through densely wooded wilderness until she came to the Buffalo River. She told me:

> I made it to the river that first day. I just remember walking and
> walking and walking, and I still had this belief that I was going to

walk myself out of the woods. And I remember there were these gnats that would fly in front of my eyes, and it was pissing me off. I was getting angry at all these bugs for flying in my eyes. So I would swat at them. And I was getting very hungry, but I didn't know if anything was safe to eat, so I didn't try to eat anything. I remember climbing down a very steep incline. I didn't know that there was a river. But I got down the incline, I walked a couple of yards, and all of a sudden through the trees I remember seeing—I probably heard it first—I could hear the water, and then I remember seeing it through the trees and seeing the light shine off the water, and I was like, Okay, river. So I went to the river. And I remember there were helicopters that were flying over. I was this inexperienced—I didn't know if it was normal for helicopters to be flying over the forest. I didn't know they were looking for me. I just thought, "Okay, well, if there are helicopters, it would probably be good if they could see me. Because this is a sign of people." So I started shouting my name, and I was throwing sand in the air to try to get them to see me, and they just never did. But then once I got to the river, I had a new plan. My plan was—and honestly, not to discount myself as a kindergartner, but I don't know how I knew this—but: rivers always eventually lead to a bridge—or civilization. So follow the river, it'll lead to a bridge, it'll lead to a road, the road will lead to a gas station, and I will call my parents. That was my plan as soon as I found the river: Follow the water.

I have been to Cloudland a number of times now, at various times of the year. It's been twenty-three years since Haley got lost there, and time has changed the trails.

I often think about trails, pathways, roads; they interest and enchant me in a vague, poetic way I have trouble articulating. If you ask me to, I will probably at some point mention Bruce Chatwin's *The Songlines* and Robert Macfarlane's *The Old Ways: A Journey on Foot*. Or Jakob von Uex-küll, the polymathic pioneer of biosemiotics, who included an elegant chapter entitled "The Familiar Path" in his quirky essay *A Foray into the Worlds of Animals and Humans*, in which he wrote, "All in all, one could say that the familiar path works like a streak of a more fluid medium in a more viscous one."

I've read deeply in psychogeography—defined by that word's coiner, Guy Debord, as "the study of the precise laws and specific effects of the geographical environment, consciously organised or not, on the emotions and behaviour of individuals," and if you read up on that word, you are sure to uncover the theories of Alfred Watkins, an early-twentieth-century British scholar who hovers in a space between legitimate archaeologist and kook, who wrote about "ley lines" in his 1925 book *The Old Straight Track: Its Mounds, Beacons, Moats, Sites and Mark Stones*: the straight lines across the countryside of the British Isles connecting long-gone historical structures or landmarks, often tracing ridges of high ground through a landscape, which he believed were the trade routes of ancient societies. It makes sense that pathways would lead from one high elevation point to the next—best to get a wide visual survey of the land, to see the weather coming in, to spot potential predators or enemies from afar—but there is another something, spooky and magical, in Watkins's tone and approach to the subject matter, which is the thing that barred him from wider scientific credence in his own lifetime and afterward and is precisely the thing that most interests me about his ley lines: He had a mystic reverence for the earth, for landscape, for land, and for the patterns and habits of the people and animals that traverse it. The rhythms of breathing and patient regular footfalls are connected to poetry and song, and when you walk along a path through the woods, you move along a line of living animal energy. A trail is made by all the bodies that have traveled it before you, and every pathway is a streamline of ghosts. Some of these streaks of "a more fluid medium in a more viscous one" are so well trodden, the stream of ghosts so thick and old, that I bet they'll still be there for at least another hundred years—like the one I drive on nearly every day, the Old Albany Post Road: one of the oldest roads in the United States, which has connected New York City to Albany since 1669; it begins in Manhattan as Broadway, and the part of it that now passes near my house a hundred miles north of the city is New York Route 9. The ghost lines in the Buffalo National River Wilderness are of course much fainter, but they are there.

The one that Jay, Joyce, Haley, and their friends took on the morning of Sunday, April 28, 2001, which once led from Doc Chester's cabin down to the unofficial part of the Hawksbill Crag Trail along the bluff to the east of the crag is not entirely there anymore; too few souls have passed along it since then to maintain its existence. About fifty feet from Hawksbill Crag there is still a trail you can just barely make out that leads up onto a shelf of higher land and passes a few firepits, but above that, it disappears into dense brush. You can't even easily follow the remnants of Hawksbill Crag Trail to what used to be Tim's house on the bluff anymore; whoever owns the house now has not kept it clear, and enough hikers obey that Private Property sign that now the only way to reach that house on foot from the trail involves shoving your way through chest-high thickets of brambles that will leave your clothes peppered with nettles that prick like thumbtacks. But the faintest phantom thread of human and animal movement through it is still there. There's still a streak of the more fluid medium there, but it is barely distinguishable from the more viscous wilderness around it, the signal nearly buried in noise. But the signal is still there. The path Haley probably took from the waterfall all the way down to the Buffalo River used to be a mule trail in the nineteenth and twentieth centuries, when there were people living down in the valley. It most likely began to vanish into brush in the 1970s after the National Park System forced the valley's residents out and people quit using it. It descends the southern slope of Dug Hollow down into the river valley through the only gap in the bluff line's sharp, rocky edge where the grade is gentle enough to traverse it without having to turn around and climb down backward using all four limbs. Tim insists that the remnant of the old mule trail has become a little game trail that runs through that gap, and although the only people with eyes trained enough to see it would probably be seasoned local hunters such as Lytle James and William Jeff Villines, he thinks it was probably that faint ley line, that almost invisibly thin streamline of ghosts, that Haley, perhaps without consciously knowing it, followed.

There used to be a shortcut right at the corner of the bluff where Tim's old house is. When he bought the property in 1990, there was still a thick old wooden ladder with rungs rubbed smooth by generations of hands permanently leaning against the edge of the cliff, welded into the rocks by time and weather, just beyond his back deck beneath the house. The people who used to live in the valley climbed into and out of it regularly on the ladder. There are still the ruins of five or six houses down there, all gone except for the foundations and chimneys half buried under the foliage. For perhaps a hundred years or so, the children who lived in the valley would go that way on their way to school: walk up the old mule trail, climb the ladder, then take the road—now the private road that leads to Tim's house—to Cave Mountain Church, later the search-and-rescue Command Center, which at the time doubled as a one-room schoolhouse during the week. That's a journey of about two miles with an eight-hundred-foot elevation gain, made by children mostly likely barefoot except in the coldest months of winter—and then back down again home after school. Tim told me that after he had first bought the property, old-timers who had grown up there, people whose families had been displaced by the government via eminent domain in the 1970s, often came out there to see the view of the valley from the high point on the bluff where the ladder led from the mule trail to the road and told him stories about it. When the water in the river was high, the mule trail that went up through Dug Hollow with the shortcut up the ladder to the top of the bluff was the only way to get out of the valley. More than one of those visitors told him an anecdote about an old man who had lived in the valley, who happened to die down there when the water was high; his family had carried his corpse on muleback up the trail, then had to carefully haul it up the ladder with a rope and pulley in order to lay him to rest in Cave Mountain Cemetery.

The route Haley walked from the waterfall to the river on that first day, if Tim's detective work is right, is only about two miles as the crow flies, but the last half mile of it involved scrabbling down a precariously steep and rocky slope of pure wilderness. Looking at a map of the terrain, one sees that Haley's hearing the river immediately after determining she had reached the bottom of the slope tracks pretty well: Cave Mountain shoots upward directly out of the west bank of the Buffalo River. And then she started walking along the river. Incredibly, she swim-waded across it several times—and again, this was in April, when the water is at its deepest and the current at its fastest. She believes she was walking in the same direction the whole time, but it is possible—especially considering she did not eat or drink anything after breakfast Sunday morning for nearly three days—she got turned around in a delirium and doubled back over the same ground more than once. Most of the ground she covered she covered on that first day: the place where James and Villines found her is not quite two miles north of the approximate spot where Tim thinks she reached the river.

Haley spent the first night lying on top of a flat-topped boulder beside the river. She said she did this because she wanted to be in the most visible place possible for the helicopters to see her. The helicopters—equipped with heat sensors—were indeed shuttling back and forth over the valley all night, but they never spotted her. (The reason the heat sensors didn't pick up Haley may have been because boulders stay warm long after nightfall—that's why cold-blooded snakes curl up on them at night—and the stored heat of the rock might have swallowed the heat signal of Haley's body.) When the sun rose, she climbed down from the rock and kept walking beside the river.

When night fell on the second day, she remembered her mother telling her that a hazy ring around the moon means that rain is coming. There was a hazy ring around the moon, so she climbed a little way up the mountain on the east bank of the Buffalo and took shelter for the night in a small cave—not even a cave, really, more of a divot in the rocks with just enough of a ceiling to keep the rain off. "I don't think it was good sleep," she said. "It was sort of more just, like, dozing, like a hypnotic. . . . It was sort of like a stupor, basically. It was not restful sleep."

The sun rose again. "And then the third day it was more of the same.

Just kept walking." At some point she began to hallucinate. "When you start to starve, when you start to dehydrate, people hallucinate all the time. I hallucinated people in the trees. I hallucinated family members. I hallucinated a valley full of flamingoes. I just remember coming around a bend in the river, and the flamingoes were everywhere. I don't know when. It could have been day two. It could have been day three. Honestly, once I got to the river, the days were kind of monotonous. I wasn't really doing anything to distinguish one from the other." Lytle James and William Jeff Villines found her at about two in the afternoon that third day, probably around the same time that Kelly, up on top of the mountain, was pleading into TV cameras, addressing an imagined stranger she feared had abducted her daughter.

Although by Tuesday afternoon Haley's parents had begun to fear the worst—a human abductor—it comforts me to remember Kelly's first reaction on the first night her daughter was missing upon learning that Colleen Nick had asked to speak with her: that surprising spark of anger. The idea that Haley might have been abducted by some pedophile was a drumbeat that began faintly the first day when Dennis Boles thought to drive back to the parking lot at the trailhead to see if any cars were missing and jot down the plate numbers, and got louder and louder until the third day, when Steve and Kelly themselves had started to become convinced of it. Kelly's first instinct was annoyance at the absurdity of the notion; it makes more sense for some predatory kidnapper to lurk around a Little League game, which was where Colleen Nick believes her daughter was taken, but why on earth would one be hiding in a remote wilderness on top of a mountain thirty miles away from the nearest traffic light? You have to start thinking in a sinister vein to even begin to come up with plausible explanations—like maybe he *followed* them there. . . . Or perhaps there did just happen to be an evil pedophile also out breathing the fresh mountain air, smelling the wildflowers, and enjoying the beauty of nature that day who had pounced on the opportunity to kidnap a lost six-year-old girl. Kelly had thought the idea absurd at first—Haley had not been abducted; she had to be right there somewhere in the woods—and in the end, the moral paranoia that imagines child rapists hiding behind trees in the forest turned out to be wrong and her initial gut instinct turned out to be absolutely right.

The scene of Steve and Kelly taking their daughter home to Fayetteville on the morning of Wednesday, May 2, 2001, is a TV cliché you can well imagine: a crowd of reporters and news anchors on the lawn, vans of many different media organizations with satellite dishes on top jamming up the ordinarily quiet suburban street, mailbox stuffed to overflowing with cards and letters from well-wishers, many from people the family knew and many not, including one from Robin Williams, who had been following the story. Haley said no to appearing on *Oprah* because she didn't know who Oprah Winfrey was. I think it is a testament to the maturity of Steve and Kelly's judgment that this decision was apparently Haley's call. They did say yes to some media coverage, like the local news outlets, and the *Dateline NBC* episode later that year. But after the initial burst of attention, they wanted more than anything else to get back to their ordinary lives. They were completely uninterested in getting famous or profiting off of their daughter.

After being home for two days, Steve and Kelly decided it would be best to leave town for a a little while, enough dead time to make the crowd of reporters on the lawn go away. They asked Haley where she wanted to go, and her favorite thing she had seen in her very short life was the Gateway Arch in St. Louis, which they had visited before on another family vacation. So they took off for St. Louis, where they spent a long weekend, and on Monday Haley was back in kindergarten, having missed only a week of kindergarten.

It was during the drive up to St. Louis, about five hours from Fayetteville, that Haley. who must have been in a very unusual state of mind after having just gone through a harrowing and physically grueling experience followed by two days of being made to feel like a superstar, told her parents—told anyone for the first time—about her "imaginary friend," Alecia.

This side of my family—my father's, the Hales—is not particularly religious, nor inclined to pay much attention to the fairies that flutter in the spiritual spectrum between brute magic and faith. My mother's parents, the Campbells, also generations-deep Arkansans, were devout Southern Baptists. But the Hale side, by far the closer and happier side, were mostly agnostics, areligious, some soft-core Easter Christians the most pious among them (i.e., a Christian who only goes to church on Easter, like a football fan who only watches the Super Bowl). My father and my uncle Jay in particular, a physicist and a mechanical engineer, respectively, being very "left-brained" people, had a pretty cold relationship with the Methodist Church they had grown up in, which crystallized into atheism in their harsher moods. Joyce also grew up attending a Methodist church, but she, too, had drifted away from it. My mother took me and my younger brother to church on Sundays—the Southern Baptist Convention she'd been raised in at first and then, as the Southern Baptists leaned righter and righter until they had politically alienated her, experimenting with other Protestant denominations, but my father wouldn't go along unless we were in Arkansas or her parents were in town, when he suffered through it politely. But as I was growing up, we began attending church with less and less frequency, and by the time my youngest brother was born, we had pretty much stopped; for a few years, I went through a hatred-of-religion phase à la Sam Harris/Christopher Hitchens in my angry-young-man days.* Haley's father, Steve, had grown up Methodist,

---

* A lot of my first book, *The Evolution of Bruno Littlemore*, was written in the thickest throes of this phase, and when I read back it, I can tell, and I'm mildly embarrassed by it. Christopher Hitchens and I had the same publisher then, and I met him a couple of times—and reveled in his riotous company like Prince Hal with an intellectual Falstaff of comparable comic genius and unwholesome habits. Of the "new atheists" of those days, Hitchens was by far the smartest and the most fun to read. My novel was published right before he died, and I was touched when my editor passed along a note from his widow, Carol, saying that it was one of the last books he read—apparently he had been reading the greenhornish rantings of a fellow pugilistic atheist while lying in his deathbed, waiting to turn into meaningless matter. My attitude toward religion has softened considerably since then, and I now believe it to

too, and their small family—Steve, Kelly, Haley—attended Methodist services sometimes, but they were not particularly regular churchgoers, either. Religion has just never been a big part of the lives of the people on that side of my family; I always thought of them as admirably sane, skeptical, rational thinkers.

According to Tim Ernst in his book, on the first night Haley was lost, Kelly called a psychic from the landline in his cabin. Here's Tim: "Then Kelly got an idea to call a psychic and wanted to know if I had a phone book. She must have detected a slight hint of skepticism in my face because she looked right at me and said, 'At this point I am willing to try *anything!*'" There are no atheists in foxholes. Tim continues: "At 11:08 p.m., she placed a call and spoke briefly with a psychic. . . . 'She is lying down next to a stream and is unhurt,' the psychic said. . . . As it turns out, this information was exactly correct."

I disagree with Tim that what the psychic said could be called "information," but it's true she happened to be right. At that moment, the first night, Haley was lying on a rock beside an inlet of the Buffalo River, hoping the helicopters would spot her. Perhaps that psychic simply possessed the same thing Lytle James and William Jeff Villines had: intuition. (As Lytle James told the *Dateline NBC* reporter whom it had apparently taken mighty persuasion to get him to talk to on camera, "Well, when an animal's hurt or lost or something like at first thing they always do is go down to the water.")

Kelly kept calling psychics throughout the ordeal, and the next day, Crow Johnson—another family friend who had come to help (Crow is a folk singer/painter/textile artist who favors long, flowy scarves and silver Navajo jewelry—a crunchy über-hippie in addition to being a dyed-in-the-wool Arkie, and of my family's friends it is thoroughly unsurprising that she would be the one to have this idea)—knew that a convention of dowsers, or "water witches," as they're sometimes called in the Ozarks,

---

be a bizarre, fascinating, and often beautiful madness the human species is probably doomed to wrestle with until its story ends, or turns into something else.

was then being held at the Crescent Hotel in Eureka Springs, and she faxed them topographical maps of the area, which they faxed back with their divined suggestions for search areas.

I distinctly remember first learning about water divination from Jay and Joyce when I was a kid, walking in the woods with them on their property in Pea Ridge. Although they were deeply mistrustful of organized religion and Christianity in particular, and though they did not exactly *believe* in water divination, they had a strange sort of respect for it, as they did a lot of the old Ozark folk wisdom. It is just as deep a part of the landscape's human psychology—its psychogeography, call it—as the tall tales and the ghost stories and the melodies in its music that have aural ancestry in the ballads of the Scottish highlands. Plus, it works sometimes. They and I know that those times when it appears to work are almost certainly just lucky accidents, the coincidences of confirmation bias that give magical thinking its power over our pattern-hungry minds. But you'd have to have the heart of a robot not to feel at least a little tingle in your spine when it does.

I think all the business with psychics and water witches all but vanished from Kelly's mind as soon as Haley had been found alive and safe. She didn't need it anymore. She was out of the foxhole.

Her own mother, on the other hand, was not only terrified for Haley during those three days, but also devastated with guilt. She still is. A part of Joyce's soul never made it out of the foxhole.

Alecia. Although Haley did not yet perfectly know how to read, from the moment Alecia first appeared in the story—as the family was driving up to St. Louis on day three after she had been rescued—she always insisted on that slightly unorthodox spelling; she pronounced it "ah-lee-see-ah." She was also insistent on other specific details. Alecia was four years old. She had long, dark hair that she wore in pigtails. She wore a red shirt with purple sleeves, red pants, and white sneakers. Haley drew a picture of her:

Alecia, Haley said, had had a flashlight with her. She had guided her to the river. Haley:

From the moment I knew I was lost, I had this imaginary friend. I have always referred to her as an imaginary friend, and I always will refer to her as an imaginary friend. Her name was Alecia. My mom has said before—and I actually don't know if I agree with her on this, I think—she said she was afraid I didn't have any imagination. She genuinely was, like, worried for me. I actually think that I had an extremely active imagination, but I was also very good at distinguishing between my imagination and reality. I had a very rich inner world. I loved to play pretend, loved to play dress-up. But I was also very like, Okay, *that* is pretend, and *this* is real. And I never had imaginary friends before this experience, and I never had any after. And I never saw this particular imaginary friend again. But I remember, her name was Alecia, she had long dark hair, she was four, she had a flashlight, and I think I specifically told my parents that she appeared to me as being four because she didn't want to scare me. I've always been someone who really likes to be in control of myself. I don't need to have control over every situation, I just need to be in control of my own faculties. So I think that her being younger than me was a way for me to still be in control. I've been asked before, "Did you think that she was another child?" And no—I was fully aware that this was a noncorporeal being that was with me. And she was a little girl, and we had conversations, we told stories, we played patty-cake, and she was just a very comforting presence. But I knew that physically, I was alone. It is hard to explain. I don't know how else to say it other that she was an imaginary friend. She did guide me. I didn't know that there was a river. But she helped me find it. And I don't know if that was just me blindly walking through the woods and finding a river and attributing that to her, or if she actually guided me to the river. . . . I did have hallucinations, but later. I had hallucinations distinctly separate from my imaginary friend that were due to the effects of exposure. I one hundred percent did not think there was another child with me. I knew, physically, I was alone.

There is a documented but scientifically unexamined phenomenon called third-man syndrome or third-man factor, which sometimes occurs when some sort of unseen or incorporeal conscious presence seems to accompany someone who is going through a long, difficult, traumatic, and frightening experience she does not know she will survive. It is not well understood. It may be some sort of emergency psychological coping mechanism. It seems to happen to people trapped for a very long time in a state of simultaneous boredom and terror. Haley says she knew she was alone, but Alecia had made her *feel* as if she was not alone. This feeling of companionship may be what helps the lost person get through the experience alive. The feeling of aloneness might lead to despair, which might lead to death; but the human consciousness in the friendly company of another soul experiencing this trial alongside her will keep on moving forward. Third-man factor was most famously experienced by Sir Ernest Shackleton during one of his expeditions to the Antarctic; the mountain climber Reinhold Messner has also reported experiencing the phenomenon, as have explorers Peter Hillary and Ann Bancroft. Shackleton writes in his 1919 memoir *South*, "during that long and racking march of thirty-six hours over the unnamed mountains and glaciers of South Georgia, it seemed to me often that we were four, not three." T. S. Eliot read that book, and with characteristic pedantry tells us in his own commentary published simultaneously with *The Waste Land* in the literary annus mirabilis 1922 that it inspired these lines, which I often reread just to feel the ominous vibration of the cosmos in my heart:

Who is the third who walks always beside you?
When I count, there are only you and I together
But when I look ahead up the white road
There is always another one walking beside you
Gliding wrapt in a brown mantle, hooded
I do not know whether a man or a woman.
—But who is that on the other side of you?

When Kelly stepped out of the car in the parking lot of Cave Mountain Church late in the afternoon of the day Haley went missing, Joyce was there to meet her. The first thing Joyce said was, "Will you ever forgive me?" And Kelly said, "There's nothing to forgive. I'm not angry at all." She was afraid that Steve would be furious with her parents, but he was not angry, either. Everyone involved with this story told me the same thing: No one ever blamed Joyce or was ever angry at her. Despite all that, Joyce could not forgive herself. By many accounts, she remained rattled and uneasy for a long time after Haley was found. One friend used the phrase "emotionally brittle." It is an understatement to say that she *could not stop thinking about it.* And soon there was a new element thrown in: in the aftermath of Haley's rescue, her "imaginary friend" made the rounds among the grown-ups, making everyone's hair stand on end. Every adult who had been closely connected to Haley, in the days and weeks following her rescue, would weather many sleepless nights, and would spend many hours staring at bedroom ceilings with a mind stuck in neutral and grinding its gears, thinking about what might have happened. Everyone was still in shellshock for a long time. None more than Joyce. There was no one else who spent more time thinking about what the world would be like now if Haley had died. Angels descend upon us in our darkest hours. When people's minds are most in turmoil is the perfect moment for a ghost to enter a story—it's when children and adults are on the same plane, inhabiting the same reality haunted and enchanted with magic.

On August 24, 2001, four months after Haley was lost and found,

Tim Ernst—now a firm friend of the family—sent Joyce an email:

> Just a tiny bit of bizarre lore that we thought about last night. Pam and I were sitting around talking about Haley's Alecia, and Pam asked me if any little girls had ever been lost or died in the wilderness near here. A huge chill ran down my spine. You may recall this too. It was twenty years ago when a little girl from Springfield of all places, was tortured, murdered, and stuffed in a pickle bucket and buried by a small group of cult members. The cult members were told to "go to the wilderness and exercise the demons" from this little girl. That location was just off of the Kapark road, which is about three or four miles from here as the crow flies. I have not decided yet if I am going to dig up the specifics of this case—wouldn't it just be CRAZY if that little girl's name was Alecia, or was anything like Haley's Alecia!!! I have not told Kelly about this, and it probably is just meaningless anyway, but just the thought of the possibilities . . .

Tim remembered that the murder had happened about twenty years earlier, but did not know the exact date. Jay and Joyce had been living in Northwest Arkansas at the time but did not know the story at all. A few days later, still thinking about the case, Tim wrote Joyce another email:

> It turns out that this cult had just moved to the woods from Rogers, and had charges pending in Benton County, and were first taken to the jail there (I'm sure there was plenty of news coverage, although we still can't find out what year it happened).

Joyce went to the Benton County Sheriff's Office and asked whether it had any records having to do with the murder of a young girl in the Buffalo Wilderness area in the 1970s, or knew anything about it. There were no records. But someone in the office did vaguely recall the case, and remembered that Judge Tom Keith had somehow been involved with it. And it just so happened that Jay and Joyce knew Tom Keith pretty well. Tom was sixty years old, about the same age as Jay and Joyce, a fellow Democrat, and by this time was a respected pillar of the community in Northwest Arkansas. Jay and Tom had served together as Justices of the Peace on the Benton County Quorum Court. Joyce called up Tom Keith. And it turned out he had been involved with that case. Before he became a judge, Keith had worked as a public defender for Benton County, and he had been one of the two lawyers on the defense counsel of one of people charged with the murder, the only defendant whose case had gone to trial: the murdered girl's mother.

Joyce wrote in an email:

When I called him, I remember a long pause before he spoke. I was afraid that client privilege was still an issue and that he wouldn't feel he could help. After a while, all he said was that I needed to research the newspapers for April, 1978. After that I should make an appointment with his secretary.

Joyce hit the microfiches at the local library and filled herself in on the broad outline of the story. Then, late that summer, taking Kelly along, she met with Judge Keith in his office. Keith told them that defending the mother of the murdered child had not been just any job for him; he believed in her innocence, and he still believed that her conviction had been a shameful and tragic miscarriage of justice. He considered losing that case the worst failure of his career, and it had haunted him ever since.

6

The Third Step to
Joyful Living

Fᴿᴇᴅ ʙᴇʟʟ, ᴀᴛ ꜰɪꜰᴛʏ-ꜰᴏᴜʀ ʏᴇᴀʀꜱ ᴏʟᴅ ɪɴ 1978, ʜᴀᴅ ʜᴇʟᴅ ᴛʜᴇ office of Newton County Game Warden with the Arkansas Game and Fish Commission for nearly three decades. A lifelong outdoorsman, he was also a much loved and respected figure in his tight-knit community in that sparsely populated part of the Ozarks, a Scoutmaster with the Boy Scouts and a deacon at First Baptist Church in Jasper. On Monday, April 24, of that year, Fred Bell and his good friend Ed Burton went turkey hunting in the Upper Buffalo Wilderness area. Around six in the morning, they drove east to west up the mountain in Fred's truck— his own vehicle but outfitted with a police radio and a stick-on beacon light—turned left on Kaypark Road, aka County Road 1410, and parked about a mile down the road in a flat, grassy clearing with a firepit in it, an area big enough to turn the truck around in, a favorite spot of theirs from which to set off hunting.

It was the middle of spring, around last frost, the time of year when the nights still get quite cold, especially at high elevations. It was below freezing when they set out just before sunrise, and by midmorning the temperatures were still in the thirties. The morning had met with success; they'd shot a nice fat bearded tom, and Ed had the big blue-headed bird, tagged and field dressed with guts scooped out, slung over his shoulder with legs trussed, dangling from a rope, the radial fan of shimmery rich russet brown plumage bouncing at his back. As the two men crunched through the springtime wilderness headed uphill back toward Kaypark Road, they were somewhat astonished to stumble across a campsite: two pitched pop-up tents, a clothesline strung between two trees, the remains of a firepit—a ring of stones around a heap of charred wood and warm ashes—and a small two-wheel aluminum camper-trailer hitched to the tow of a tan Jeep Wagoneer with wood paneling, which Fred was a little amazed anyone had managed to get all the way down into those woods. It was a very remote and odd place to be camping: pretty far from the road, not within sight of a trail, and not very close to any water source. The choice of campsite was odd, and so was the group of campers. There were six of them, all white. One was a man about Fred's own age, early to midfifties, perhaps balding, lean, clean shaven, narrow eyes with one slightly droopy lid, gold-rimmed aviator glasses, jeans, tucked-in flannel shirt, and denim jacket; he looked like a high school football coach, and he was by far the oldest person there. There was a much younger man in his early thirties, maybe, who looked like a hippie: bushy beard and long, straggly brown hair; a woman of about the same age with long black hair, pale, thin; another very young and very pretty woman who couldn't have been older than her early twenties, trembly and fragile looking, with long, dark hair and big black eyes; and a kid: a timid, skinny blond girl who looked perhaps nine or ten years old.

Fred immediately sensed something off about the group. The young long-haired hippie-looking guy in jeans and jean jacket stepped forward to speak for everyone, and shook hands with Fred and Ed. This guy was doing all the talking; there was a nervous, jittery energy about him that Fred mistrusted; he was acting too chummy and gregarious, like he was covering for something, and the others were cagey, hanging back at a distance, unnervingly silent. The older man, taciturn and stone faced, glowered at them from a distance, standing like a scarecrow, didn't say a word. The younger of the two women in particular, the very young one, had a dazed, empty look in her face. It would have looked less weird if these campers had been a family—say, a mother and father with little children—or a group of teenagers. The adults didn't look related to one another, and none of them looked very healthy; they looked sickly, skinny, and ashen, and there were strange social tensions going on between them; Fred didn't know what they were, but he could feel them. These people clearly were not expecting to meet two strangers out here in these woods, and they were visibly anxious for them to go away. Fred, after all, was a kind of cop, and although his purview was violations of hunting and fishing regulations, he had a cop's well-trained nose for fear. The two men talked with the motley crew of campers for a while, and Fred showed them his game warden's badge. They did not appear to be doing anything illegal, but Fred silently flash froze the license plate number of the Jeep Wagoneer in his memory, told them to have a nice day, and as soon as he and Ed were out of their sight wrote it down on a scrap of paper with the pencil stub he kept in his pocket for marking game tags. Fred and Ed climbed with their turkey up the steep hill, emerged from the woods onto Kaypark Road, glanced back down the steep slope behind them, and saw something even more bizarre: Somebody had managed to drive a twenty-four-foot U-Haul moving truck all the way up the mountain and down onto this tiny Forest Service road that you really wouldn't be wisely driving on in anything but an ATV. Fred and Ed walked down to the U-Haul to look at it more closely. One of its back wheels was lodged deep in a rut, and the mud spray on the back of the truck and deep cuts in the road indicated that someone had gotten the truck stuck, mightily but unsuccessfully tried to get it unstuck, and given up. The alarm bells in Fred's mind were sounding louder and louder. Something strange and most likely not good was up. He jotted down the plate number of the stuck U-Haul, too, and he and Ed headed up Kaypark Road to the grassy clearing where they'd parked the truck earlier that morning. As Ed loaded the dead turkey into the truck bed and tied it down, Fred sat behind the wheel in the cab, switched on the radio, and called the Newton County Sheriff's Office in Jasper. The radio squealed and crunched, and Sheriff's Deputy Ray Watkins answered. Ray, who would later serve as Sheriff himself, has long since retired from law enforcement and now works at Bob's Do It Best Hardware and Lumber in Jasper, said that Fred thought the folks he had encountered were "acting kinda funny."

Fred read off the license plate numbers he'd written down and asked Ray to run them. His instincts had been right. Ray ran the plate numbers and got back to him a few minutes later: they were vehicles linked to several people who had an active warrant out for their arrest in Benton County on suspicion of child abuse. They also supposedly had two young children with them, a little girl probably not older than five, and another girl a little older, maybe about ten.

It had looked to Fred that they only had one kid with them, the older one.

He agreed that he and Bill would stay where they were to make sure the people in the woods didn't leave. Ray and the Sheriff would be there as soon as they could to make the arrests.

The Sheriff of Newton County, Earl Hurchal Fowler, who hadn't come in to work yet, lived on Cave Mountain Road, just a few miles away from Fred's approximate location on Kaypark Road. At the sheriff's office in Jasper, Ray finished his coffee, strapped on his Colt Python, pinned his badge to his shirt—that was the extent of his sheriff's deputy's uniform—got in his car (he didn't have an official vehicle; like Fred, Ray drove his own car, a tan Ford LTD outfitted with a police radio and a beacon light to stick on the roof), and drove at law enforcement prerogative speeds the half hour west on AR-74. When he pulled into Hurchal's driveway, the sheriff was standing there talking with his twenty-year-old son, Eddy, who had a volunteer sheriff's deputy card. They decided he would come along that day to help make the arrests. Hurchal wore a mesh-sided baseball cap and had his six-pointed metal star pinned to the breast of his flannel shirt. The Fowlers have lived in that part of the Arkansas Ozarks for many generations going back to the early 1800s, and jowly, heavyset Hurchal Fowler in his bottle green aviator sunglasses was about as local a boy as you could get. Fifty-eight years old, Hurchal had served as Newton County sheriff for six years. Not counting the volunteer deputies who would assist as needed, Newton County employed exactly three police officers in 1978: Fred Bell, Hurchal Fowler, and Ray Watkins, who with his two-year associate's degree in administration of justice was the only one of them who had any formal training in law enforcement. Ray had served as a reserve deputy part-time for the county's previous sheriff, Toot Wagner, but his primary source of income had been a gas station and repair garage he ran in Jasper. Hurchal, a road grader operator and chairman of the Democratic Party in Newton County, had beaten Toot Wagner for sheriff in the 1972 election and offered Ray a full-time job as deputy. The Sheriff's Office also assessed and collected taxes, and that was the part of the job that interested Hurchal; he and Ray had a gentleman's agreement that Hurchal would deal with the taxes and Ray would do most of the actual work of enforcing the law. So Ray sold the garage and gas station and for the past six years had been the county's only full-time cop. Hurchal would step down from his position later that year, Ray would run uncontested to replace him, and following the election that November, he would go on to serve as sheriff for twelve years. Hurchal Fowler died in May 2001, and he's buried in his family's large plot in Cave Mountain Cemetery, next to the church—a couple of miles, as the crow flies, from the spot where the three men—Hurchal, Ray, and Hurchal's son, Eddy—met Fred Bell and Ed Burton in the clearing off Kaypark Road. Fred and Ed led the caravan of three vehicles a little way down Kaypark Road—a very primitive Forest Service road so seldom traveled that a strip of tall grass runs through the middle of it—to the place where the twenty-four-foot U-Haul moving truck was parked in absurd incongruity with its surroundings in the rugged and empty wilderness. They could see the tracks that the campers had made eking that Jeep Wagoneer into the woods. They parked their vehicles in a row behind the U-Haul.

Fred and Ed led them from there into the dark springtime woods, five pairs of boots crunching on the leaf litter: Fred and Ed in their hunting camo cradle carrying their shotguns, Hurchal and Ray armed with handguns in their hip holsters (unusual for Hurchal, who didn't ordinarily carry a weapon and would retire from his six-year stint as sheriff without having fired a single shot in the line of duty). They found the campsite perhaps a hundred feet from the road: the pile of pale gray ashes ringed with stones, the two tents, the bight of laundry line strung between two trees, the aluminum camper-trailer hitched to the brown Jeep Wagoneer with wood side paneling. The trunk of the Wagoneer was packed to the ceiling. No one was about, but the curtains in the windows of the camper-trailer were drawn, and they could see shadows of movement behind them. It was about nine in the morning now, and the sunshine had burnt away the frost. A beautiful midspring day. Shooting stars and pink azaleas were at their height. The sheriff and deputy unsnapped their holsters and put their palms on the gun handles. The five men on foot surrounded the car and the camper-trailer. Approaching the vehicle, they could hear voices inside; not talking, but several voices speaking in unison in the murmuring cadence of a chant, as if they were reciting something. Hurchal stood back a bit and with a nod gave Ray the go-ahead. Ray banged with his knuckles three times on the door of the camper-trailer. The voices inside went silent.

"Police," Ray said. "Open up."

A long time passed. Sounds ds of weight shifting inside the trailer. Nothing. He banged on the door again. "Police. Please step out of the vehicle."

After a very long while, he heard a latch lifting, and the trailer door squealed open. The older man of the group stepped into the doorway and looked around. Thin, tall with a bald crown ringed with short, sandy iron gray hair, a lean, gaunt face, gold-rimmed glasses, one slightly droopy eyelid. The man wore the unmistakable look of someone who knows this is the moment everything changes. He looked sick, haggard, tired. Ray could see at once that he knew the general reason why there were armed men knocking on the door of his trailer. Ray drew his gun, but didn't point it at him. "Turn around please, sir, and place your hands against the vehicle."

He did as he was told without a word. Hurchal's son, Eddy, patted him down, and they had him stand back a ways from the camper-trailer with his hands up.

Next, one of the women came out—youngish, very pale, long black hair, barely taller than five feet, and skinny, probably not much more than a hundred pounds. One of the two children they were supposed to have with them followed her out; that had to be the nine-year-old girl. Ray figured the woman was her mother. There was no fight in the woman, either; she came out with her hands up. Eddy patted her down, and they made her stand off to the side next to the older man. Eddy took the child by the hand—she let it be taken—and guided her away from the others. He told her to sit down on the ground, and she did.

The door opened again, and the wiry young guy who looked like a hippie came out—long brown hair and beard, jeans and jean jacket, cowboy boots—already talking, saying something like, "Now, Officer, look—"

He was the healthiest looking and most able-bodied person to emerge from the trailer yet. There was a jumpy energy in his body, and wildness in his eyes. He immediately made Ray nervous in a way the others hadn't; if there was anyone here he might need to be rough with, it was going to be this guy. Ray shushed him and jerked his gun at him.

Turn around and place your hands against the vehicle."

He did as he was told, but he was still trying to talk.

"Shut up."

Ray quickly patted him down. Clean.

The Newton County Sheriff's Office possessed only one pair of handcuffs, which Ray had clipped to his belt. This guy was the only fish that had tugged back against the line, and he decided to put the cuffs on him. He holstered his gun, grabbed the man's arms, pinned them behind his back, and ratcheted the cuffs onto his wrists. Hurchal guided him by the elbow to stand beside the others.

The camper-trailer door swung and banged shut and opened again. A fragile, frightened-looking, pretty young woman with big quivery eyes came out of the trailer next. No fight whatsoever in her. Ray handled her gently, and in a moment she was standing beside the other three with her hands up.

Then: a long nothing. Silence.

A tableau of ten people: Fred and Ed standing back cradling their shotguns, Hurchal and his son Eddy standing with hands on hips, Ray with his hand on his holstered gun, four others standing quietly in a row, one handcuffed, the others with their hands up, and one little girl sitting by herself off to the side. Spring sunlight dappling the shady green forest, the crisp midmorning mountain air still cold enough their breaths came out as faintly visible fog, the songbirds singing.

Ray looked at Hurchal. Hurchal was looking at the camper-trailer. The bulletin from Benton County had said three men, two women, two children. That left one man and one child unaccounted for. Ray could sense that the camper-trailer wasn't empty. He banged on the door again. "Police. Come on out of there."

A long time passed—perhaps five, ten minutes. Every once in a while Ray would walk over, bang his fist on the door of the camper-trailer, and shout, "Police, open up." Then more silence. They could hear movement, weight shifting now and then, and the trailer would wobble slightly and creak. But the door was shut, and the curtains remained drawn over the windows. Hurchal and Ray came together for a sotto voce private palaver about whether or not they were going to have to go in there. While Ray kept periodically banging on the trailer door and shouting, Ed Burton, who had just been out for turkey hunting, made himself useful and took care of the child; he walked her through the woods back to the road and put her in the backseat of one of the vehicles. Eddy stood watch over the detainees while Hurchal did a quick cursory sweep of the Wagoneer; he found a Remington .32 pistol in the glove box and a Ruger Mini .223 in a compartment in the driver's-side door, both loaded. He unloaded the guns and placed them on the hood of the car. An anominous sign. Most of the law-enforcing these backcountry cops did in the day-to-day was writing tickets, and the most adventuresome police work Newton County typically required of them involved busting illegal marijuana farms—that is to say, dealing with ordinary human criminals motivated by the most ordinary of human motives: money. They knew they were dealing with something dark and strange and very out of the ordinary.

Considering the arrest warrants and the guns Hurchal had just found in the car, they had no doubt they could claim probable cause to enter the camper-trailer. That wasn't the issue. If they had loaded firearms in the car, there was a good chance there were more in the trailer. Ray wasn't going to just open the door and stick his head inside.

Again, Ray banged on the door. This time he said, "Listen. There's a warrant out for you. If you don't get out of there, I'm gonna shoot you and pull you out."

Silence. The trailer creaked and wobbled. At long last, the door opened. Ray Watkins drew his gun, stepped back, and kept it pointed at the trailer. "Come out of there with your hands up."

A lanky, gangly teenage boy in jeans and a tight red-and-white-striped T-shirt appeared in the doorway. He had a mop of curly brown hair and prickles of acne on his cheeks; he was still awkwardly growing into his body, the features of childhood and adulthood jumbled together: big hands but rail-thin wrists, broad shoulders but a skinny chest, girlishly pretty eyelashes, a man's Adam's apple bobbing in a long, slender neck. He had wild, wide-open eyes, and he looked, if anything, confused to be there.

With all five adults accounted for, Ray felt safe enough to open the camper-trailer door and peek inside: a lot of boxes full of stuff heaped atop one another, a sleeping cot folded out on the floor, pillows, blankets, books—and most notably, a .44 Magnum lying on one of the benches, which Ray suspected that the last of them to come out—that gangly teenager—had been spending all those long minutes of silence contemplating using, and a thin chill scissored through him as he briefly imagined a more interesting way the morning could have gone just moments ago. But he could tell at a glance that the trailer was now empty of human occupants.

Ray Watkins was certain that the arrest warrant from Benton County he'd seen had mentioned that the group consisted of five adults with two young children with them: two girls, one about nine or ten years old, the other not older than five. The older girl was accounted for; they were going to have to get Social Services to come get her after they had the adults locked up. But the younger one—she wasn't there. There was no sign of her.

They questioned the five detainees about the missing child, the little girl. None would talk. It was clear they would be getting nothing out of them. Hurchal and Ray conferred and decided it was time to take them to jail. It was about half a mile to get out of the woods and back up Kaypark Road to where the vehicles were parked, a good fifteen minutes or so of walking. They went single file: the older man and the two women in front, Fred and Eddy following them, then the jumpy young long-haired guy in cuffs, then Ray, then the teenage boy, and Hurchal bringing up the rear. Ray's spider sense kept tingling with that teenager walking behind him. Several times he felt him get too close, and he turned around and barked at him to stay back.

"He kept easing up behind me," Ray told me. "I have a wide peripheral vision. And I could see him easing up, easing up. And I turned around and told him, 'Stay back.' And he said, 'No.' And I pushed him. I said, 'Stay back. I want you *this* far back. I don't want you up behind me like that.' And so then we walked another, oh, probably from here to that tree out there, and he was up behind me again. He was about two and a half feet from me. If he had made a lunge, he might have been able to get ahold of the gun—which he hadn't, but that was beside the point. I turned around, and I'm left-handed. I turned around, and I hit him right there." Ray pointed to the spot on himself, where the neck meets the shoulder. "Took him to the ground. And I told him, Now that is your last warning. You get up behind me again, I'm going to turn around, and you're going to have this here pistol. It's going to be *pow*. I said, Always go right. And so he stayed back then, but I had to watch him every step of the way until we got him into the car."

Sheriff Fowler entrusted Fred, Ray, and Eddy to take the detainees to jail in Jasper. Hurchal said he wanted to stay there and look around the campsite. They put the two women into the back of Eddy's car and the older man and the teenager into the back seat of Ray's, with Fred Bell sitting in the back to keep an eye on them; and the young man in hand-cuffs they put up front in the passenger seat. Ed Burton drove the little girl in Fred's truck, with the gutted turkey trussed up in the bed. The three vehicles pulled into Jasper about forty minutes later. Ray locked the three men in one jail cell and the two women in another. There were logistics to figure out after that. The child must have been placed in some kind of emergency state custody, and somebody had to have notified the police in Benton County. Someone else—Ray doesn't remember who—must have driven the five detainees to Benton County later that day, because there are records of them being booked and processed there that afternoon.

The five people who were arrested in Newton County that day and taken to Benton County, where there was an active warrant for their arrest on suspicion of child abuse, were Royal Harris, fifty-one years old; his stepson, Winston Van Harris, thirty-one; his son, Mark Harris, seventeen; Suzette Freeman, thirty-one; and Lucy Clark, twenty-two. Once the five were locked up in Newton County Jail awaiting transfer to Benton County, Ray got back in his car and headed back out to Kaypark Road on Cave Mountain to rejoin Hurchal. When he made it back to that scraggly forest service road in that remote wilderness area, the sheriff had bad news.

After the others left, Sheriff Fowler stood alone on Kaypark Road with a heavy feeling in his gut. He hiked the half mile or so down the road and through the woods back to the campsite: the camper-trailer hitched to the Wagoneer, the tents, the clothesline, the firepit. He noticed a shovel leaning against a tree near the camper-trailer with dirt on its blade; that told him to look for a place where it looked like someone had dug a hole, buried something, and filled it in. Hurchal had grown up on Cave Mountain—his mother's father had been the first person buried in Cave Mountain Cemetery—and he knew these woods in his bones; like Fred Bell and Ray Watkins, he was a hunter and an experienced woodsman who knew how to read signs. He paced around the campsite and swept in widening circles out into the woods surrounding it, looking for some kind of sign. After perhaps an hour of crunching through the woods scanning the ground, about fifty feet away from the firepit, the tents, and the Jeep and the trailer, just out of sight of them, at the bottom of a swale in the ground in the mulchy leaf litter on the forest floor, he found a mound of dark, freshly overturned dirt with a few dead logs that appeared to have been deliberately dragged over the spot. He rolled the logs aside and with the same shovel that had probably been used to dig the hole and fill it back up, he started digging. The soil was loose, and it didn't take long to get down about thirty inches, when the blade of the shovel hit something that wasn't dirt. He squatted over the hole in the ground and started digging with his hands. His fingers found the thin wire handle of a bucket. He scooped handfuls of mud away from the bucket and found a black plastic garbage bag inside it. He ripped it open and saw two small feet sticking up, wearing little white sneakers.

Forensics would later determine that Bethany Alana Clark, three and a half years old, had been shot eight times with a .22, stuffed in a plastic garbage bag that had then been stuffed in a five-gallon plastic paint bucket, and buried (very recently) a foot and a half deep and fifty feet away from where the other six people had been found. Among other things, Newton County sheriff's officers would confiscate from the Jeep Wagoneer, the camper-trailer, and the rented U-Haul truck: twenty-two firearms, more than two thousand rounds of ammunition, an enormous quantity of dry goods and canned food, and three copies of a book titled *The Third Step to Joyful Living, or How to Stop Worrying*, by Royal and Edith Harris.

Edith Otellia Aaron—later Edith Smith, later Edith Harris—was born in 1926 in the tiny East Texas town of Navarro. She was the daughter of a Methodist minister, and she would later claim to have been ordained as a Methodist minister herself. Edith married her first husband, a US Army captain from Augusta, Georgia, named Gobe Smith, Jr., in Dallas on June 11, 1944, in a ceremony officiated by her father, the Reverend James Aaron. The couple's son, Gobe Smith III, was born in November 1946. They were an army family, moving every few years whenever the father was assigned to a new base. By all accounts, Edith was a woman who held "tremendous domination" over her son, —called by the nickname "Buster" from an early age—and was, to put it mildly, "an excessively religious person." Many years later, Douglas Wilson, a public defender, would recall in court that Gobe Smith, Jr., had told him that during the twelve years of their marriage, "they would join one church, and then another, and after a short period of time she would find herself in disagreement with whatever doctrine prevailed in that church, and would attempt to tell them what the true path was, and they didn't agree with it, so she would cut herself off from it. And eventually, it led to the founding of her own church where she could have total dominion over the doctrine." In 1956, when their son was nine years old, "it had become clear" to Edith that her husband "was just not in agreement with every pronouncement in terms of religion that she made," she left him, cut off all communication with him, and took their son with her back to Texas. Gobe Smith, Jr., would have no more contact with Buster until twenty-two years later, when his deceased ex-wife's brother called him in April 1978 to tell him that his son had been arrested for murder in Arkansas.

Soon after Edith Smith returned to Texas with her nine-year-old son, she met a fellow Texan, Royal Winston Harris.

I know only the sparest details of how these two met each other. I know that Royal Harris was born on January 27, 1928, and grew up on a farm near Tyler, Texas, a city of about 50,000 at the time, halfway between Dallas and Shreveport, Louisiana. I know he must have grown up deep in the sticks because the home address listed on his draft card and on his father's draft card is a Rural Free Delivery number. I know he graduated from John Tyler High School in 1945; next to a picture of a lean-faced teenager with center-parted hair in his senior high school yearbook: "How could he possibly be so shy/And also retain the twinkle in his eye?" I know he enlisted in the US Air Force's Air Mobility Command Reserve while a student at Texas A&M. Years later, in court, he would claim to be a veteran of World War II, though I don't see how that could possibly fit with the timeline. He graduated with an engineering degree in 1949. After that, I know from census data that he was living with his parents and much younger brother on the farm he had grown up on and working as a clerk in the country grocery store his family owned—eighty-four hours a week, which must mean that he was working grueling twelve-to-fourteen-hour shifts nearly every day, a schedule with barely enough time left over for eating and sleeping.

I am looking at his face now as it must have looked around this time, his senior picture in his college yearbook. His mouth is flat and serious, and he's wearing his AMC dress uniform: a not unhandsome twenty-one-year-old man with a neck beefed out a bit since high school. He frankly looks a little dumb: big ears and narrow eyes set close together, something asymmetrical about them—one lid droops lower than the other. He looks exactly like an East Texas farm boy in 1949.

Where Edith and Royal met, the countryside beyond Tyler, is a flat, brown place dotted with trees, a quiet place with big open skies where oil derricks creak and bob their mechanical beaks up and down in the distance and a building taller than one story is an unusual sight. You may picture it in black and white, and you may hear Hank Williams playing from the radio of a Studebaker pickup with stake siding. How they met is a mystery. Royal Harris is twenty-eight years old, still living on his family's farm and working long hours in their little country grocery store. The meat and milk and eggs and a lot of the produce for sale probably come from the family's own farm. A thirty-year-old woman shows up in the area in 1956. She has family nearby, but not that near—closer to Dallas, about an hour and a half away. She has a nine-year-old son with her. She's been a young army wife for ten years, bouncing around the South from base to base every few years, most recently in South Carolina, but she divorced her husband and has come back to Texas. Perhaps they met at the grocery store. It was a small store at the intersection of two country roads, probably still the old-fashioned kind where all the goods are stored in inventory and you have to tell the guy behind the counter what you want, and he goes and gets it for you and rings you up. The guy behind the counter is Royal Harris, working eighty-four hours a week (or at least that's what he reported to the government). Everyone describes him as shy and taciturn—though he would have to interact with people to sell them food. Was a thirty-year-old recently divorced single woman with a nine-year-old kid in rural Texas in the 1950s unusual enough that the neighbors whispered about her? Probably. The young man fetching groceries down from the shelves for the stranger new to town, the single mother with her little boy with her who answers to the fairly odd name of "Gobe." They get to talking; one thing leads to another. Or perhaps they met in church. Religion must have been a key component of their becoming a couple. It couldn't not have been; Edith was obsessed with religion. Her first husband's insufficient piety had been the reason she'd divorced him. So now I imagine they meet in church on a Sunday morning, mingling after the services, the Sabbath being Royal's only day off, he in his Sunday best with hair combed, there with his family, young still but getting old enough to be a little embarrassed about still roosting in the nest.

Edith is forceful, a big personality by all accounts, domineering, a dynamo. She is also two years older, has already known marriage and motherhood, and has seen much more of the world. Royal, by contrast, is shy and quiet, lets his family work him like a mule, the obedient and faithful older son who never leaves and never gets a fatted calf slain in his honor, who doesn't need to be found because he's never been lost, still living in the farmhouse he was born in and still toiling for his father seven years after graduating from college with the engineering degree he's put to precisely zero use in the grocery store.

Whatever happened between them, it happened fast, because Edith left her first husband and moved back to Texas in 1956, and she married Royal Harris at Bethany Baptist Church in Chapel Hill, a small town outside Tyler, on April 26, 1957. Edith took Royal's surname and changed her son's name, rechristening him with Royal's middle name: Winston Van Harris.

———

They lived in Tyler in the late 1950s and early 1960s. That was where Edith and Royal's own son, Mark, was born in 1960. In the early 1960s, Royal landed a job as a systems analyst at Ethyl Corporation, a manufacturer of lead gasoline additives based in Baton Rouge, Louisiana. So the family moved to Baton Rouge, and except for his years in college, Royal was living away from his parents for the first time in his life. Winston Van Harris, formerly Gobe Smith III, aka Buster, graduated from high school in Baton Rouge in 1964, enrolled as a student at Harding College, a small private Christian college in Searcy, Arkansas, for two years in 1964–1966, dropped out, joined the army, trained as a reconnaissance ranger, rose to the rank of first lieutenant, and served three years at the Demilitarized Zone in Korea, where he racked up an exemplary record of service, received an honorable discharge at the end of his tour, and returned home to Texas with his wife, Mia, a Korean national.

Meanwhile, Edith Harris was becoming increasingly isolated from her family and increasingly obsessed with some fringe interpretations of Christianity that they found worrisome and bizarre. Royal's parents had started a trucking company, which by the late 1960s had begun to do pretty well. Royal quit his job at Ethyl, and the small family sold their house in Baton Rouge and moved into a trailer on his parents' property in Tyler, behind their house. Royal got his trucker's license, and for the next few years he was often on the road, driving a truck for his father's company. Edith stayed at home in the trailer parked behind her in-laws' house and obsessed over Christian doctrine, poring over the Bible for clues, listening to gospel on the radio.

Edith's brother, Paul Aaron—the same brother who would call Gobe Smith, Jr. many years later to tell him that his son had been arrested—when asked if his sister and her second husband had had any "unusual religious beliefs," would tell a courtroom:

> They became involved in unusual religious beliefs that, in my opinion,
> amounted to a cult. . . . I won't go into the religious doctrine unless
> you want me to, but the results was that they should consider the
> whole family that did not go along with them in this belief as their

enemy. At this point, which was after Van had returned from the military and married, they began to put themselves in seclusion from the family and practically from the rest of the world.

When asked about their beliefs, Paul mentioned that they were adherents of British Israelism, a crackpot theory with racist and anti-Semitic overtures that has been kicked around on the pseudohistorical fringes of dubious Christian scholarship since the seventeenth century, positing that the Ten Lost Tribes of Israel, said to have been exiled from the Promised Land after the conquest of the Neo-Assyrian Empire in 722 BC, eventually resettled in the British Isles and northern Europe—i.e., Celtic, Nordic, and Germanic people; meaning that the white Anglo-Saxon Protestant settlers of North America directly descended from Jacob, Isaac, and Abraham: the true-born chosen people, the bloodline of the Messiah. This notion essentially combines colonial apologia with Christian atavism—the quest to return to early Christianity as it was practiced in the first century AD, before the Devil in the disguise of what's now called the Catholic Church took over and started twisting everything around—and its first major wave of popularity hit the United States in the mid–nineteenth century, where it influenced both Mormonism and Pentecostalism. Biblical genealogical nonsense and its intersection with global politics—wars and empires and the migrations of tribes—continued to influence Royal's religious thinking up until the end. Royal and Edith may have believed they were the true descendants of the people God gifted with the power of prophecy, and it's worth keeping in mind that those who wish to revive the earliest form of Christianity believe the Book of Acts to be their best record and model (KJV, Acts 4:30): "By stretching forth thine hand to heal; and that signs and wonders may be done by the name of thy holy child Jesus." It's not just narrative, and it's certainly not metaphor: in the Book of Acts—the story of the formation of the Christian Church at Antioch in the days after Christ's Ascension and the first apostolic missions of Peter and Paul—God appears as a blinding flash of light and speaks directly to Saul of Tarsus on the road to Damascus; when Peter gets thrown in jail, angels come in the night to melt his chains and bust him out; Paul's hands heal the sick just as Jesus's had. The yearning for the uncorrupted early Church is also a sincere yearning for a human world in which God can and will directly and visibly intervene.

In Tyler, Texas, in the late 1960s and very early 1970s, this "cult" described by Paul Aaron was just a family: Royal and Edith and their young son, Mark; Edith's first son, Winston Van, who was then living in Dallas and whose marriage to Mia was already failing after less than a year since they had returned from Korea, could maybe be counted as a peripheral member. Most of Edith's family also lived in the Dallas area, but by the late 1960s, Edith had cut off all contact with her mother and siblings. Paul Aaron would testify that when Edith and Paul's mother died in 1971, Edith, Royal, Mark, and Winston Van did not attend her funeral, but waited outside the gates of the cemetery until all the mourners had dispersed from the graveside ceremony; when everyone had gone, they approached the yet-uncovered grave, and each of them tossed a pebble onto the casket—and, Paul said, "they pronounced an anathema on my mother and her mother and Van's grandmother." That testimony comes from an appeal to Winston Van's sentence four years after his conviction, in 1984; the lawyer for the defense asked Paul Aaron about the word *anathema*. "It's a curse," he said. "The entire meaning is not clear to me except that I suppose one who has received this curse is supposed to lose his soul. I think that would be the bible definition of it."

That same year that Edith made her husband and sons pronounce anathema upon her recently dead mother, Royal had some sort of ugly falling-out with his father over something related to the trucking business. Royal liquified all the family's assets and took out a bank loan, and the family, with resources considerably reduced, moved back to Baton Rouge. He managed to scrape together enough money to buy a trailer, and they moved it into a trailer park on the outskirts of the city. For whatever reason, the Ethyl Corporation wouldn't rehire him. After that, Royal struggled to find work, and the family's finances dwindled. The following year, 1972, they "founded" their church and simultaneously registered it as an corporation, presumably for tax purposes: the Church of God in Christ through the Holy Spirit, Inc. It was the same year that Royal and Edith self-published a book titled *The Third Step to Joyful Living, or How to Stop Worrying* and registered the copyright with the Library of Congress. I have tried to track down a copy of it, with no success yet. (The Library of Congress keeps all publishing records but throws away some books after a certain number of years, this title unsurprisingly being one of them.) 1972 was also the year when Edith Harris, who had declared herself a prophet, prophesized that her younger son, Mark, then twelve years old, was also destined to be a prophet.

At some point in the mid-1970s—all I know is that it happened after 1972 and before 1976—the claustrophobically close-knit group began to expand, and here the story begins to emerge more clearly out of the dark. Edith's first son, Winston Van, had recently moved to Houston and found work at an insurance firm and a part-time job teaching karate; he wasn't there long before his wife, Mia, divorced him and he lost his primary job. He joined his family in Baton Rouge, where he briefly worked for another insurance company before landing a job as an assistant bookkeeper at Lynch Freight, a trucking company, which he held for a couple of years. There he met and married his second wife, June, who joined his parents' church. Also in Baton Rouge around this time, the mid-1970s, two outsiders, Larry and Suzette Freeman, joined the Church of God in Christ through the Holy Spirit, Inc.

Barbara Suzette Kleinpeter was born on February 27, 1947 in Grosse Tête, Louisiana, the first of nine children. The Kleinpeters are a prominent and sprawling family in southern Louisiana, with roots that go back to German émigrés who settled in New France in the late seventeenth century. Another branch of the family owns a large, successful, more than century-old dairy farm on the other side of the Mississippi, and the red-and-white Valentine-heart logo of Kleinpeter Farms Dairy is a ubiquitous sight in the refrigerators of Louisiana's groceries and convenience stores. Suzette's grandfather, William Sidney Kleinpeter, made a fortune in logging, acquired a great acreage of land and twelve hundred head of cattle, and today the main artery that runs through Grosse Tête—Sidney Road—is named after him. Grosse Tête, a village of about seven hundred residents, straddles a bayou seventeen miles west of Baton Rouge. It is a picturesque place that looks like a romantic exaggeration of southern Louisiana: verdant showers of Spanish moss hanging from the witchy claws of live oaks; fields of sugarcane. Alligators can sometimes be seen sliding through the film of fungal muck on the glassy surface of the bayou; and the night air in the summer, when I saw it, is enchanted with the phosphorescent twinkling of lightning bugs. That Kleinpeter patriarch with all the land and cattle and logging money left three farms situated all in a row to his three sons, each of whom married and was fruitful, multiplied: three sets of cousins, altogether twenty-two kids growing up in the middle of the century on the country road named after their grandfather.

There was something dark and rotten between Suzette and her mother, Barbara Landry Kleinpeter (the Landrys are another big old Louisiana family). Barbara was an alcoholic whose drinking worsened throughout her life until she died of complications of diabetes brought on by her alcoholism in 1975. Suzette would often tell her brother Jerry and her sister Freida—the second and third oldest siblings, with whom she was closest—that her mother was jealous of her. "I don't know if she was talking about looks or what," Jerry Kleinpeter told me. "I don't know. It was kind of strange. They kinda had a strange relationship." (Several people have mentioned Suzette's physical beauty to me; it seems to have been an important part of the story. In a high school yearbook photo she looks a lot like Natalie Wood in *Splendor in the Grass*.) The friction between Suzette and her mother was so bad that Suzette moved out, and she spent most of her childhood living with her mother's parents down the road. She moved back in with her parents and siblings only after both her maternal grandparents had died, when she was in high school.

When Suzette was twenty years old, she married a fellow Grosse Tête native, Robert Dardenne, a Vietnam veteran recently returned from the war; their daughter, Desha, was born in 1970, and the couple divorced not long after that. A few years later, Suzette met and soon married Thomas Larry Freeman—also a native Louisianan, also a Vietnam vet, and also a divorcé, with two young sons from his previous marriage.

Like many Cajun families, the Kleinpeters and the Landrys were Catholics, and Suzette and her many siblings grew up attending Mass at St. Joseph Church in Grosse Tête, where all her brothers were altar boys. But when she got together with Larry Freeman, who had grown up Southern Baptist in a more northerly part of the state,* she drifted away from Catholicism and toward nondenominational evangelical Christianity. She and Larry began attending church at the Family Worship Center Church in Baton Rouge, headed by the helmet-haired pioneering radio minister (and first cousin of rock and roll great Jerry Lee Lewis) Jimmy Swaggart, who would later go on to become famous as a televangelist, and then infamous as a hypocrite and charlatan when he was defrocked after several prostitution scandals in the late 1980s. Jerry Kleinpeter thinks his sister and her second husband may have met the Harrises through Jimmy Swaggart's church in what had to have been 1975 or the first months of 1976.

Suzette Kleinpeter and Larry Freeman married in 1976. Suzette's semiestranged and long-suffering mother, with whom she'd had a deeply troubled relationship, had drunk herself to death at the age of fifty-one less than a year before, and later that year, Edith Harris—the founder, matriarch, and first prophet of the Church of God in Christ through the Holy Spirit, Inc.—Edith Harris, died of a heart attack at the age of fifty.

Larry and Suzette joined the church shortly before Edith's death. After Edith died, the small group probably would have been reeling in

---

* A famous anecdote about Louisiana's Protestant/Catholic, north/south divide from T. Harry Williams's biography of Huey P. Long: "It is said that while campaigning in southern Louisiana, Huey Long was told that many voters were Catholic. 'When I was a boy,' he began speeches, 'I would get up at six o'clock in the morning on Sunday, and I would take my Catholic grandparents to mass. I would bring them home, and at ten o'clock I would hitch the old horse up again, and I would take my Baptist parents to church.' A colleague later said, 'I didn't know you had any Catholic grandparents.' To which he replied, 'Don't be a damned fool. We didn't even have a horse.'"

uncertainty, destabilized by the abrupt passing of the woman who had been their main driving force. I have encountered many different sources describing Edith Harris as a figure of almost terrifying dominance and control, and I believe her death created a sudden, sucking power vacuum, which Suzette Freeman adroitly stepped into; she quickly and radically changed the social dynamics of what by now could surely be termed a cult.

Now they were a group of eight: Royal; his son, Mark; his stepson, Winston Van and his second wife, June, who had just given birth to a son, Matthew David; Larry and Suzette Freeman; and her young daughter, Desha. Soon afterward, two more would join them: a lost and confused young man named Johnny Stablier, and a psychologically broken, penniless, and desperate twenty-year-old woman with an infant daughter who had just been abandoned by her abusive husband. Her name was Lucy Clark, and her daughter was named Bethany Alana.*

---

* I have changed the first and last names of Lucy and her daughter, but for reasons that will become clear much later, her daughter's middle name, Alana, remains unaltered. I have also changed the names of other people and places connected to Lucy Clark.

7

The Tribulation

Lucy clark was born in baton rouge in 1956 and grew up near there on her family's farm in Camden, Louisiana, the youngest of five children. They grew up "on the old home place," Lucy said, and a lot of native blood ran in her family. "I am French and Indian," she wrote. "My great-grandfather on Mama's side was full-blooded Choctaw whose tribe came down the Trail of Tears in North Carolina. My great-grandpa on Daddy's side was full-blooded Cherokee. My mother's dad was French. My oldest sister Emma and I are the only ones with light blonde/brown hair. All the rest have black hair. I was born black-headed, but didn't stay that way though." Lucy grew up in a musical family. "My grandpas on both sides played the fiddle. All of my mother's brothers played also. My uncle Billy had a bluegrass band and had a show on the radio when I was younger. The same person who played for Hank Williams, Lum York, also played the bass fiddle for Uncle Billy. I learned how to play the guitar when I was eight years old. I would play with my uncle. I couldn't read a note of music if my life depended on it, though. My uncle always used to tell me that if you hear it in your mind and heart, then you could play it with your hands."[*]

---

[*] The bass fiddler she mentioned, Lum York, was one of Hank Williams's Drifting Cowboys from 1944 to 1949 and went on to play in bands with Lefty Frizzell and

Camden is a small town spread out along I-12 in a wide stretch of verdant and pancake-flat land between Baton Rouge and the swamplands at the edges of Lake Pontchartrain, and it's another quaint, rural place where everyone knows everyone. When she was a freshman at Camden High School, Lucy fell in love with her schoolmate Gary Clark, a year older than her. She married him shortly after graduating from high school at the age of eighteen. Soon after, Gary began beating and otherwise abusing her. "I was not allowed to see my family even though they only lived 3 miles from me," Lucy wrote. "Many times my Dad would come by my house and I would pretend I was not at home because I did not want him to see my face black and blue and eyes swollen shut. I was not raised in a family that was abusive like that. At that time, I was pregnant with Bethany." She gave birth to their daughter, Bethany, on November 2, 1974. Her husband left her for another woman when Bethany was a few months old. "So here I was a child with a child devastated and just didn't know where to go."

Lucy and her daughter moved back in with her family for about a year, and they helped her care for the baby. She was psychologically damaged by the domestic abuse, heartbroken, dependent upon her family, and dirt broke. A couple of months after her divorce from Gary was finalized in 1976, she went to an employment agency in Baton Rouge, seeking temp work. That was where she met June Harris, Winston Van Harris's wife, and Suzette Freeman, who were working there. An employment agency is a good place to meet desperate people. Abused, broken down and brokenhearted, taking care of her infant daughter, twenty years old and desperate for money, Lucy was in a dangerously vulnerable

---

Bill Monroe. But my favorite factoid about Lum York: Legend has it that late one night, while driving back from a gig, Hank Williams, his wife, Audrey, and all four Drifting Cowboys were crammed into their 1942 Chevy Fleetline, trying to get some rest; Lum glanced out the window, saw the beacon light outside town they used as a landmark, and lay back down, saying "We're gettin' close to Montgomery. I saw the light." Hank remarked that the phrase was a good title for a song, and wrote the signature tune the next day.

and emotionally fragile state.—exactly the sort of person cults prey upon. "They sent me on a couple of interviews," Lucy told me, "and I think I got a job. I can't even remember where the hell it was at now. But then they would start wanting to know how I was doing, because they knew the situation I was in, and they knew that I had a baby—and they kind of drew me in, and I went to Suzette's house, and they were talking about their church, and I . . . at the time I was so beaten down by my husband, and then you have this little light. That's how they kind of put me in there. How I got involved with them. . . . I was young, stupid and had been in a beating relationship, and just so far down that I didn't even hardly know my own damn name. And so it was, like, they just kind of sucked me in there." Lucy became more and more closely involved with the church over the next year. She had moved out of her family's home again and was living on her own with Bethany in an apartment in Camden. Throughout 1976 and the beginning of 1977, the Church of God in Christ through the Holy Spirit, Inc., gradually isolated her from her friends and family. "It was days that I sat in the chair, and it was like that toward right before we left. 'Your parents don't love you and they're bad for you and you can't talk to them and you can't go around them and you can't see them.'" Lucy did not join the church until after Edith Harris died. By the time she did, Royal was still the church's "Pastor," but the position of "Prophet" had been passed down after his mother's death to her son, the then-fifteen-year-old boy, Mark Harris. Suzette Freeman was called the "Interpreter." I believe that by this point she had become the church's real leader. And when Lucy had been with the church for over a year, in the winter to early spring of 1977, "all of a sudden we were supposed to be going to Arkansas," she told me, "because of such-and-such tribulation and this kind of stuff. All the bad stuff didn't happen until we got to Arkansas." The Church of Christ in God through the Holy Spirit, Inc., moved from the Baton Rouge area to Northwest Arkansas; the wilderness of the Ozarks was their eventual destination. They towed up the trailer that Royal owned and parked it in the Midway Trailer Park in Springdale, rented another trailer next door to it, and rented an apartment not far away in Rogers. For a time, Royal and Mark were living in one trailer, Winston Van and June with their young son in the other, Lucy and her daughter, Bethany, in a small camper-trailer parked in the driveway, and everyone else—the Freemans and Johnny Stablier—in the apartment in Rogers. At some point, Suzette ordered Lucy and her daughter to move into the apartment with them.

Jesus prophesizes the Great Tribulation in the Olivet Discourse, which appears in all three synoptic Gospels, and in Matthew (chapter 24) it is the final speech he makes to his disciples before the narrative of the Passion, the crucifixion, and the resurrection. "Tell us," the disciples ask of Jesus, "when shall these things be? and what shall be the sign of thy coming, and of the end of the world?" . . . "Ye shall hear of wars and rumors of wars," he answers—many false prophets, nation rising against nation, kingdom against kingdom, famines, pestilences, and earthquakes, and then the end shall come. "Then let them which be in Judaea flee into the mountains. . . . For then shall be great tribulation, such as was not since the beginning of the world to this time, no, nor ever shall be."

The Church of God in Christ through the Holy Spirit, Inc., relocated from Baton Rouge, Louisiana, to Northwest Arkansas because its leaders intended it to serve as their way station and jumping-off point before moving into the sparsely populated Ozarks to wait out the imminent nuclear war they believed would kick off the Great Tribulation, and then to hide from the roving bandits and warlords and such in the three and a half years (Revelation: "a time, times, and half a time") to follow before the second coming of Christ and the end of the world.

During their year and several months in Arkansas, Lucy worked almost constantly. She had three different jobs. She worked for one of the area's biggest employers, Tyson, at a poultry-processing plant, and at a Long John Silver's, and waitressed at a diner, and she turned all of the money she earned over to the church. Winton Van Harris also worked at the Tyson plant, and also gave everything he earned to the church. None of the other members of the cult worked, and the toddler, Bethany, was often left in the care of the others. One of the other cult members—

usually Royal, Winston Van, Larry, or Suzette—would drive Lucy to her various jobs, pick her up at the end of her shift, and take her to the next one, or back home.

"I was so scared of these people," Lucy told me. "You couldn't go nowhere. You couldn't call your family. My family did not know where I was at. And I had wrote letters. Even after all this happened, I know I told my sister, I wrote you letters. And she said, I never got them. So I wrote the letters, but they wouldn't send them. They would destroy them. They took all my stuff. I come home from work one day, and Suzette had sold my wedding ring and my graduation ring and all my clothes."

Some horrific anecdotes about that time surfaced in Lucy's trial and are mentioned in the newspaper coverage of it—for example, that one of Suzette's adages to justify the beating and torturing of children was, "It's better to be black and blue on the outside than black on the inside." From the September 13, 1978, *Blytheville Courier News*, concerning June Harris's testimony in court:

> Mrs. Harris said sometime in late March, a meeting was called concerning Bethany.
>
> At that meeting, Mark Harris placed a pot on the coffee table in one of the members' homes in Rogers and started a fire in it. He ordered Mrs. Clark to get some pictures and Bethany's doll and threw them into the fire, she said.
>
> Mrs. Clark tore the clothes off the doll and threw them and pieces of the pictures into the fire, Mrs. Harris testified. When flames shot up out of the pot, Mrs. Harris recalled that Mrs. Freeman said, "That's what it's going to be like, Bethany, in hell."
>
> She then screamed to Bethany, "Put your hand in the fire," Mrs. Harris testified.
>
> She said Winston Van Harris took the child's hand and placed it into the flames. Mrs. Clark did not try to stop them; she only called out, "Van," Mrs. Harris testified.
>
> Mrs. Freeman then held Bethany over the fire, Mrs. Harris

recalled. She said that afterward Bethany's hand was black and blistered.

The hand was placed in ice water, then wrapped in gauze, but no other medical attention was given, she testified.

Everyone seemed to live in terror of Mark Harris and Suzette Freeman—the "Prophet" and the "Interpreter." The founding member of the church, Royal Harris, appears to have taken on a secondary role: His job was not to make decisions but to enforce Mark and Suzette's rule over the others. At one point in one of the court transcripts, Richard Parker, the public defender appointed to defend Mark Harris, arguing for a lighter sentence for his client, said, "We would ask you to consider that if a seventeen-year-old boy orders or tells his father and his brother who is almost twice his age to go out and shoot a child, and they actually go do it, who should owe the greater responsibility or draw the greater penalty, the boy for telling them to do so, or the father and the brother for actually going out and doing it?" It is disturbing how Mark Harris acquired this seemingly absolute—divine—power over the others. His mother Edith declared her son to be a prophet in 1972, when he was twelve years old, and she died not long afterward. The boy seems to have been in control of everyone else, including his father, since then. The lion shall lie down with the lamb, and a little child will lead them. "Since Suzette supposedly was an 'interpreter,'" Lucy wrote in an email, "and Mark the 'prophet,' I was always afraid of God. Many, many times I would have sat in a straight back chair in the middle of the floor, after coming home at night from work and listening to them tell me what God was going to do to me. Over and over and over." Later in the same email: "At that time my fear of those people and God was so great it was like I was nobody. I honestly believed that they were getting messages and if I did anything, they would know about it because God would tell them. I was doomed any way I went."

The series of events that led to their arrest in the woods began some-time in mid-April 1978, when Mark Harris and Suzette Freeman de-clared June Harris—Winston Van Harris's wife, who had been in the church longer than Suzette had—to be "anathema," accused her of having an affair with a woman who lived nearby, accused her of worshipping the Devil, and cast her out of the church—keeping her son, Matthew David, who was two years old and who may have been suffering from the same routine physical abuse on Mark and Suzette's orders as Bethany was. Her husband gave her some money and let her take their car. Distraught and panicked, June drove all night back to Baton Rouge, but when she got there, she had second thoughts, turned around, and drove all the way back to Rogers to try to get her son back. (That's about a ten-hour drive both ways.) She met with James Mixon, a family law attorney in Bentonville, and explained at least some part of the situation to him.

Mixon's reaction to June's story was: This is not a hire-a-lawyer problem you have here, this is a call-the-cops problem. He called the police and told them that he was almost certain that something dark and crazy and deeply fuckedup and involving young children was happening in that trailer park and they had better look into it—and he had a woman right there in his office who needed to get her son out of there right now. Because they believed that it might be an urgent matter of the child's safety, before they had the arrest warrant, some Benton County sheriff's officers escorted June Harris to the two trailers in Springdale, from which they took Matthew David and returned him to June.

Lucy and Bethany were inside the trailer when the police knocked on the door. "And they would not let me go outside, because I would've left them," Lucy told me. "I said, 'Just let me go home, just let me go home.' 'Okay,' [Suzette said.] 'We'll let you go home.' But when the cops came to get Matthew, they refused to let me go out of the room. And the cops never came in the trailer. So it was like, oh my God, that was my chance."

When the police retrieved Matthew David Harris from Royal's trailer in the Midway Trailer Park, they also wrote down the license plate numbers of the cars parked outside. Benton County issued a warrant for the arrests of Royal, Winston Van and Mark Harris, Larry and Suzette Freeman, Johnny Stablier, and Lucy Clark for suspected child abuse. But by the time the police returned to the trailer park later that day with the warrant, they had all fled, and one of the two trailers was on fire.

After the visit from the police, Suzette Freeman told everyone that Mark Harris had received a message from God, which she believed she had successfully interpreted; it was that the time of the Great Tribulation had been "moved up." The apocalypse had been rescheduled, and they had no time to waste. The catastrophic nuclear war that was going to inaugurate the end times would begin at any moment, and the time to flee into the mountains was now.

That night, the church checked Lucy and her daughter into a motel somewhere outside Fayetteville under a fictitious name, while, according to Lucy, "they got all their stuff together, I guess with the guns and the trailer, the U-Haul and all that stuff." Lucy knows now that the night alone with her daughter in the motel was another lost opportunity to escape. "I've had many people ask me, why didn't you leave? Why didn't you leave? I don't know why. I didn't leave 'cause I was scared. 'Cause they watched me all the time." And the next morning, "they come got me." Then Royal, Van, Mark, Suzette, Suzette's daughter, Desha, Lucy, and Bethany, in Royal's Jeep Wagoneer towing the aluminum camper-trailer that Lucy and Bethany had been living in before they moved in with Suzette, Larry, Johnny, and Desha, and a rented twenty-four-foot U-Haul moving truck, drove from Northwest Arkansas to Cave Mountain in the Upper Buffalo Wilderness; they climbed a few miles up Cave Mountain Road, turned down Kaypark Road, and rumbled down the tiny forest service road until the U-Haul got stuck. They did manage to drive the Jeep towing the camper-trailer a good way into the woods, though, and found a spot near Kaypark Cemetery to camp for the night.

The place where they were camped is about two miles, as the crow flies, from the place where Haley would get lost in the woods twenty-three years and five days later.

Meanwhile, Suzette's husband, Larry Freeman, and Johnny

Stablier—also on Mark and Suzette's orders—drove up to Columbia, Missouri, where Larry's ex-wife, Dinah Turnbull, lived with their two sons—four and seven years old—to kidnap the children and take them to the place where the others were bivouacked in order to await the Tribulation.

Larry Freeman and Johnny Stablier broke into Larry's ex-wife's home in Columbia, tied her to a chair, and successfully kidnapped their two kids. But Dinah Turnbull managed to untie herself and called the police, and the two men were arrested on the highway an hour later. This is from an article in the *Columbia Missourian* covering Larry Freeman's trial that summer:

> Freeman was arrested in April less than an hour after he and a fellow religious cult member, John Stablier, allegedly tied up Freeman's ex-wife, Mrs. Turnbull, and took Freeman's two sons from their mother's Columbia home.
>
> Freeman said the leader of the cult told him to go to Columbia to bring his sons to the hills of Arkansas in preparation for the end of the world.

Unbeknownst to the other members of the church, Larry Freeman and Johnny Stablier were arrested on April 21, two days before the murder of Bethany Clark.

Bethany Alana Clark was killed because Mark Harris said that the voice of God had told him —and Suzette had agreed via "interpretation"— that Bethany was "anathema" and had to die. That is the reason Mark Harris still gave later in court during his sentencing. One particularly disturbing thing about the court transcripts is that Royal and Winston Van Harris seem to be aware that the jig is up—they understand that they're about to be sentenced for murder, and are no longer in make-believe land—but Mark Harris does not. He still believes. He also still believes he is a prophet. He sometimes floats off on irrelevant flights of insane, quasi-Christian mystical gobbledygook that the judge frequently interrupts with comments such as "Mr. Harris, at this time I do not want to get into the philosophy of the church." Mark is still, so to speak, drinking the Kool-Aid—his own. (That wasn't an idiom yet, because the Jonestown massacre would happen a little less than two months after the trial ended.)

In court Royal Harris would offer another explanation, which was that they all seriously believed that a three-and-a-half-year period of the apocalyptic collapse of human civilization loomed on the horizon and that three-year-old Bethany Alana would not survive it, anyway; it had been a mercy killing. An excerpt of Royal's remarks to the judge prior to sentencing:

> I was acting in the belief that tribulation was starting in, and that we would in a matter of hours be in nuclear war, and that I was going in as a military commander of the group and responsible for the protection of the whole group, and I am an Air Force veteran and am very familiar with nuclear bombs and effects or results, and have studied extensively what happened in Germany during World War II and I know what happens when there is a war and law and order breaks down, and I watched the movie *Exodus* just a few nights before this happened and we went in the wilderness. . . . My actions were for the protection of the overall group and having a small child with us was a liability which endangered the whole group and we thought that she could not survive anyway and it would be more merciful to her to be out of it.

My first thought reading this was that it was a piece of self-palliative bullshit that had entered Royal's head when he was in jail long after the fact, before a weird detail he had thought relevant to bring up in court—"and I watched the movie *Exodus* just a few nights before this happened"—prompted me to watch the movie myself to try to glean some guess as to what the flying fuck Royal Harris thought he had gotten out of it. Otto Preminger's film came out in 1960, so Royal must have seen it on TV or something. It's an interesting movie for several reasons, one of them being that it was the first script Dalton Trumbo wrote under his own name after his decade of exile on the Hollywood blacklist. Nominated for seven Academy Awards, of which it won five, it's a three-hour-long historical epic based on the novel by Leon Uris about the founding of the state of Israel. Paul Newman stars as Ari Ben Canaan, a decorated former officer of the Jewish Brigade in the British Army during World War II who tricks the British military into letting 611 Jewish refugees, most of them Holocaust survivors, being held in the Karaolos internment camp on Cyprus board a decrepit cargo ship to be sent back to Germany, which he intends to redirect instead to the British Mandate of Palestine; the British realize they've been duped after the refugees board the ship but before it leaves, so they block it from the harbor; then there's a long standoff as the people on the ship dump their provisions over the sides and declare a hunger strike; on the ship there's a lot of back-and-forth about the ethics of including the children with them in the hunger strike: at one point a doctor on board says to Ben Canaan, "We've made a mistake—a bad mistake in letting the children be part of this. A child's body grows every hour. They need food more than adults. Their bladders require more sugar." The doctor convinces Ben Canaan to let the children off the ship, but their mothers band together and patriotically refuse. "I will not take him back to Karaolos," one says while holding her infant. "He will go to Palestine with me, or right here on the ship we will die together. I will not take him back." So: Huh—thoughts about the extraprecarious health of children in times of crisis—and the harsh but supposedly noble necessity of sacrificing them, for their own good or for a higher cause—may actually have been bouncing around in Royal's deeply deluded mind in the days before Bethany's murder.

That the film so clearly resonated with Royal Harris may have had something to do with his wife's earlier obsession with British Israelism. I personally believe that there is an element in the Abrahamic religions that tickles a certain romantic itch for historical fantasy. I first had something like that thought as a child at Bethany Baptist's Summer Bible

Day Camp, when the counselors told those of us assembled in the pews that we were about to go back in time. The magic school bus drove us to some kid's house, where his parents were waiting in the backyard, dressed in impressively professional-looking Bible-times costumes, with a pre–Columbian Exchange Levantine lunch arranged on blankets on the ground, ready with a lesson in Ancient Aramaic table manners—the ritual significance of washing feet and breaking bread and so on. I suspect that this LARPing element of Christianity might even go back to the Middle Ages, when painters felt free to anachronistically depict Classical and Ancient Hebraic subjects such as Hercules and Samson in clothing or armor that was contemporary for them, but when depicting Jesus, Mary, or the apostles, they usually remembered those characters' historical, cultural, and geographical contexts as distinct from those of the artists or the worshippers looking at their paintings: robes and sandals and so on. This historical fantasy reaches out from the holy texts and touches the fingers of the present via apocalyptic prophecy—absolutely essential to the theological structure of the religion—that has been foretold but not yet come to pass: the long-awaited return to the land promised to the descendants of Abraham, lost at a time when armies fought with bows and arrows and swords and regained in the time of tanks and machine guns, but continuous within the same story. This emotional narrative, built on a foundation of romantic fantasy and essential to the self-mythology of Israel, is connected with a mystical umbilical cord to the Christian Revelation, a scriptural mirror that reflects your own times' nightmares, whatever they are, whenever you are: a flash, a ring of fire, a mushroom cloud rising over the plains of Gomorrah, a sea of blood reaching high as the horses' bridles.

Who actually murdered Bethany is a matter of some dispute. "Each one of 'em had shot her," Ray Watkins said. "That's what the prophet wanted to do, have each one of 'em shoot that little girl. That's what the others told me." With all respect due to Ray, I think his imagination invented that in the intervening years. In court, the narrative solidified into this: On Monday morning, Royal Harris and Winston Van Harris took Bethany out of sight about fifty feet away from the campsite, and about an hour later they returned without her. Throughout her trial Lucy maintained that she had never heard the gunshots. Though the three were not very far away, this isn't implausible; sound does not travel very far in the Buffalo National River Wilderness in late April, with full foliage on the trees. Plus, a .22 is a very small-bore weapon that doesn't make much noise. That may have even been precisely why they used it; as Ray Watkins duly noted, they had plenty more powerful firearms with them. It may have also been the reason it took eight shots to kill her.* In court, Royal insisted that he had been the one who had pulled the trigger—eight times—but that may have been a story they'd agreed on in the hope that the much older man, rather than his thirty-one-year-old stepson or his seventeen-year-old son, would get the longer prison sentence.

Forty-six years later, Lucy's memory of the sequence of events is a bit muddled, and she contradicted what she had said in court about not hearing the gunshots. She told me that she and Bethany had spent the first night in the woods in a tent with Suzette and Desha, and the next morning, "Suzette said Van and Royal were going to get some water and they wanted Bethany to go with them. . . . He [Royal or Van] took her by the hand and said, 'We'll be right back.' And then I'm sittin' on this log, and that's when I heard the shots. . . . They came back, they didn't have her. And I wanted to know where they were, and Suzette kept telling me, 'You sit down and hush, just sit down and hush. It's okay. It's okay.'" She does not remember what happened the rest of that day or the following night, but the next morning was when Fred Bell and Ed Burton discovered their campsite and the Sheriff's officers later arrived to arrest them; she does remember that all of them were holed up in the

---

* When I was a kid learning to shoot with Jay and my dad on Jay and Joyce's plot of land in Fourmile Canyon, they started me with a .22 rifle—aka a "peashooter"—because a kid can fire it fairly safely: very little recoil. I remember picking up the Coke cans I'd just shot off a log and hearing the bullets still rattling around inside them: the gun was powerful enough to blow through one side but not the other; the aluminum cans had no "exit wounds."

camper-trailer when the police got there, and that Van was sitting beside her with a .357 Magnum pointed at her. "They knocked on the door, and Van said, 'Shut up, don't say nothing.' And we opened the door and went outside. And that's when all they got us." She told me that she was in retrospect grateful that the sheriff's officers arrested them when they did, because if they hadn't, she was sure "they would've killed me, too."

8

The Child Is Not Alive

Newton county sheriff hurchal fowler and deputy ray Watkins arrested five people that day: Royal, Winston Van and Mark Harris, Suzette Freeman, and Lucy Clark. Within one day of the arrests, 19th Judicial District Judge W. H. Enfield in Benton County had granted Suzette Freeman immunity from prosecution in exchange for her agreement to testify as a witness for the state of Arkansas. The other four entered pleas of not guilty, but Royal and Mark would later switch their pleas to nolo contendere, or no contest, and Winston Van Harris would switch his plea to guilty. Only Lucy Clark maintained her plea of not guilty; thus hers was the only case that went to trial.

Why Suzette was allowed to walk while Lucy was put on trial was totally unclear to me when I first began researching this story, but it was tempting to put it down to the very facts that make it seem the opposite outcome would have been more just. Suzette was much older and more experienced; had made herself powerful enough in the cult's leadership that she apparently had more standing in it than Royal's stepson's wife, June Harris; and by most accounts was a terrifyingly forceful and manipulative person. Lucy, on the other hand, was a twenty-two-year-old single mother, a woman who had been badly abused and then abandoned by her husband before she had joined a cult, and who had been terrified of disobeying Mark and Suzette because she seriously believed if she did that omniscient God would tell them. That is to say, Suzette was probably a lot better than Lucy at talking people into things.

When I first spoke with her, Lucy had no idea why Suzette had been granted immunity. "Suzette was a whiz at this stuff," was all she could guess about it. "The very person who gave them the order to kill that baby and to kill me was the one who got immunity and got off scot-free."

I first met Ray Watkins in December 2022. I had gone to the Newton County Sheriff's Office in Jasper, arrived near the end of the day, and caught Sheriff's Deputy J. D. Harper just as he was trying to lock up and slip out a little early at 4:30 on a Friday afternoon. He was more friendly and accommodating than he needed to be to the stranger who pulled up half an hour before the beginning of his weekend, asking to see police records from 1978. He led me into a storage room full of cheap metal shelving units, fetched a cardboard box from on top of one that was hand labeled in Sharpie "1976–1980," and sat chatting with me at a conference table while I flipped through manila folders, each of which contained one slip of yellow legal paper torn in half with ghostly minimal notes jotted on it by hand in pen and sometimes pencil about bad checks and stolen canoes: there was nothing in it about the murder in the woods near Kaypark Cemetery.

Harper apologized. "They weren't too good about writing stuff down back in those days," he said. But he later recalled that Ray Watkins, who had served as deputy sheriff and later sheriff of Newton County back in the 1970s and '80s, was now working at the hardware store, and suggested I ask him about it. "If you go down there now, you might still catch him."

So I thanked him, ran back to my rental car, and drove the two minutes from the Sheriff's Office to Bob's Do It Best Hardware and Lumber just outside town—which thankfully closes at 5:30—and found the eighty-five-year-old Ray Watkins sitting behind the counter in a plaid flannel shirt and green John Deere cap. I introduced myself and asked if he remembered what had happened on Cave Mountain on April 24, 1978. Indeed he did. Pausing a couple of times to ring up customers, he told me the story. This is the end of it:

> We brought 'em out and took 'em to jail and they went to court and they entered pleas. I believe they got life, and some a little less. And the mother, she—the prosecuting attorney gave her immunity because he was gonna have her testify. But we really didn't need her, we had enough evidence to hang 'em all. But she got off, did the deal, and the other three went to penitentiary, and I don't know what happened to 'em after they went down there. They were all charged except for that Clark lady, and the sheriff was pretty upset that the prosecutor gave her immunity, because she was just as guilty as they were—lettin' 'em kill her daughter.

Watkins was right to say they were "armed to the hilt." This is what the *Blytheville Courier News* reported in its coverage of the trial on September 5, 1978: "Newton County Sheriff E. H. [Hershel] Fowler said in April authorities confiscated 15 to 20 weapons and 'something like 2,000 rounds of ammunition' from a van belonging to the sect. The weapons included seven or eight rifles and pistols of assorted calibers, he said." The van also contained food, clothing and several copies of a book

---

* For the sake of completeness, here is the official list of weapons police confiscated from the U-Haul, the Jeep Wagoneer, and the camper-trailer:
  5 boxes .357 mag. Remington (50 rounds per box)
  4 boxes .357 mag. High velocity Federal (50 rounds per box)
  1 box .357 mag. Smith & Wesson (50 rounds per box)
  4 boxes .223 Super X Remington (50 rounds per box)
  4 boxes .223 Remington .55 grams (50 rounds per box)
  10 boxes .223 military steel jacketed (50 rounds per box)
  4 boxes .357 mag. shells (Remington)
  3 20-round Ruger 14 clips
  50 rounds of military .223 ammunition
  2 boxes CC1 mm. mag. .22 (100 rounds per box)

entitled 'The Third Step to Joyful Living, or How to Stop Worrying' by Royal and Edith Harris."

There are a few things Ray misremembered that day—understandably, as it happened forty-six years ago, and although Ray is a rather astoundingly healthy and lucid eighty-five-year-old man, he's still an eighty-five-year-old man. For one thing, it was Benton County, not Washington County, that put out the warrant for the arrests. And most notably, it was Suzette Freeman, not Lucy Clark, who was offered immunity. Ray said

---

1 box Super X 35753 .223 (20 rounds per box)

2 boxes .44 mag. 240 grams Federal

1 box of .32 cal. Remington Arms, fully loaded

1 Walmart bag with misc. .22 shells (37 rounds)

2 sling belts 1" wide and 2 leather holsters 6.5" Blackhawk

3 .357 rounds of ammunition in right pocket of tan vinyl jacket

7 Ruger mini 14s in boxes (.223 cal.)

1 Crossman 1400 .22 cal. air rifle

1 Crossman 760 air rifle

1 .22 Stevens Model 871 auto., recently fired; 3 shells in magazine, 1 in chamber

1 .22 auto. Ranger 101-11

1 Hawes 5 single action .44 mag. Silver City Mars (in box)

1 .357 mag. Ruger Security 6" barrel (in box)

1 .25 cal. auto. pistol, made in Czechoslovakia, marked with "2" on handle and sides, "2-1-58" scratched on the frame, with 4 rounds in clip

1 .22 cal. pistol mod. P44. Johnson Arms & Cycle Work. 8 shot with 6 spent cartridges in it, in black holster (gun appears to have been recently fired)

1 .32 cal. auto. Colt, loaded with 6 rounds of R&R .32 auto. ammunition

1 empty box fox 6" barrel Colt Trooper Mark 3

3 machetes, two in leather cases, one in canvas case

1 High Standard .357 in black holster, Centennial Model Mark II revolver (loaded)

1 .22 Ruger single .22 cal. 6" barrel (loaded)

1 Remington Sportsman 16-gauge model .58 auto. shotgun

1 12-gauge single-shot Ward Hercules shotgun with barrel and stock both sawed off

1 set of black nylon num-chuks

1 set walnut num-chuks

1 hunting knife with 9" blade and holster

1 hunting knife with 12" blade and holster

1 bow, with quiver and 47 arrows

"four people" but then listed them as Clark, the Harrises (three people), and "this other lady." He conflated Lucy Clark and Suzette Freeman, and Suzette faded into the background

Ray misremembered it being Lucy who had been offered immunity, rather than Suzette, but I do believe him that the Sheriff was pissed off at the prosecuting attorney for offering any of them immunity, because he thought they were all equally guilty and furthermore they didn't need the additional evidence of her testimony to convict them.

One thing that Ray was absolutely certain of, however—and he remained so when I returned to Jasper to interview him several more times—is that Hurchal Fowler discovered the body of Bethany Alana Clark later on the same day that they made the arrests. He said he remembers very distinctly that Hurchal had found the body by the time he returned to the campsite after taking the detainees to jail. Days like that one did not happen very often.

"Hurchal, he's a woodsman like I am," Ray told me in a later interview. "He was born and raised in the woods. So he noticed things as different. And so he went looking around, and he found a spot that had fresh dirt on it. It was over by a creek bank, and it shouldn't have been there. So he dug down there, and that's where he found the bucket. It had the little girl in it. Five-gallon bucket with a little girl stuffed in there. And then, when I got back up there after I got 'em in and got 'em locked up, he was still down there. And he came up from the creek, and told me he found the little girl. 'She is dead.'"

In 1978, Jerry Patterson was Arkansas's 14th Judicial Circuit prosecutor. He is still alive, and it took some doing to track him down. While in Arkansas in the summer of 2023, I sent him an email and left him a voicemail, neither of which he responded to. Eventually, with uncharacteristic boldness and unforgiveable rudeness, I simply drove to his address listed in the white pages—a house perched on a hill high up in the Ozarks on a rural road outside the near-ghost town of Marshall in Searcy County—and knocked on the door. No one answered. I was sitting on the front steps of his porch writing him a note when the eighty-year-old man with a face belying understandable confusion and suspicion roared into the driveway in an enormous silver pickup truck with a dog in the back seat of the cab barking her head off at the stranger. Jerry Patterson was shirtless in shorts and flip-flops, with long, wild gray hair and a woolly white goatee. It was midafternoon on the first day of July, and the sunlight bathed the Ozarks in a buttery glow in the wake of a brief but torrential midsummer rainstorm—puddles flashing everywhere—and Jerry's dog paced circles around me and growled. When I introduced myself and told him what I'd come to ask about, he nodded in recognition and invited me inside. The reason he hadn't returned my call or answered my email was because he and his wife had been off the grid the past few days at their lakeside cabin, fishing. They had just come back earlier that day. I sat in his living room—gold-lettered stippled-leatherbound law books on the shelves, rifles mounted on the walls, his dog in the backyard still barking at me, chess set on the coffee table, backyard and beautiful view of the mountains through the sliding glass door to the back porch—and Jerry poured me a glass of water, half buttoned on a shirt, flopped into a tan leather recliner as cracked and worn as the palm of a baseball mitt with one leg over its arm, and began to speak.

"Here's the way it all began," he said. "There was a bulletin that was put out by the law enforcement agencies up in Northwest Arkansas. The reason that there was a bulletin put out is because the father of the child who was killed was very concerned about the welfare of his daughter, and he had requested a welfare check. And when they attempted to make their welfare check, there was nobody there." (It's possible that this also happened, but I think Jerry's memory made it up; everything else indicates that the cult's undoing began when June Harris met with the lawyer James Mixon. Human fallibility and forty-six years tend to pepper fact with fiction, sometimes in fairly banal ways.) "In the meantime, unknown to the father, the religious group that the child was with thought that the world was coming to an end and that Christ was coming to take his 'bride,' they called it, to Paradise or—whatever. So this religious group decided through their prophet, who was a seventeen-year-old boy, that they needed to stockpile food, clothes, guns, whatever they could get ahold of, to carry them over until Christ got here. So they started writing hot checks and they started using credit cards and extending over the limits—they did everything except steal, I guess, and maybe that's what they were doing, too—but whatever they were doing, it was justified because Christ was gonna come and take them to Paradise. So they had all this stuff stockpiled, and there was a very—the most in-strumental person in that was a lady called Suzette Freeman. Suzette Freeman was kind of the mentor for the prophet. The prophet's dad was the preacher, but the prophet talked to God and Suzette Freeman talked to the prophet. I think there's a little more to that, but I'm not positive."

"What do you mean, 'more to that'?" I asked.

Jerry paused for a while, squinted and drummed his fingers on the arm of his chair. "I think she was screwing him."

"Really?" I said. That was new.

"Yeah," said Jerry. "I think so."

"The seventeen-year-old kid?"

"Yeah. Because everything, anything she suggested, that's what he prophesied, see? And so I think there was a really close bond between those two. I don't even want to call it a 'bond,' because that gives some legitimacy to what their relationship was. So anyway. They've got all this stuff stockpiled, and now they're moving out of there. They're trying to find a place to go to. The prophet says that they need to go to the wil-derness in Newton County. And that's what they were going to do, go to the wilderness in Newton County over in the National Forest. So they take their truck, and a big U-Haul truck, and go to the wilderness. And this little girl, precious child . . . apparently Suzette Freeman didn't *like* her. So anytime anything happened that, let's say, didn't facilitate what the prophet was saying, she blamed that little girl. And the prophet, then—he blamed the little girl, too."

According to Jerry, prior to their abrupt relocation to Newton County, back when they had still been in the Springdale/Rogers area, the prophet, through Suzette, had prophesied that there was some sort of treasure buried in a grave somewhere on Cherokee Mountain in Tennessee. So Suzette's husband, Larry, and Johnny Stablier—those two guys seem to have been the group's gofers for such out-of-state missions—drove out to Cherokee Mountain, went looking for the buried treasure, didn't find it, and returned to Arkansas empty handed.

"So they run out there," Jerry said, "and of course they don't find this grave. And so they come back, and the little girl gets blamed for all this. It's because of her they can't find the grave. Suzette and the prophet blame the little girl. And so now they get past that problem, and now they're headed into Newton County and they get into the National Forest, and they have a flat, or they get stuck. I can't remember. Anyway, Suzette and the prophet announce that it's because of the Devil in this little girl. It's trying to keep them from greeting Jesus and going to the ever-ever good land."

"Like it's her fault," I said. "It's her fault that the truck got stuck."

"Yeah. I can't remember exactly, but it was a flat or they got stuck. So anyway, they blame this on the little girl. She's got the Devil in her, and she and the Devil are preventing them from accomplishing their goal to go to the wonderful land with Jesus. So the prophet tells Suzette Freeman and she tells the men that they have to kill the Devil, and in order to kill the Devil they have to kill the little girl. So they take her out and they kill her. Then they stuff her in a five-gallon bucket. They bury her. They shot her with a .22 Ruger. So they come back and they've accomplished it. But now in the meantime, you've got the police up in Northwest Arkansas searching for these folks."

Let's leave Jerry Patterson for now, to return later.

In the Upper Buffalo Wilderness Area on Cave Mountain, in the woods near a Forestry Service road near Kaypark Cemetery, around midmorning on Monday, April 24, 1978, Newton County Sheriff Hurchal Fowler, Game Warden Fred Bell, and Sheriff's Deputy Ray Watkins, with the assistance of Hurchal's son, Eddy, and Fred's friend Ed Burton, arrested

Royal Harris, Winston Van Harris, Mark Harris, Suzette Freeman, and Lucy Clark. Suzette's nine-year-old daughter, Desha, was placed in temporary police custody. (Larry Freeman and Johnny Stablier were also named in the warrant; they had been arrested in Missouri while trying to kidnap Larry's children three days earlier.) According to the arrest warrant issued by Benton County, the group had another young child with them, a girl under five years old. Wherever the second girl was, she wasn't there.

While Hurchal stayed behind to look around their campsite, Ray, Fred, Eddy, and Ed took the four adults, one juvenile, and nine-year-old child to Newton County Jail. Ray then returned to Cave Mountain to rejoin Hurchal. Someone told the Sheriff's Office at Benton County Jail that they had their suspects, and then someone drove the suspects there—a trip of a little over two hours rolling through the Ozarks from Jasper to Bentonville—where the five detainees were fingerprinted, photographed, booked, locked in separate cells, and each allowed to make one phone call. Neither Royal nor Winston nor Mark nor Lucy exercised their right to make a phone call, because none of them had anyone to call. Suzette Freeman, however, called her lawyer, David Matthews.

Matthews, in Jerry Patterson's words, was "a damn good lawyer. He reminded me of Bill Clinton, 'cause he had a hell of a gab." Matthews would later be elected state representative in 1983 and he represented Benton County in Arkansas's House of Representatives until 1990. A Democrat, his career was in fact closely connected with that of Clinton, who had been his professor at the University of Arkansas School of Law and would appoint him special justice to the Arkansas Supreme Court in 1991.* At the time of the murder, Matthews was a young lawyer still

---

* Clinton was first elected governor of Arkansas in 1978 at the age of thirty-one. A photograph that ran beside one of the newspaper articles about the murder shows him at a Friday-night fish fry in a lunch-lady apron and with vestiges of baby fat in his face, captioned "Democratic gubernatorial candidate Bill Clinton took a turn on a fish fry serving line last night at Walker Park. Some 1,000 MissCo residents turned out for the cookout sponsored by the Mississippi County Democratic Central Committee."

in his twenties; he had been licensed in 1976 and had been running a private family law practice in his hometown of Lowell, a little town between Rogers and Springdale, for not quite two years.

Suzette Freeman was already his client; he had represented her not long before in a custody battle over her daughter with her ex-husband, Robert Dardenne. Matthews recalled that sometime in the fall of 1977, Suzette had come to him with "a pretty straightforward case": She was divorced and had custody of her daughter, Desha, who lived with her and her second husband, Larry, in Rogers. Her ex-husband, who lived down in Baton Rouge, wanted visitation rights, and Suzette told Matthews that "her daughter was terrified terrified terrified of her daddy." Matthews lost that case, and the judge ordered that Desha's father was entitled to visitation rights. Matthews vividly recalled that the first handoff happened in the parking lot of his family law office in Lowell: "[Desha] was screaming, kicking, crying, hollering, hitting, begging, 'Please don't make me go, please don't make me go.' Suzette's crying and raising Cain and accusing her ex-husband of torturing their daughter. And he literally physically grabbed her and threw her into the backseat of the car." That histrionic scene in the parking lot of his office was the last time he saw or heard from Suzette Freeman until about six months later on a Monday afternoon in late April, when she called him from the Benton County Jail.

The following day, Tuesday, April 25, 1978, Matthews drove to meet Freeman in a small conference room in the jail and spoke with her for several hours. He recalled that the urgent concern of the police was where the missing little girl was. Nobody knew, and none of the detainees was talking, including Suzette, at first. "She was not being straightforward with me or anyone else," Matthews told me. "But the prosecutor was saying,], we really, really, really need to know where the child is, what's going on. And I spent several hours talking with her and finally said, 'I might be able to get you immunity if you tell them what you know.' And at that time I didn't know what she knew. She wasn't telling me, either.

But anyway, we negotiated the immunity deal with Gary Kennan, the Benton County prosecuting attorney."

The first document in the paper trail of the Harris/Freeman/Clark case is dated April 24, 1978, the day they were arrested and taken back to Benton County, recording the arrests and charges filed against Royal, Winston Van and Mark Harris, Suzette Freeman, and Lucy Clark. The second document is also dated April 24, an appointment of counsel, appointing Tom J. Keith, public defender, to represent Lucy Clark. The third document, a grant of immunity and order to testify giving Suzette Freeman immunity from prosecution in exchange for her testimony in a court of law, is dated April 25, 1978.

Matthews negotiated the plea deal on Suzette's behalf with prosecutor Gary Kennan, the judge signed it, and then—he remembered that they were all sitting around a table in a conference room somewhere in the Benton County Jail: him, Suzette, Gary, and a State Police detective (whose name David couldn't remember)—as the ink of the judge's signature may have still been drying, Suzette said to him and the other two men, "The child is not alive."

David Matthews said that at the time he negotiated the plea deal, he had had no idea whether the child was dead or alive, though the language in the first paragraph of the grant of immunity and order to testify seems to indicate that the Benton County police at the time figured it a high likelihood the missing girl was dead, but they didn't know for sure: "The Prosecuting Attorney seeks to immunize B. Suzette Freeman from prosecution for any matter divulge[d] by her in the course of her testimony concerning the investigation of the battery and possible homicide of Bethany Alana Clark."

Suzette told David Matthews, Gary Kennan, and the State Police detective that Bethany was buried near the area where they had been arrested the day before. I asked David if Suzette had actually gone with the police back to Newton County to show them where the body was buried or if she had just told them where to look. He said he didn't remember.

Here we reach the knot of confusion. Ray Watkins remains adamantly certain that Hurchal Fowler found the body on his own on Monday, and about that I myself believe he is correct; it would have been, to say the least, a memorable day. But Suzette was given immunity on Tuesday, when the Benton County police did not know where Bethany Clark was and were desperate to find her. Why did the police in Benton County not know that the body had already been found the day before?

I held a second and much longer interview with Ray Watkins in October 2023, and the eureka moment hit me in the middle of our conversation. I had called Ray earlier in the day to ask when we could talk, and he had told me to meet him at the hardware store at 5:30. He was closing the store that day, and we could talk after he finished work. After he locked up the store, we sat at a lone wooden picnic table on an interstitial afterthought of lawn between the hardware store's entrance and its empty parking lot and went over the events of Monday, April 24, 1978, in much more fastidious detail than we had before.

After making the arrests, "we was probably back here [in Jasper] at nine thirty, ten o'clock," Ray said. "And I went back probably about eleven o'clock. It was about eleven thirty when I got back over there."

"And when you got back up there," I said, "Hurchal had already found the body."

"Yep. He had already found the body."

"Okay, and that was about eleven thirty, close to noon. And then you—"

"And as far as I know, he didn't have no communication with anybody after that," Ray added. "Except to our office. And we called the coroner, and the coroner would have come right out and done their investigation."

"So he didn't tell anybody that he'd dug up the body except you and the coroner," I said. "And I guess the coroner didn't tell anybody, either. So that's the reason why the cops in Benton County didn't know. Nobody had told them."

"Yeah," Ray said. "That's very possible."

———

Back in Jerry Patterson's living room on the first day of July 2023, Jerry had let his dog in from the backyard, and now she lay curled placidly asleep on the rug between us with damp fur faintly stinking. The sliding glass patio door was open to the humid midsummer's early-evening air, and we were drinking bottles of Budweiser he'd fetched from the fridge.

"The deal they cut was," Jerry said, "was 'we'll give you all the information you want if you'll wave prosecution of Suzette Freeman.' Well, how wonderful. They did it."

On April 24, Benton County charged Royal, Mark and Winston Van Harris, Suzette Freeman, and Lucy Clark with battery in the second degree, "said to have been committed on or about April 7, 1978." The charge was for beating Bethany and Matthew David and burning Bethany's hand, which June Harris had told the Benton County police about. Several days later, once the confusion had cleared up some, it was obvious that the body had been discovered in Newton County and that the murder had almost certainly taken place there; at least the crime of trying to cover it up indisputably had. Jerry Patterson—who was thirty-five at the time and had only recently been elected prosecuting attorney for Arkansas's 14th Judicial Circuit, comprising the four mostly rural counties of Boone, Baxter, Marion, and Newton, filed charges of first-degree murder against all five defendants in Newton County later that week.

Over the course of the coming months, Arkansas's 14th and 19th West (Benton County) Circuits palavered back and forth about it, and the 19th West would drop second-degree battery charges in order for the 14th to focus on the much more serious first-degree murder charges. The defendants were transferred to Boone County Jail in Harrison by the end of the summer.

Sometime before that was settled—Jerry remembered it as having been in mid-May—Suzette's lawyer, David Matthews, drove out to Jerry's office in Jasper to tell him he had to drop the charge against his client Suzette Freeman because of the plea deal Circuit Court Judge Enfield had signed in Benton County on April 25. Jerry remembers it being a tense and contentious meeting. He had mixed feelings toward

David Matthews, the man he called "a damn good lawyer" with "a hell of a gab—just a natural politician." He had a lot of professional respect for him, seasoned with some irritation that Matthews was younger than him and, he could tell, charismatic, well connected, and well positioned to rise in Arkansas politics; Matthews was based much closer to the university and comparatively cosmopolitan Fayetteville than Jerry, who was posted out in the boondocks of the Ozarks. Furthermore, Matthews had him bested, as he had already won this legal proxy battle before he even stepped into Jerry's office; the language of the grant of immunity and order to testify is clear as day: "The Prosecuting Attorney seeks to immunize B. Suzette K. Freeman from prosecution for any matter divulged by her in the course of her testimony concerning the investigation of the battery and possible homicide of Bethany Alana Clark." If the words "and possible homicide" had not been included in that sentence, Jerry would have had solid grounds for filing the first-degree murder charge against Suzette. But they were, and there was nothing he could do about it.

"I wanted to file charges against Suzette Freeman," Jerry said, "and he comes down here and says, 'You can't, because we've made a deal. And you'd have never found this child had it not been for her.'" Jerry rolled his eyes remembering. "That's just—puff, you know."

With all the confusion and lack of communication between law enforcement agencies in Newton and Benton counties, Matthews probably still didn't understand that the body had been discovered *before* he had negotiated the plea deal with the Benton County prosecutor. (Today, Matthews says he doesn't remember whether or not he knew it, but he does remember making the trip to Jerry's office in Jasper to tell him that he had to drop the murder charge against Suzette.)

Remembering that meeting with Matthews raises Jerry's hackles even now. He was outraged that one of the defendants in his murder case had escaped justice so easily and incensed at his being hamstrung to do anything about it. For his part, Matthews expressed some regret about his involvement in the case but can't imagine that he would have done anything differently, considering what he knew at the time and his position as Suzette's attorney. He was only doing his job. Forty-six years have gone by since then, and both he and Jerry rose up the ladder afterward: Jerry went on to serve as a judge for most of his career, and Matthews went on to hold office in the Arkansas House of Representatives and later served as a justice on the Arkansas Supreme Court. Both men have now returned to private practice, and still have mostly complimentary things to say about each other.

"To me, Jerry was a good lawyer, a good guy," Matthews said. "He was outraged at what had happened, of course. Jerry Patterson really, really hated the fact that—I can't emphasize that enough—he *hated* the fact that she got immunity." Not only that; as the prosecuting attorney, he was now going to have to work with her as a witness.

Suzette Freeman spent the tail end of April and the month of May in Benton County Jail, and on June 1 she was released "into the custody and care of her father, Leo Jerome Kleinpeter, Sr., who agrees to supervise the Defendant and assist her in appearing in this Court and any other Court in the State of Arkansas. . . . The Defendant may leave the State of Arkansas and return to her home in Grosse Tete, Iberville Parish, Louisiana."

A few days before the trial began, Suzette—apparently alone, despite the order of release mandating her father to supervise and assist her in appearing in court—traveled back up to Arkansas to testify as a witness for the state. According to Jerry Patterson:

I never will forget my first meeting with Suzette Freeman. I immediately did not like her. I could see that she was a manipulator. And that she had abused the system to save her own ass, and everybody else could go to hell in a handbasket as far as she was concerned. I did not like the woman. At all.

So we're getting ready to go to trial, and I meet with her. She's got a motel room in Harrison. She didn't wanna tell me where she's at. I said, "Well, how in the hell am I supposed to visit with you to find out what you're gonna be doing?" And this is *after* I'd visited with her before. "We've got a trial coming up, I need to sit down with you to get a feel for how to present you as a witness."

She said she didn't want me to know where she was at because she was afraid that somebody would be out looking for her and then possibly kill her. She just fed me—she tried to feed me so full of shit.

And so I said, "All right, you don't want me to know where you're at. I'm the prosecuting attorney. If somebody's gonna kill you, it would be a pretty damn stupid thing for them to do, or even try to do." I said, "You're up! You're under a subpoena. You've gotta come to trial tomorrow."

"Oh, well, oh, well, that's why I came up here. I wanted to visit with you."

And I said, "Well, tell me where in the hell you're at!"

Well, I finally got her to tell me where she was at. It was some motel, some seedy little place, and I . . . damn, I hate that bitch. Brings back a lot of bad memories. Anyway, so she's saying "Well, am I gonna have escorts?"

And I said, "Why would you need an escort?"

"Protection! I need protection."

"Really?" I said. "I don't think you need protection." I said, "Hell, you're gonna be testifying for the state, who's gonna to hurt you?"

"Well, somebody might be mad because I gave information about Lucy and Winston and Mark and their daddy."

I said, "I don't think so."

Oh, well. Here we are, we're getting our preliminaries the day of trial, I'm in my office getting everything ready, and somebody from the clerk's office comes up, knocks on my door, and says, "There's a Mrs. Freeman down here that needs to talk to you."

"That's my witness, Suzette Freeman."

"She needs to talk to you."

I said, "I talked to her last night."

"Well, she needs to talk to you now."

So I go down there: Hollywood! She's got on this damn—some

big old hat. Sunglasses about *this* big. Like some movie star. And of course she's got on some nice dress and everything. But you could see she's trying to hide her face.

And I said, "Well, what is it that you need?"

She said, "How can I get in there without anybody seeing me?"

And I said, "What the—?" I said, "Why are you worried?"

"Well, I just, I'm just *apprehensive*." Da da da dee da.

And I said, "Well, if you feel that badly, there's a staircase through the clerk's office that comes out in the courtroom, over at the far end by the bench. You can come in that way."

So I go back up there, and she follows me up there. And so she's sitting there, and we qualify the jury and do our preliminaries. . . . And I felt so damn mad about the deal. I can tell you that before that trial, I didn't sleep. I bet I didn't sleep three hours. The little girl, the tragedy about the way she was killed, stuffed her in a damn bucket, the Suzette Freeman shit—it troubled me a lot.

Anyway, the record will bear out that we worked a plea deal for Dad and the prophet and Winston. The only person that we had that didn't plead was Lucy. The thing that troubled me about it was, here I am prosecuting this poor girl—and she was . . . she was just a flower girl. She was so timid, so easily manipulated—and it just didn't seem fair to me to be prosecuting her. But that's my job, so I did it.

There was probable cause to charge Lucy, because she was aware of what was going to happen and she didn't stop it. But I'm the prosecutor. So my job was to present the evidence in the best possible way that I could to show the jury that she was guilty. And I did. I didn't like it, but being a prosecutor, it's not what you like and don't like, it's what you have to do. And you know, I would've loved to've just stood up there in front of that jury and point at Suzette Freeman sitting behind me and say, "*That's* the bitch *right there* that you need to send to prison!" But I couldn't.

"But I got the bitch later on," he said—with a vengeful twinkle in his eye—and he told me an interesting coda to the story of what had happened between him and Suzette Freeman.

About four months after Lucy's trial—it would have been in January or February 1979—Jerry got a call from a lawyer who was representing Suzette's ex-husband, Robert Dardenne, in the still ongoing legal fight over custody of their daughter, Desha, who had been living with her father in Grosse Tête since the arrests in April.

"I'd like to subpoena you to come to Louisiana and testify," the lawyer said.

"Yeah," said Jerry. "I'd be happy to."

The lawyer bought him a plane ticket and booked him a hotel room, and the next week Jerry flew from Little Rock to Baton Rouge on a drizzly afternoon. Robert Dardenne's lawyer picked him up from the airport and along with a few colleagues from his law firm took him out for drinks and the most quintessentially Cajun of dinners, a giant heap of boiled crawfish served on a sheet of newspaper, dripping with butter and mouth numbing with capsaicin. "I'd never eaten crawfish before," Jerry said. "It was him, a couple of friends, and me, and I thought, man, no *way* can we eat all that stuff." (This is a thought that often occurs to someone about to eat crawfish for the first time; it looks like a lot more food than it really is because each crawfish, when snapped in half, has only about a teaspoonful of meat in the tail, though you can also slurp the guts out of the head, which is not for the squeamish. It's a messy meal involving frequent minor injuries to the fingers and a lot of spatter—bib recommended.)

The courthouse the following morning was a scene "I'll never forget," Jerry said. "Big-ass courtroom, big window overlooking the Mississippi River, and it's raining. I'm standing there looking out the window, and I hear this commotion behind me. When I turned around, there was Suzette Freeman with a whole gaggle of people. Her new church. Well, course, they're really happy and joyful, and everything just seems to be going along just great for them, until she sees me. When she does, she stops right there."

Suzette had showed up to the custody hearing with a cohort of enthusiastic supporters in colorful holiday dress—fellow worshipers at the church she had joined since returning to Grosse Tête, Sunnyside Apostolic (it, too, it turns out, is an institution embracing of doctrine considerably beyond the theological pale of mainstream Christianity). She had planned to have them all sitting in the public gallery cheering her on, but upon seeing Jerry Patterson standing there in his suit and tie, watching the rain sprinkle the Mississippi through the grand courtroom windows, she stepped aside and said something to her lawyer, who had come in alongside her. Suzette's lawyer then knocked on the door of the judge's chambers, and the clerk let him in. After a few minutes, the clerk came out and asked Robert Dardenne's lawyer to join the conference. A little while later, both of them emerged from the judge's chambers, and the lawyer who'd subpoenaed Jerry and flown him down to Baton Rouge came up to him and told him that Suzette's lawyer had asked the judge to close the proceedings to the public, and he had complied. "You scared the shit out of her," he said. That made Jerry smile.

So the custody hearing proceeded, and the only people in the stately courtroom overlooking the Mississippi River on that rainy winter morning were the judge, the two lawyers, the clerk, the court reporter, Suzette Freeman, Robert Dardenne, their lawyers, and Jerry Patterson. The sizable Sunnyside Apostolic contingent was forced to wait in the hallway outside. Jerry was the first and only witness called that day. He swore the oath, took the stand, and told the lofty and nearly empty room the whole story about everything that had happened the previous year in Arkansas.

During cross-examination, Suzette's lawyer asked him exactly one question: "You don't *like* my client, do you, Mr. Patterson?"

"You're exactly right," said Jerry. "I don't like your client. I don't like anybody who abuses the system in order to save their own ass and let everybody else go to hell."

The judge awarded permanent custody to Desha's father, allowing Suzette Freeman, after she completed "three or four different programs," supervised visitation once a month.

When it was over, Robert Dardenne's lawyer patted Jerry on the back and said, "You did a hell of a job for me."

"Thank you very much," Jerry told him. "I can't tell you how much pleasure that gave me." And then, he said, "I took an airplane back to Arkansas."

Losing custody of her daughter certainly wasn't the lifelong prison sentence Jerry thought Suzette Freeman deserved, but it was at least a small morsel of revenge.

The midsummer sky was now rosy with the beginnings of the late sunset, the dog was asleep on the floor, and the coffee table between us was piled with memorabilia from Jerry's career as a prosecutor, including a 1996 issue of *Playboy* with a paparazzi snap of Uma Thurman on the cover, which quoted Jerry in an article about the right-wing separatist militia the Freemen (he had received death threats for prosecuting one of its members for the rather quaint crime of refusing to register his car; Jerry's job had led him into entanglements with several more cults and extremist organizations over the years). He had returned to thinking about the Church of God in Christ through the Holy Spirit, Inc.

"The boy, that poor boy," said Jerry.

"The teenager, you mean," I said. "Mark Harris."

"Man, he didn't know where he *was*. That's about all I can tell you about him. That's all I can remember. And I *still* hate that bitch."

"Do you think that Suzette was really the main one telling everybody else what to do?"

"Yeah," Jerry said. "She was running the show. She didn't want to take credit for it. 'I don't want to take credit for it, but I *suggested* we do this. I *suggested* we do that. I wasn't in charge, but I *suggested* . . .' She was so full of herself. Whatever happened to her, whatever it was, if it wasn't bad, it was too good for her."

A little later, our conversation turned to Larry Freeman and Johnny Stablier getting arrested in Missouri for tying up Larry's ex-wife and kidnapping their two children while the others were camping in the woods on Cave Mountain.

"Now," Jerry said, "I think those were the same two guys that went to that place in Tennessee. I think those were the same two folks."

"Do you think that she might have been sending her husband off on these crazy missions because she was having this relationship with the prophet, with the teenage kid—just to get him out of the way for a while?"

"Well, kidnapping will get him outta the way for a *long* time, won't it? . . . Yeah, well, I think that's plausible. I sure do. But she was running the show, man. She was the mentor for the prophet. Basically whatever she said, he said, and that was the golden rule. And she made sure, this is God's word. God's word through the prophet."

"Did it come up in the trial? Like what else they believed and how this church had started and so on?"

"No, it did not. The only thing we did is, we presented our case about the murder, about the involvement of poor little old Lucy. She was just *sold*, man, she was just passing on their shit. You know?"

"Yeah."

"I hope her life was better after that."

"And Royal, Winston, Mark—those guys got long sentences. Were you involved with that, or was that just between them and the judge?"

"No, no, I was involved in that. I wanted more time on the boys. But the dad said, 'I'll take the big sentence for a lesser sentence on the boys.' I thought it over and decided that's probably a good thing, 'cause they're gonna get fifty years at least, and Daddy's gonna die in prison. I didn't hate those guys, either, Daddy and the two boys . . . I guess if I ever hated anybody, I hated her."

"You didn't hate Royal."

"I hated Suzette Freeman."

"And you didn't feel the same way about Royal Harris?"

"No. Oh, no. No. I mean, I can't tell you how bad I disliked that woman."

"Do you think that Royal Harris had been manipulated by her, too?"

"Yeah. I think she manipulated everybody. I honestly think that she got involved with this church and she was smarter than everyone else, and she just took charge. But she's smart enough to push others out in front of her. She'd make the decisions, but the actions were done by somebody else, just like the two guys that killed that little girl. She didn't go out there. She made sure that the prophet made the pronouncement and sent those other two guys out there to do it."

"So she just orchestrated the whole thing. She manipulated everybody."

"That's exactly right."

"That's really incredible."

"It's hard to imagine how somebody could do that. I mean, *how*? But then you gotta think about how friggin' bizarre their religion was—to think that they got a *prophet*? That's like *Moses*? He's talking to *God*? You mean the big guy up there?"

"Do you think that Suzette actually believed these things? That she believed that the Devil being in the little girl was somehow responsible for the truck getting stuck, or for their not finding the grave in Tennessee?"

"No."

"You don't think she believed it at all?"

"Right."

"But you think everybody else believed it."

"Yeah, they did. I think she just didn't *like* that kid. That's the reason it happened."

"Do you think that she believed that the second coming was about to happen, and the end of the world was coming?"

Jerry paused, stroked his beard, thought about for a while. "Do I think she thought that? I think that might have been in the back of her mind in a way."

We laughed about that. Then Jerry asked me, "Do you read the Bible?"

"I've read it," I said.

"I have, too. And I'll go to Sunday school, and I enjoy Sunday school—but I don't believe that stuff. I don't believe there was a Moses. I don't believe that the Israelites crossed the Red Sea. I'm not real sure that Jesus Christ was the son of God. I have a lot of questions. And when anybody answers them, they say, 'Well, it's in the Bible.'"

"There are a lot of things in the Bible."

"Yeah. No shit, man," Jerry said. "So what I mean is—if you really believe in all that, well, you can get into some bizarre situations. *They* believed in all that. I don't think Suzette Freeman really did, not hook, line, and sinker like they did. I think that Suzette Freeman had picked up on some stuff, and I think she saw that she was smarter than the rest of them. She was the person that was really making decisions, pulling the strings on the puppets. There you go."

9

Anathema

ROYAL HARRIS, MARK HARRIS, WINSTON VAN HARRIS, AND LUCY Clark spent a little over four months in jail awaiting their trial, first in Benton County Jail, where they were charged with second-degree battery, which was what they had been arrested for, and then, after Jerry Patterson filed the murder charges against them in Newton County, in Boone County Jail in Harrison, which was within the 14th Judicial Circuit but bigger and better staffed and equipped than the tiny jail in Newton County.

Royal, Mark, Winston Van, and Lucy were all appointed public defenders. Tom Keith was appointed to defend Lucy on the day they were arrested. I don't know the reason for the delay with the others, but they weren't appointed counsel until May 26. All four entered pleas of not guilty on June 13 and again at their omnibus hearing on July 6. The court ordered psychiatric evaluations for Royal, Mark, and Lucy. For some reason it never ordered one for Winston Van. Everyone I've talked to who knew Winston Van described him as an extremely garrulous, headstrong, assertive guy; it's possible that his personality did him no favors in the justice system; there were moments when it would have been wiser of him to keep his mouth shut. Dr. Travis Jenkins, the clinical director of the Ozark Guidance Center, evaluated Lucy and Mark. Dr.

Jenkins reported to the court that Lucy was competent to stand trial: "In my opinion there is no evidence to suggest that she is psychotic at the time of my interview with her nor was there any evidence to suggest that she was psychotic at the time of the alleged offense." But Jenkins wrote of the seventeen-year-old Mark Harris:

> I have seen Mark Harris today in psychiatric consultation. The background situation, as well as his current mental status, is very complicated. It is difficult for me to make the usual determination regarding competency and the presence of psychosis based on this one visit.
>
> Therefore, I would like to recommend further observation and evaluation at the Arkansas State Hospital.

The judge in Benton County, W. H. Enfield, had already decided to bypass the Ozark Guidance Center and send Royal straight to the Arkansas State Hospital in Little Rock for his evaluation. Royal and Mark were both examined that summer at the Arkansas State Hospital, whose doctors ultimately declared them both competent to stand trial.

The four months in jail awaiting sentencing were grueling. For one thing, they were all underfed; Mark Harris—a tall, skinny teenager—lost forty pounds in the months before the trial. But Lucy's experience was particularly harrowing. After being terrorized, beaten, and abandoned by her husband, Lucy—still only twenty-two years old—had endured three years of more terror, brainwashing, and physical abuse in the cult, at the end of which they murdered her daughter, and then she spent several months after Suzette's release as the only woman being held in the two Arkansas county jails.

Cops often make under-the-table quid pro quo deals with inmates, offering favors for information having to do with other cases. Lucy told me that one of the deputies in the Benton County Jail unlocked her cell and let in one of the male inmates, who raped her: "The deputy let him in there in my cell one morning. I know the deputy got fired, but hey, you didn't hear about that in the paper, did you? Nope." She said the same thing happened again after she had been transferred to Boone County Jail—that time without anyone being reprimanded for it, apparently.

During the same time, late in the summer of 1978, another inmate started a fire in the Boone County jail in an attempt at escape, and while the fire was being extinguished and the damage repaired, the sheriff's officers rounded up all the inmates and crammed them all into the same cell. Lucy, again, was the only woman. "They put me in the cell with all these guys around me," she said. "And these guys pissed on me and they spit at me, and there was piss all over the floor, and they just left me there all day."

Lucy believes that the Boone County sheriff's officers felt justified in their degrading and contemptuous treatment of her because of their indignant moral disgust at the woman who allowed her three-year-old daughter to be murdered. (I hear a note of this in Ray Watkins's voice even now: "She was just as guilty as they were, lettin' 'em kill her daughter—helpless.") Allowing male inmates to rape her, shutting her in a cell with them—whatever she got she had coming to her, including starvation and sexual humiliation at the hands of the officers themselves. Lucy told me:

> The way the cell was fixed was that they had a door to come into the hallway, and at the end of the hallway was the shower, which had no curtain on it. And I would ask [the sheriff's officer] for a shower, and he would stand at that door and watch me while I took a shower with just a washcloth. . . . And then in the morning they would give me breakfast. I had a spoonful of eggs and a piece of toast, and they would pour half of the coffee out, and I wouldn't get any lunch, I wouldn't get any supper. Because it was like, "Oh my God, this is the worst person in the world."

Tom Keith had been assigned to Lucy's defense when she and the others had been taken to Benton County; early on, she had established a rapport with him, and toward the end of the summer she'd had to write a letter to the judge presiding over her trial for murder in Newton County to allow Keith to continue representing her. "He was my rock," she said of Keith. Newton County also appointed its own public defender, Buford Gardner, to represent her, and from then on, she had a legal defense team of two; Tom Keith was doing it pro bono. Lucy didn't trust Gardner, and she said he screwed her over, too:

> From those jobs that I did—he wanted to know what jobs I had done, and it was like, income tax time. So he had got the papers and figured out where I had worked, and whenever I got my income tax, when it came in, it'd come to him. And he says, "Well, I'm going to keep this." I think it was like six hundred dollars or something. He says, "Well, I'm gonna keep this, but you owe me a lot more."

Tom Keith was young and idealistic. Defending Lucy was a moral crusade for him; he strongly believed that she was innocent. For Buford Gardner, it was a job, and he squeezed every cent he could out of it (which wasn't much). Gardner was a lot older and more experienced than Keith, and another source of tension between the two men arose from the fact that country mouse Gardner was on his home turf, Newton County— the absolute sticks—whereas town mouse Keith was visiting with the judge's special permission from Benton County in the northwest corner of the state, where the university is, a much more populous place abustle with all the economic activity that Walmart, Tyson, and Daisy bring in. The two lawyers didn't know each other well, but they had been friendly before Lucy's trial. During the trial, something happened between them that tore a permanent rift in their friendship, and afterward they never spoke again. Unfortunately I can't ask either of them about it; Keith died five years ago in June 2020, and Gardner died more than twenty years ago in January 2004.

Lucy also had to endure the humiliating ordeal of the trial and the local press's callous and often incorrect sensationalism of it. Suzette's lawyer, David Matthews* ("hell of a gab"), put it most colorfully:

> I did not see anything except the first few opening minutes, but I'll
> never forget those. It was like a scene out of *To Kill a Mockingbird*.
> They obviously did not have cable television in Jasper, Arkansas. That
> courthouse square was packed, I mean, *packed* with people. There
> were folks that had brought up the equivalent of what we'd call a
> food truck now, that were selling concessions on the square. The
> courthouse itself was packed full, full, full. And when Lucy was led
> in to start the trial, this murmur went through the crowd. "There she
> is. There she is. There she is." It was creepy.

"Everyone has his 'own' idea about my case which was sensational-
ized by the newspapers and TV media," Lucy wrote in an email years
later to Joyce. "They know nothing of the horror, nothing. I never knew
who killed my daughter until the trial was almost over."

Tom Keith later came to believe that if all this had happened after the Jonestown massacre—which did more than any other event to
change the public's understanding of cult psychology—the jury and the
press covering Lucy's trial might have better understood the power of
brainwashing and the impossibly weak position she had been in and had
more sympathy for her. Of course, that's possible—but as we've seen recently with a tabloid fixation from a few years ago, Casey Anthony, there
is absolutely nothing that incites the rabble to misogynist wrath more
than a mother who somehow causes or permits the death of her own
child. It scratches at some instinctual horror lodged deep in our mam-
malian middle brain. Milk and motherhood are in the very name of our
warm-blooded taxonomic stratum. It's the nightmare on the other side

---

* Matthews was there to counsel Suzette Freeman and testify if needed, but as soon
as the proceedings began, Jerry Patterson motioned to bar him from the courtroom,
which Matthews had been fully expecting him to do.

of what Colleen Nick would tell Kelly twenty-three years later, advising her to emote like hell for the cameras: "There is nothing stronger and more understood by people than a bond between a mother and child." There is something about these cases people find so horrible that perhaps they perversely crave for the charges to be true. No, Keith thought, Lucy Clark was not guilty of complicity in her daughter's murder, but the shocked outsider's salacious imagination is, and cries out for catharsis.

All four remaining defendants maintained their pleas of not guilty until the morning the trial was set to begin at the Newton County Courthouse in Jasper: Tuesday, September 12, 1978. All three of the men had clashed with their initial court-appointed defense lawyers. All of them had requested to be appointed a new lawyer before the trial, and their requests had been granted. The motion terminating the relationship between Royal Harris and his defense counsel, Donald Bishop, during a pretrial hearing on August 8 was hastily jotted down by hand, apparently the result of a decision Royal had abruptly made that day. By the time of the trial a month later, Royal and Mark had switched defense counsel several times and were represented by attorneys they had met with only once or twice.

Because Winston Van Harris appealed his sentence twice in the decade that followed, the court records in his case were preserved in the Arkansas Supreme Court archive, so I have the most documentation about him. He appealed his case the first time in 1981, alleging inadequacy of counsel, which was denied. He tried again in 1987 and ultimately won a half victory, getting part of his sentence reduced. Because the appeal centered around his claims of inadequacy of counsel, most of the court record is the testimony of his second court-appointed defense lawyer, Doug Wilson, talking about his attempt to represent him in the lead-up to the trial in 1978. Again Winston Van's ego—and mouth—got in his way. At first Wilson figured the best strategy would be to try to present him as a victim, a brainwashed cult member in a weak position, but Winston Van kept undermining that strategy by insisting that he was one of the leaders of the group. "He was not, therefore," Wilson said in court, "in the position of a subordinate adherent to his being brainwashed by the leaders, he was a leader." Throughout his testimony in the appellate case, Wilson vented the frustration he remembered representing a client who wasn't being cooperative and who he strongly suspected wasn't being fully truthful with him. The story that Royal, Winston Van, and Mark had stuck to from nearly the beginning was that Mark had given the order that the child be put to death, Suzette had confirmed that through interpretation, and then Royal and Winston Van had taken her into the woods, away from the others. Royal had been the one to pull the trigger, and Winston Van had helped him bury her. Wilson knew there was almost no chance that his client would not be convicted of a crime and sentenced to significant time in prison; the best he could hope for was to lessen the sentence with the argument that he had been an accomplice who had not directly committed the murder. That strategy deflated after Wilson received the ballistics report on August 8, indicating that two guns, not one, had been used to shoot Bethany Clark; she had been shot eight times, four times with each weapon. The ballistics report prompted Doug Wilson to send Winston Van a (surprisingly funny, considering the circumstances) letter the following day (as a writer, I particularly applaud the sardonic flourish of capitalizing the pronouns referring to God):

Dear Van:

As you may know, the ballistics report is in and shows that two guns were used in the murder. Of course, this pretty well turns your story into a fairy tale. Unless Royal comes up with a new version, that he was aspiring to be a cowboy and packed a couple of sixguns or rifles or whatever for the fun of it. What I am trying to say, as before, is that the jury will in all likelihood include a few people of at least normal intelligence who will listen to your version and get some good laughs out of it before they send you to the penitentiary for the rest of your natural life.

As I have said repeatedly, I'll advocate strongly whatever story you tell me to be true. It doesn't matter that your present version has got more holes in it than a country club golf course. But it does occur to me that one possibility is that you may be doing what you honestly believe God Almighty wants you to do. If that is the case, my advice is to get in touch with God as soon as possible and ask Him if it is all right if you follow your lawyer's advice. Of course, it is also possible that He wants you to work among the prisoners for the rest of your life, in which case He definitely has you on the right track. . . .

I wish I could be more encouraging and less sarcastic, but I really have no reason for either at this point. I'll just say what I've said before—I'll do the very best I can, and that as matters stand, it won't be near enough.

Sincerely,

Douglas L. Wilson

Trial preliminaries began on Tuesday, September 2, 1978, and the trial date was set for September 12. The court-appointed lawyers for the three male defendants—Doug Wilson, Richard Parker (who represented Mark Harris), and Tommy Martin (who represented Royal Harris)—went into it knowing there was virtually no hope of winning the case, but they would try as hard as they could with what they had. They knew that their main job was going to be to try to mitigate the sentences their clients would receive. The jury selection was a long and arduous process that took up most of the week before the trial. Newton County is a thinly populated place where everybody knows everybody, and obviously everybody had been talking for months about the cult that had murdered the little girl and buried her in a bucket in the woods. Here's Jerry Patterson dramatizing a dialogue with a potential juror:

"Mr. Brown?"

"Yeah."

"Do you live in Newton County?"

"Yes."

"How long have you lived here?

"All my life."

"Have you heard about this case that we're about to try, State of Arkansas versus Lucy da da da?"

"No. Haven't heard a word about it."

"*Really?* Not a word? You read the newspapers?"

"I, uh, sometimes watch the news on TV. Well, not hardly ever."

"A lot of people wanted to be on that jury," Jerry said. "Out of curiosity, for one thing, but also because they saw this as a shocking situation they wanted to help cure. Let's just say that most of the people that we called as jurors had the propensity to find them guilty." Which was a situation that was fine with him, as the prosecutor. But the defense counsel had their work cut out for them. They knew that winnowing the jury pool down to twelve people who either hadn't heard much about the case—fat chance of that—or who might have the slightest chance of sympathizing with their clients was probably going to be the biggest and most difficult job they would have to do.

The three male defendants were transferred from the Boone County Jail to the Newton County Jail in Jasper on Monday, September 11. Jury selection had taken up the previous week, and the trial was set to begin on Tuesday morning. The three were housed in the same cell, and it was the first time since their arrests that Royal and his stepson and son had been together. The old Newton County Jail, built of local stone in 1902, has four cells in it and looks like a place to lock up Jesse James. It was in continual use until 2009, when construction was completed on a new, less picturesque, and more functional jail next door. The old one, sitting empty and semiderelict, is now listed on the National Register of Historic Places. During one of my recent visits to Jasper, in October 2023, it had been tricked out into a haunted house for Halloween, with spooky cotton cobwebs stretched across the doorways and mannequins in striped jumpsuits lying on the cots.

In the early-morning hours before their trial was to begin, Royal, Mark, and Winston Van Harris were caught attempting to escape from this jail. Winston Van—and exactly how this happened no one

remembers—had somehow managed to get ahold of a hacksaw blade, and he used it to saw through one of the bars on one of the upper windows of the jail. They were caught when the warden on the graveyard shift at the jail heard the sawing, stepped outside, and saw Winston Van with his hand out the window, trying to cut through the bars. From the *Blytheville Courier News* of September 13, 1978:

Three Defendants Attempt Escape

Jasper, Ark. (AP)—Prosecutor Jerry Patterson confirmed Tuesday night that three defendants in the first-degree murder trial of Bethany Clark, 3, tried to escape Monday evening.

Royal Harris, 51, Winston Van Harris, 31, and Mark Harris, 18, tried to pry open a window in a communal cell where they were held in the Newton County jail here, authorities said. . . .

The second story window of the jail had a bar removed and wire mesh covering the window had been rolled up in one corner, authorities said.

Newton County deputies said the three were caught before they managed to break out of the cell. There were several remarks made in Newton County Circuit Court Tuesday that referred to the "incident" at the jail Monday evening.

Attorneys for the defense Douglas Wilson, Tommy Martin, and Richard Parker arrived at the Newton County Courthouse for the trial on Tuesday morning to learn first thing that their clients, after all their fastidious work selecting the jury the week before, had pretty much torpedoed their case overnight by getting caught trying to break out of the jail. Suffice it to say, an escape attempt does not reflect well on defendants who have entered not guilty pleas. The three lawyers met separately with their clients to regroup. "There was a great deal of turmoil among all the defendants," Doug Wilson recalled. "Everybody was agitated about the overnight developments."

After meeting with their lawyers, Royal and Mark Harris decided, against the advice of their respective counsel, to switch their pleas from not guilty to nolo contendere, or no contest. A plea of no contest means that the defendant does not admit guilt but does not contest the charges; it is effectively a guilty plea, with the slight difference that there is technically no admission of guilt. For instance, a defendant might plead no contest on principle if he maintains his innocence but has given up hope of not being convicted. However, a prosecutor is more likely to offer a plea deal to a defendant who pleads guilty, and the judge is more likely to be lenient in sentencing. There is virtually no advantage for the defendant in a criminal case to pleading no contest as opposed to guilty. The only perk of a no contest plea is between the defendant and God.

In court, Royal and Mark's lawyers, Thomas Martin and Richard Parker, respectively, made it very clear to the judge that their clients had made this decision—which left their sentencing totally to the judge's discretion—against their advice. I think I can also hear in the lawyers' comments a note of their exasperation with their clients, almost a relief to wash their hands of these people. When Judge Kenneth Smith asked Royal if he understands that by pleading nolo condendere he is waiving his right to a trial by jury, he answered, "Yes sir. There is no reason to drag it out. I do not wish to smear the church." The judge repeatedly asked him if he understood what he was doing—that he was waiving his right to testify, waiving his right to confront his accusers in court, waiving his right to appeal to a higher court in the event the jury should find him guilty—and Royal continued to answer that he did not believe the jury could give him a fair trial (to which Jerry Patterson objected each time), that "it would do [him] no good." The exchange ended:

> **The Court:**   And you state that you have discussed this fully with your attorney?
>
> **Mr. Harris:**   Yes sir, he has discussed it with me.
>
> **The Court:**   Are you satisfied with his services and his advice in this case?
>
> **Mr. Harris:**   Yes sir, it has nothing to do with his advice. It is contrary to his advice, but that is my decision.
>
> **The Court:**   Mr. Harris, the Court accepts your plea.

With that, the judge dismissed the jury, and Richard Parker, Mark Harris's attorney, told the judge that his client would also like to change his plea. Mark Harris went forward, was put to the exact same barrage of questions that his father had been just before him, to which he answered only "Yes sir" or "No sir," without commentary or elaboration, and the court accepted his plea. Then Deputy Prosecutor Gary Isbell requested that some record be made of the factual basis of the pleas, and Judge Smith dismissed the public from the courtroom and reconvened in chambers. There Tommy Martin presented four factual bases of Royal Harris's no contest plea: (1) that he did "with leaded bullets end the life of Miss Bethany Clark"; (2) that he recognizes that it was "an unlawful act and a sinful act"; (3) that "the jury would upon hearing the evidence inevitably give him a life sentence"; and (4) that "he has no wish to spend the State's time and money or undergo the ordeal of reliving these moments" and "he has no wish to participate in any way in the slandering and tearing down of his church and his religion." The court accepted these factual bases. At the end of all that, when Royal was asked if there was anything else he wished to say, he left them with only, "I believe that covers it."

Mark Harris, in chambers, had somewhat more to say. Mark's lawyer, Richard Parker, presented two factual bases for his client's no contest plea. The first was that "as the recognized Prophet of the Church of God in Christ through the Holy Spirit, he did in fact make a prophecy that Bethany Clark was to be shot and that in fact is what occurred as a result of this prophecy." The second was that Mark Harris believed the jury would in all likelihood return a verdict of life imprisonment and that by making this plea and arguments for mitigation at the time of sentencing, he might hope for a lesser sentence.

The Court: Mr. Mark Harris, do you concur in the statement that your attorney has made to the court?

Mark Harris: Yes sir, all but one.

The Court: Tell me at which point you do not concur.

Mark Harris: I do not concur—yes, I guess that is right, because that was changed.

The Court: Would you explain, I don't understand.

Mark Harris: I don't really understand myself. I would like to give a brief statement about the people and the prophecy to add more emphasis to the fact that it does still exist and the fact that it is here today and also the fact that tribulations will occur very, very soon. When Edith received the gift of prophecy she was a Methodist Minister and also the daughter of a Methodist Minister and she was baptized when she was three years old.

The Court: Mr. Harris, at this time I do not want to get into the philosophy of the church. If there is any part of your attorney's statement that you disagree with, as you indicated you might, I would like to know what it is. I will give you an opportunity at another time to make all the statements that you want to along this line.

Mark Harris: What I am saying . . .

Mr. Parker: Do you agree or disagree with any of the words I said?

Mark Harris: What I am saying is what is written down in the message some months back that what is written down in the record books of life, you know what happened here on earth is what we have been telling everyone. And also that if we lied in Court we would be anathema, so that is why we have maintained what we have told. Also it is a fact that if it was not changed I would have just went ahead and pleaded guilty and gotten it over with. I have really no wish to continue this or have not wished in the past to continue this any longer, but since this is the Lord's will, so be it.

Mr. Parker: It is my client's religious belief that the events that occurred in the Kay-Park area that involved the death of Bethany Clark have been changed by God and in God's eyes they did not happen.

The Court: Very well. I think the Court is clear on it at this time.

Mark Harris: May I state something. Bethany was an anathema. This church is based on free choice. That is why it is such small numbers, because in the past we have observed the Commandments and we have not diverted from them without express orders from God Himself, through prophecy and interpretation, over which Suzette is the interpreter for the church.

The Court: All right, I will hear anything else you want to say at a later time. Does the State desire to make any statement at this time?

Mr. Patterson: Not now, your Honor.

Mr. Martin: Your Honor, we will waive any demand for immediate sentencing and let the Court sentence at the discretion of the Court.

The Court: The defendants may be returned to jail.

Several different and perhaps contradictory ideas jostle against one another in Mark Harris's confusing remarks to the judge, which his lawyer, Richard Parker, tried to clarify: one is that he, Royal, and Winston Van are not guilty of murder because the events leading to the death of Bethany Clark had been "changed by God and in God's eyes they did not happen." Therefore, were they to plead guilty, that would be a lie, and "if we lied in Court we would be anathema. But then right after that he said, "Bethany was an anathema." I think, squinting through the fog of Mark's delusory thinking muddled with ecclesiastical language, that he was trying to explain that his choice to plead no contest instead of guilty is due to this: Although here on man's Earth they may be guilty of murdering a three-year-old girl, he and God know that what they really killed was an unsalvageable human body possessed by the Devil. I do not think Mark's comparatively taciturn father still believed that four and a half months later, with their interpreter having turned witness for the state against them and the Tribulation still unbegun—but Mark does.

The consequences of Royal and Mark Harris's decisions to plead no contest rather than guilty would last for the rest of their lives.

Court returned to session, and the trial began. Now it was only two defendants on trial, those who maintained their pleas of not guilty: Winston Van Harris and Lucy Clark. Two witnesses took the stand in the beginning; the records have unfortunately been destroyed, but I believe, based on newspaper coverage of the trial, that the two witnesses were Suzette Freeman and June Harris. The trial broke for recess late in the morning. Lucy's trial kept going later that afternoon, but at that point, Doug Wilson, along with Winston Van's biological father, Gobe Smith, with whom Winston Van was now in contact for the first time in twenty-two years, closeted with Winston Van and explained to him that considering their deplorably idiotic escape attempt the night before, he was going to have to reassess his options. Wilson recalled his conversation in private with Winston Van Harris and Gobe Smith while the court was in recess:

> To me it was clear that the escape was an additional circumstance, which, while I was going to object to any reference to it as not being relevant to the trial, we were running the risk that the judge was going to rule, as a matter of law of evidence, that testimony could be induced about that escape attempt. And that it would substantially undermine whatever presentation Van was going to put on. . . . This was a very unfortunate development, and we really needed to be thinking about how we were going to get out of this prosecution with less than the maximum. . . . I said words to the effect of, "You've had me barking up the wrong tree all along, and I have not been able to prepare the defense as effectively as I might have, and now for your own sake, it's time for you to tell me the truth. Did you do this? Should I be talking about a guilty plea, or should we just sail into that courtroom full of denial and hope for the best?" Finally he said, in his father's presence, "Yes, it's all true. I was very actively involved. I went out there with the child, with Royal." . . . He said that there was only one gun, but that he was right there and assisted Royal in putting the child to death. And that's when I said, "Okay, now, we've got to start talking about how many years we're going to accept."

When the trial resumed after the recess, Doug Wilson requested a private conference with Jerry Patterson. The two lawyers stepped aside, and Wilson told him that his client was prepared to change his plea to guilty. Jerry told him he would recommend a sentence of fifty years.

"I'm going to save you a big prosecution," Wilson recalled saying. "You ought to think about something less than fifty."

"Forget it, Doug," Jerry said. "Fifty or nothing."

Wilson returned to the defendant's table, where he remembers saying to Van, "This [fifty years] is what he's offering. We don't have much to bargain with. I can in good conscience recommend to you that this is better than life in prison, and I recommend that you take it."

Van agreed to plead guilty in exchange for the fifty-year sentence the prosecution offered. Wilson then returned to the private conference with Jerry Patterson and told him that his client would accept the fifty years. Then Jerry told him he wanted to add another fifteen years on top of that for a separate charge of illegal possession of a firearm.

"Oh, come on, Jerry," Wilson said, "you know you're really warping me on this."

"That's the way it is," Jerry said. "Take it or leave it."

From Doug Wilson's testimony in the appeal years later:

So I went back to my client, and I said, "This is not fair, it is not the way he led us to believe he was going to deal with us, but he's in the driver's seat, and he wants the additional 15 years." . . . He didn't like it any better than I did, but at that point, I think he was pretty well aware that the options were diminishing, and that he was running a very serious risk of getting the maximum imposed, and so he reluctantly accepted the offer of the prosecutor.

After those negotiations—wherein the prosecution, which had the decisive upper hand, got everything it wanted—Winston Van Harris switched his plea from not guilty to guilty and furthermore entered a plea of guilty to the additional charge of illegal possession of a firearm. He kept his answers to the judge's questions to "Yes sir," and "No sir." The judge ordered him taken back to jail, and the trial resumed for the only defendant not to switch her plea from not guilty to guilty, Lucy Clark.

The records of what was said during the rest of Lucy's trial, which are of course the ones I am most interested in reading, do not appear to exist any longer. Donnie Davis, the Newton County Court clerk in Jasper, seemed a bit befuddled himself as to why there were no records of the trial. Jerry Patterson used to have a copy of them, but some years after the trial, Buford Gardner had told him he was writing a book about this case and asked if he could borrow his records. Jerry gave Buford all his documents pertaining to the case. Buford never wrote that book. He died twenty years ago, and his two adult children have no idea what became of those documents. All I have to go on are the memories of the people who were there who are still alive—Jerry Patterson; Lucy Clark; the forewoman of the jury, Katherine Nance—and what was reported in the newspapers. June Harris testified. Suzette Freeman testified. Fred Bell, Hurchal Fowler, and Ray Watkins testified.

Katherine Nance is now eighty-nine years old. She was born on her family's homestead on the bank of the Buffalo River, at a time when they were living in "an old tin camp house," while her father was building the house she would grow up in (the homestead is long gone, and the ruins of her childhood home are now on federal land in the Buffalo National River Wilderness). Katherine and her husband, Joe, lived for many years in a big, beautiful stone house they built on a large plot of land that her husband's great-grandfather had homesteaded after the Civil War on Mill Creek, a tributary of the Buffalo. Including Joe and Katherine's great-grandchildren, the property saw seven generations of the same family through 160 years of continuous ownership, and when I met them, they had just sold it to Johnny Morris, the billionaire founder and majority owner of Bass Pro Shops, who had also recently purchased the adjoining property of Dogpatch, USA, the ruins of a Li'l Abner theme park that operated from 1968 to 1993.* Katherine told me this about

---

* In one of our conversations, Ray Watkins also mentioned these two significant land deals, then the subject of much gossip in Newton County. He believed Morris intended to donate the massive combined plots of land—about 1,400 acres—to the government for an enormous tax break, toward the federal government's plan to eventually expand the Buffalo National River Wilderness into a national park. According to NPR affiliate KUAF Public Radio, Morris in fact building a private nature reserve, which will include a network of hiking trails, a trout hatchery, and a restaurant.

serving on the jury in Lucy's trial:

> It was a long, long jury. Lots of evidence and the horrible pictures and
> everything. All but one person on that jury knew that she was guilty.
> But we had one girl on the jury that was in doubt that the lady was
> guilty. Why? I don't know. But anyway, we ended up, we came out of
> the jury room two times with a hung jury, and the judge would send
> us back in there. So we'd go back and go over our notes and go over
> our notes and everything. And then I would ask finally, the last time
> he sent us in there—I remember now, her name was Sharon Pierce—I
> said, "You convince us, the rest of us, that she is not guilty." Well, she
> started crying, and we finally got a jury.

Sharon Pierce was a public elementary school teacher; she taught for
nearly thirty years at Mount Judea School in the tiny town of Mount
Judea, about ten miles south of Jasper. She also founded the Mount Judea
Volunteer Fire Department and worked at the town's post office after she
retired from teaching. She died of covid-19 in October 2020 at the age of
sixty-eight. She would have been twenty-six when she served on the jury
in 1978—the youngest person on it, not much older than Lucy. She was
the reason the jury's deliberations lasted so long, resulting in two hung
juries before she finally broke down in tears and went along with the
verdict finding Lucy Clark guilty of her daughter's murder.

Royal Harris and his son Mark Harris, who had turned eighteen while
in jail awaiting sentencing, were both sentenced to life in prison without
the possibility of parole. Winston Van Harris, one of the two people
who had directly committed the murder and buried the body, was given
fifty years plus another fifteen for the illegal possession of a firearm.
Although sixty-five years might seem effectively a life sentence for a
thirty-one-year-old man, it was in fact a significant compromise with
the prosecution, his recompense for pleading guilty; it was a sentence
that could potentially be appealed, reduced, paroled—none of which was

a possibility for Royal or Mark.

Meanwhile, up in Missouri, Larry Freeman and Johnny Stablier had been charged with kidnapping and the lesser charge of child enticement—i.e., convincing Larry's two young sons to get into the car with them. Johnny Stablier, who was apparently considered more of an accessory to the crime, was released from jail on $500 bond shortly after his arrest. Larry Freeman's bail was set at $40,000. In a deal with the judge that August, upon paying 10 percent of his bail, he was released and given permission to live with Suzette in Louisiana before returning to Missouri for his trial in October. The court seems to have gone easy on both of them; they had otherwise clean records, Larry Freeman was a Vietnam War vet, and it seems the deluded but good-hearted intentionality of the crime's bizarre motive (they believed they were saving the children from dying in a nuclear war) also factored in winning them leniency. The more serious kidnapping charges were dropped for both defendants in exchange for their pleading guilty to the lesser enticement charge. They were both given probationary sentences and served no prison time.

Lucy Clark was sentenced to five years in prison.

In February 1983, at the age of fifty-six, Royal Harris—who was suffering from prostate cancer that would go in and out of remission for the rest of his life and would eventually kill him—was transferred from the Cummins Unit prison to the Diagnostic Unit Hospital in Pine Bluff—that is, the hospital within the Arkansas Department of Corrections where inmates too ill to be held in the general prison population are taken—and remained there until he died at the age of seventy in 1998.

Winston Van Harris appealed his case twice, the second time with some success, and managed to get the additional fifteen years taken off his sentence. He was released on parole in 1993 and discharged from the system in 2003. He changed his name to Daniel Gobe Smith and moved to Alpharetta, Georgia. He died of cancer and septic shock in 2022 at the age of seventy-five. This is from his obituary from Covenant Funeral

& Crematory in Alpharetta (which doesn't mention his prison sentence):

> After his discharge [from the military], Daniel worked in a wide range of areas in the civilian business sector, and was a dedicated employee. Daniels [*sic*] Christian faith was very deep and strong, and his determination to adhere to the doctrines of his faith was absolute.
>
> Daniel married Robin Lynn Holt, and they enjoyed a strongly loving marriage for 25 years. During the final 7 years of their marriage, Robin developed senile dementia, and Daniel took care of her until her death with love, compassion and unswerving loyalty. When Robin passed away on November 8, 2020, Daniel was devasted, and tried to go on, but he was never quite the same. He looked forward daily to rejoining his beloved wife in heaven.

In 2017, the state of Arkansas passed a statute eliminating life without parole for juvenile offenders, which provides that juveniles convicted of capital murder are subject to a sentence of life with eligibility for parole after thirty years. Mark Harris, who had been a juvenile at the time of the crime for which he was serving a life sentence, appealed under the new statute in 2018 and was paroled out of state to Georgia after serving forty years.

After testifying in Lucy's trial, Suzette Freeman returned to her hometown, Grosse Tête, Louisiana, with her husband, Larry, who was serving five years of probation for the child enticement charge. The couple later moved to Baton Rouge, where they owned and operated Advantage Personnel—a temp agency—for over three decades. Larry died in 2013 at the age of sixty-seven. Suzette died in 2019 at the age of seventy-two. This is from her obituary:

> Suzette had a strong Christian faith and a positive outlook—always quick with a bright smile and words of encouragement to everyone she encountered. Throughout her life, she shared God's blessings and love in her service to others, both in her business, Advantage Personnel, and in the community, teaching Sunday School and

volunteering to help those in need. She was happiest in her beautiful flower garden and with her beloved dogs. She was a beautiful soul and will be greatly missed.

The day after Lucy Clark's conviction for second-degree murder, Katherine Nance visited her in Boone County Jail, where she was being held. The jury had found her guilty knowing she would probably receive a fairly lenient sentence, and the five-year sentence was determined by the judge. Nance's decision to visit Lucy in jail was unusual, unnecessary, and legally a little unorthodox. When I asked Nance why she had visited her, she simply said, "Because I am a Christian."

"She wasn't mean," Lucy said, "she was nice. She was compassionate. But she said, 'We didn't find you guilty of murder. We found you guilty because you couldn't tell the future.' I should have known what they were doing. I should have foretold, should have seen better than what I did. . . . And she brought me some books. I kept those books for a long time. And then one day I just threw them all away."

Lucy's father, with whom she was very close, died not long after Lucy began serving her sentence. When it became clear that her father was gravely ill, she was given a temporary furlough from prison, which she spent at Tom Keith's home, but was ultimately denied permission to leave the state of Arkansas to visit him. She wrote:

My dad passed away September 27, 1979. He was a very soft spoken and caring man. He never raised his voice and his relationship with Bethany was a close one. It is true they would not let me come home when he passed. They considered me a flight risk and because I had been convicted of murder, they would not allow it and neither did they care. Before he was taken to the hospital, he told [my sister] Billie Jean that he did not want to die with me in that place (meaning prison). I was on furlough at Tom's house. When we got to his office, Tom called the hospital for me. My dad had not spoken to anyone.

When Bennie Faye told him that I was on the phone, he grabbed the phone from her and talked to me and my sister told me he never spoke again. That was on Monday afternoon. My dad died early Thursday morning. After I came home, my mother was telling me a few weeks before my dad died, that she would hear him talking in his bedroom. She said that once she stood in the doorway and saw him looking up past where Bethany's picture was on the dresser and talking. She said he was talking with Bethany. He kept saying, "PaPaw loves you and PaPaw is coming to be with you in just a little while." So, to my daddy's prayer, I was not in prison on the day he died.

When Lucy was released from prison in April 1980, after serving two years of her sentence, it was Tom Keith who drove her home to her hometown of Camden, Louisiana, and he stayed in regular touch with her afterward. Lucy married again and gave birth to another daughter, whom she and her husband raised on the same family farm Lucy had grown up on, and who now has her own children. Lucy worked as a court reporter for many years. She and her husband still live on her family's land in Camden. A few of the people closest to her, including her husband, know about her past, but most of those in her general social orbit do not.

Tom Keith died a few years before I began writing this, but everyone who knew him said that as a public defender and later as a judge, he was a markedly compassionate person of deep convictions about justice. And Tom was an ardent and loyal friend to Lucy from the day he met her—the day she and the others were arrested and returned to Benton County—until the day he died. The bond between Tom and Lucy was adamantine; Tom was "her rock," Lucy said of him. For decades after her release, Tom stayed in touch with her by phone and mail and then by email. In the decades that followed her trial, he remained outraged and adamant in his belief that Lucy had been innocent and should never have been convicted or served any prison time.

And then, late in the summer of 2001, twenty-three years after the trial, Tom Keith got a phone call from his friend Joyce Hale, asking him if he knew anything about a certain murder case from 1978 involving a cult and a little girl found buried in a paint bucket on Cave Mountain.

10

Nothing to Forgive

EDITH HARRIS FOUNDED THIS CULT—WHICH OF COURSE DIDN'T think of itself as a "cult" but a "church"—and led it from the beginning. She was its prime mover going all the way back to the '50s, when she left her first husband and met a more sympathetic spiritual journeyer—and probably a more pliant soul—in Royal Harris. Edith was the one making decisions, the one laying out the doctrine of their church, and its first "prophet." Her husband Royal was really the first member of the cult— her first acolyte, the first weak mind she found susceptible to brain-washing, the first person who believed her when she told him she could communicate directly with God. And she declared their teenage son, Mark, to be a prophet, too, perhaps grooming him for leadership. It was her son, not her husband, she was preparing to take her place; Royal was more of an acquiescent, slow-witted Joseph figure in the Bible story she was telling about their family. (That sad-sack dupe leaning on his crook in the manger, cuckolded by God, gazing down at that miracle glowing in the hay he knows had nothing to do with him. Why is he even in the story at all?) Sometime in the process of Royal and Edith's family expanding into a small cult—the foundational moment would have been 1972, the year they self-published their book and registered their church as a corporation—Royal and her first son, Winston Van, acquired official titles, "Pastor" and "Assistant Pastor," both of them decidedly below Edith and Mark in the hierarchy she had established. While Mark was touched with the same spiritual power she declared that she herself had, Winston Van was assigned an administrative job, to use the labor of his body to raise silver shekels for them after the move to Arkansas (he also worked at the Tyson poultry plant with Lucy) and to use his more earthly mind for the humdrum logistical tasks of paying bills and filling out legal paperwork and whatnot—positioned thus because, as Doug Wilson would later say, "he was less fortunate than Royal and Mark because, as I understood it, in his mother's eyes, he was tainted with the blood of his natural father, who was not one of the faithful."

Larry and Suzette Freeman joined the group while Edith was still alive. And although Jerry Patterson suspected that there was some sort of sexual relationship going on between Suzette and Mark, at least near the end, two of Suzette's siblings recalled that Suzette had actually dated Winston Van Harris; they had been a couple for a time. The time after the end of their relationship and before Winston Van's marriage to June and Suzette's marriage to Larry must have been fairly brief. Suzette married Larry Freeman in 1976, and I don't have a record of when Van and June married. The detail of Winston Van and Suzette's previous relationship adds an interesting layer of possible sexual jealousy to the dynamics between Suzette and June, perhaps coloring in that critical moment that led to the cult's downfall, when Suzette declared June to "anathema" and cast her out of the church sometime in mid-April, 1978. Suzette's brother Jerry Kleinpeter is pretty sure that all of these people met one another at the future televangelist Jimmy Swaggart's flagship megachurch in Baton Rouge, the Family Worship Center. For some period of time in the mid-1970s, the Church of God in Christ through the Holy Spirit, Inc., was apparently an intensely fanatical but almost "normal" evangelical Bible study group. Three couples—Royal and Edith, Van and June, Larry and Suzette—plus the teenage Mark would meet either at Royal and Edith's home or at Larry and Suzette's, to read aloud to one another from the Bible, sing hymns, discuss scriptural hermeneutics, and talk about the problems in their lives—all with Edith Harris leading the discussions.

In 1976, at the age of fifty, Edith died of a heart attack, and that was when things started getting weirder and decidedly darker. It was, of course, Edith who had introduced the weirdness and darkness before her death—with her claims to the power of prophecy, her declaring Mark to have the power of prophecy, her declaring people "anathema," her inventing creepy, arcane rituals like the time they had sneaked into the cemetery after her mother's funeral and she had everyone toss pebbles into her uncovered grave; but she apparently had control over the situation and control over all the others. Edith had been the power that held the group together. Without her, the power dynamics within the group splintered in several different directions, and the members' theology, what they understood they were supposed to believe, became scrambled and confused. Edith's widower, Royal, the cofounder of the group and now the oldest among them, would naturally have been in the best position to assume its leadership, but I don't think he was terribly smart or charismatic or even very confident in himself; he was not a natural leader as his wife had been. Furthermore, he and the others truly believed in his son's power of divine prophecy, which left the fifteen-year-old boy occupying the center of their universe.

Jerry Patterson believes that this was the moment when Suzette Freeman seized control of the group, using the teenage prophet as a puppet. And that was the situation that Johnny Stablier and Lucy Clark got sucked into. In Jerry's view, the other people who were arrested that day—especially Royal, Winston Van, and Lucy—had been motivated to do what they did by the sincere belief that an apocalyptic nuclear war was about to commence at any moment, that Mark and Suzette had direct access to the mind of God, and that the Devil was trying to thwart them and had entered Lucy's three-year-old daughter. One testament to the sincerity of their beliefs is that according to Dr. David Pritchard, a psychologist who testified as an expert witness at the appeal of Winston Van's sentence, in the days immediately after their arrest, he was seriously panicked because now he was going to be stuck in jail and utterly defenseless when the nuclear weapons started raining down, obliterating human civilization in a daylong storm of radioactive fire. Jerry, of course, does not think that Suzette ever really believed any of it. Although the end of the world and the second coming of Christ "might have been in the back of her mind in a way," as he put it, she didn't seriously believe it—as evidenced by the fact that while the others were despairing about being stuck in jail during the apocalypse, she called her lawyer.

What was Suzette's motivation, then? What did she get out of it? Did she just get some sort of high off of manipulating people, sending them out on childish treasure hunts, ordering them to commit kidnapping and, ultimately to murder a three-year-old girl? In Jerry's opinion, yes; it was a game to her, a power trip that lasted several years until it collapsed and ended in murder, after which she slipped out the back door.

The prosecution's situation in 1978 was: They had a particularly horrific murder—could you possibly have a more innocent victim than a three-year-old girl?—and justice had to be done. And while the one person Jerry believed bore the most responsibility for the crime had been rendered legally untouchable, they had four other people about to stand trial for it: the two adult men who had actually shot Bethany and buried her, a teenage boy who had supposedly ordered them to do it—who was so disconnected from reality that the local legal shrink had sent him up to the next level for psychological evaluation (Jerry on Mark: "That kid didn't even know where he was.")—and a twenty-two-year-old woman, the mother who had apparently been complicit in her own daughter's murder, the "flower girl" who had somehow gotten mixed up with these people.

I have changed my mind about one aspect of this story. Before I met Lucy, I mostly shared Tom Keith's opinion of things, mainly that she should not have been convicted, and should not have even served the two years of her five-year prison sentence that she did. Tom considered her conviction a cruel and shameful miscarriage of justice tainted with ignorance, hot-blooded vengeance, and misogyny. There was one juror—Sharon Pierce, the youngest person on the jury—who believed in her innocence; the jury twice went back to the courtroom hung before the other eleven jurors finally convinced her to convict, and she broke down into tears as she agreed to join their decision of guilty. And the judge was sympathetic enough to Lucy to sentence her to only five years in prison. But Tom was still pissed off about it. As he told Joyce and Kelly in his office in 2001, he considered losing Lucy's trial the worst failure of his career and felt that he had failed her personally. Tom's caring mentorship of and stewardship over her, which continued for the rest of his life, may in some way have been a kind of atonement for what he saw as his great failure.

But when I finally spoke with Lucy, I found her attitude about her conviction and prison sentence much more contemplative and penitent than I had expected. She is still angry about Suzette Freeman's being given immunity, but she seems at peace with her own conviction and full of genuine and terrible remorse. She is not angry about it at all. Those two and a half years in the women's prison in Pine Bluff afforded her safety and stability, and she spoke of them in a tone almost of serenity and gratitude. Her time in prison was the first time in more than five years—her husband, the cult, the jail—that she had been in a relatively safe place.

"You would think it's a college campus," she said about arriving at the women's prison. "There's no bars, there's all glass. Everybody wore their clothes. So it wasn't like one of these dark places you see on TV with the bars and all that. It was none of that. And I got an education. I had graduated from high school, but I did another course there, it was a two-year course. I finished it in a year. So that place wasn't all bad. You had bad people there, but basically it was okay. It looked basically like a college dorm. The only thing is that they lock you in at night."

Lucy's prison sentence gave her time to recover and recalibrate after the bizarre nightmare that her life had been before. She even came out of it with an associate's degree. Who knows what might have happened if she had been found innocent and immediately cast back into the wider world so freshly and severely traumatized? Is it possible she might have careened off into some other new insanity without any time to heal her badly damaged soul? On the whole, I think the rest of her life was in fact probably made much better by her prison sentence. I've now come to think it was probably a good thing the jury found her guilty. Although Tom Keith did not believe she was guilty at all, Lucy herself said something to me that is strikingly similar to what Ray Watkins said: "But I was just as guilty, because I was there, and I've had to live with that." If she had been found not guilty, she might not have been able to begin to cope with the guilt she felt.

After his first meeting with Joyce and Kelly in late August 2001, Tom Keith emailed Lucy, asking if she minded him giving Joyce her email address. He was one of the very few people whom Lucy had kept in touch with who knew about her past and whom she trusted. Keith told her she could trust Joyce. For various reasons—mainly, I understand, long gaps in the correspondence between her and Tom on Lucy's end—it would be another three years before she gave Tom the green light. Joyce emailed Lucy. Lucy emailed her back. And thus began an extremely unlikely long-distance friendship between the two women.

The heart of their friendship was built from the beginning upon the resonances between Haley's disappearance and Bethany's murder; several astounding coincidences lined up, starting with the facts that the two incidents had both happened in late April and had happened within about two miles of each other. The world is old and a lot of things have happened in a lot of same places, but that particular place happens to be an extraordinarily remote, *very* sparsely populated area. As Ray Watkins put it, "A wilderness area, really, there ain't nothin' in there."* Then there was the fact that Haley said that her imaginary friend had dark hair she wore in pigtails, as Bethany had and often did, and that she was four

---

* As Haley said when I asked her if she had kept up afterward with the men who had rescued her, "People who live in Newton County live there because they want to be left alone."

years old (Bethany was three and a half years old when she was killed). As Joyce and Lucy emailed back and forth, other connections inevitably surfaced: Haley said that Alecia had a flashlight with her, which would have been useful in those dark woods if Haley had actually had one; one time, Lucy wrote, Suzette took away one of Bethany's only cherished and comforting possessions, a cloth Raggedy Ann doll (possibly the same doll June Harris mentioned in her testimony) because it was demonic idolatry or something, and the best thing Lucy could replace it with was a flashlight, which the child thereafter always held on to and clutched under the covers in bed at night as she had done her doll. "[Suzette] would just turn the lights off," Lucy said, "and I had to give Bethany a flashlight. So she wouldn't be so scared." There were other felicitous connections like that, but in my opinion everything that travels further afield from objective recorded facts—such as the time and place where these events happened—feels more and more to me like finding new breadcrumbs leading to an answer already decided upon.

I, myself, am a skeptic—in this, and in most things. I do not believe—as Lucy believes and as I think Joyce sort-of-maybe-kind-of believes—that Haley's imaginary friend was the ghost or spirit or something of Bethany Alana Clark come to comfort and guide her when she was lost. (For one thing, "guide"? Guide her *where*? Really far away from almost all of the hundreds of people who were out looking for her?) Haley does not believe this , either. As with admirable wisdom and maturity she said to me, "There are things that I will never know, and that's okay." But one of the emails Lucy wrote to Joyce contained something that gives even me the willies: "Bethany's middle name is Alana. Sometimes she would say her name is Alasee (al a see). I would tell her no it's Alana. She would laugh. I would think how funny she even came up with that name as it was a little different than her own." Imagine a toddler with a southern accent saying the words "all I see," giving the last word a slight extra half syllable, a diphthong it's called in linguistics. Stretched out phonetically: *all ah see-ah*.

Alecia?

For a long time, Haley did not know much about what had happened in the Upper Buffalo Wilderness in 1978. She was ambivalently aware of the rabbit hole Joyce had gone down, but she had never asked her mother or her grandmother about it. I was the first person to tell her that part of the story in much detail, over a beer at Maxine's Tap Room in Fayetteville sometime in the spring of 2023. Her hesitancy to ask about it for the past two decades had come not from incuriosity but from respect, a disinclination to tread into a story that wasn't hers. Her wariness of trespassing on someone else's story comes in part from her irritation at other people's trespassing on hers, glomming their imaginations onto her experience, altering things with their invasive interpretations.

"A lot of people have used my story to say, 'This is proof of angels, this is proof of this or that' or whatever fits their belief system," Haley told me some months later. "I'm not going to say, 'Don't do that.' Where I draw the line is when people try to say definitively, '*This* is what it is, you should believe this.' The truth of the matter is nobody was out there. It was just me. I'm not saying it wasn't some metaphysical—whatever— but I'm the one who experienced it. I don't need anybody to tell me like 'It was an angel, it was an alien, it was a ghost.' I've had all these people on the internet co-opt my story and essentially tell whatever story they want to tell and then attach my name to it. Which really pisses me off. I can't fucking stand that shit, because it causes people to come to me and be like 'You told it wrong.'"

All this is why I also do not want to dwell too long on the ghost story. At worst this paranormal element is just stupid, and at best there is something interesting in it about the moment when the rational mind turns a corner and enters a realm where, although it's possible that most of the human beings who have ever lived on this planet have been there, I just cannot allow myself to go. It's a place where the most abstract ideas of God hover at its heights, and there's a slumber party going on down on its floor, where the planchette slides around on the Ouija board.

Confirmation bias happens when two shapes in the disorderly chaos of reality line up in an astounding coincidence, like a stopped clock that tells the right time the moment we happen to look at it.

A ghost haunts not when it manifests visibly right before our eyes, rattling chains and moaning our names, but when it evades us, when it stays just out of sight, when we think we just saw it flit past a window. A ghost we can clearly see probably is "an undigested bit of beef," as Scrooge called Marley's apparition, "a blot of mustard, a crumb of cheese, a fragment of an underdone potato"—or a mental illness, or a tab of LSD—but to be believed, a ghost must not perfectly appear.

There is something tantalizing about how Alecia's crux of coincidences *almost* snaps into focus and then blurs again. The coincidences are uncannily close, but not exact. Bethany Clark was killed on April 24, and Haley got lost on April 29. The two incidents happened not in exactly the same place, but about two miles apart. Haley's Alecia was four years old; at the time of her death, Bethany was not quite three and a half. Alecia's flashlight and Bethany's flashlight—well, that one is pretty goose-pimply. As is "All I see ah."

Ghosts are much less interesting to me than why we want to believe in them. I have not asked Joyce if or how concretely she believes in this ghost, because I don't really want to know the answer. I have no desire to try to peek under the eyeholes in the bedsheet.

In the early 1980s, a woman named Dina Williams, then a graduate student at the School of Social Work at Stephen F. Austin State University in Nacogdoches, Texas, visited Arkansas's Cummins Unit prison about a dozen times as a volunteer assistant therapist. She helped lead group therapy sessions with the prisoners and met frequently one-on-one with one of the patients she knew from this group, Winston Van Harris. Dina was young and attractive, and Winston Van was in prison; he fell in love with her and mailed her a lot of long, rambling letters. Many years and several moves and lives later, Dina and her husband, Jeff, landed in Fayetteville, where they became friends with Jay and Joyce through the Sierra Club. When Joyce became obsessed with this case, Dina gave her the letters. When I began researching this book, Joyce, not wanting them or seeing any use for them, gave them to me. The original and only copies of these letters are now in my possession.

Dina wrote in an email:

> *I was teaching inmates how to be innovative about connecting with*
> *their children and previous partners, so as to both participate as parents*
> *and to encourage their visiting. Van was one of the inmates who had*
> *elected to work on himself in the Therapeutic Community. I heard his*
> *history and was sick about what had happened to the child in the cult.*
> *But as a newcomer to prison therapy, I was fascinated with how someone*
> *could look so normal in the prison, but have done such horrifying things*
> *on the outside, and Van was a case in point. Except for his appearing*
> *intense and very focused on things he planned to do with his life in the*
> *future, he seemed to be a fairly normal young man. He was nice-looking,*
> *black-haired, fit-bodied and a little cocky, well-groomed, and was*
> *interested in martial arts. We got along immediately: he was not shy.*

In his letters to Dina, Winston Van is mostly saying things just to have something to say. One gets the impression of a man infatuated with a woman, trying not to succumb to despair at his situation, and who has a lot of time on his hands. One learns that in prison he was listening to J. J. Cale ("boy, he's a down-soundin' dude"), Rita Coolidge's cover of "Fever," and Anne Murray's "Could I Have This Dance." One learns about the details of his workout regimens: "I work w/ weights about 11/2 hours ea. day: I work on my arms, shoulders and lats. on M-W-F and on T & TH I work on my stomach, chest and legs. Before I hurt my shoulder I was doing 240 lbs. on the bench but that was 3 months ago. Now I'm sticking w/ light weights and a lot of reps." One learns of his artistic and literary ambitions: "That's why I wanna go ahead and get my degree, finish my book and hope I can get something going in that direction before I get out. Don't know any Norman Mailers out there do you? HA!" He shares his aesthetic judgments, including this one I happen to agree with: "Stephen King. Super writer when he hits. Funny thing about him though, he'll write a simple book that's a 'blockbuster' like 'Fire Starter' and then write a piece of shit." He gives the impression of an impatient, shallow mind with a lot of jittery energy, obsessed with measuring value in numbers, bragging about how many pounds he can bench and how many book pages he reads in a day. He occasionally writes alarming sentences like (suddenly, on the fourth page of a letter that has no trace of anything else amorous in it): "If you were here I'd grab your blouse with my hand push you [carated in: "gently"] up against a wall, look real mean, then kiss the hell out of you." And one learns that a man convicted of murdering a child four years earlier began a letter with this:

"Dear Di," it reads, "A fuzzy hug for ya." In all these letters, he never once mentioned the murder. I asked Dina if the letters had creeped her out. Not really, she said. She'd done a lot of counseling work with prisoners and had gotten used to their falling in love with her. Like a lot of people who work with prisoners, she was accustomed to compartmentalizing, keeping her life on the outside strictly separate. She had genuine affection for Winston Van—a goofy guy who was boyishly obsessed with karate and country music. She soon graduated from the social work program, moved to Florida, became busy with other things, and the correspondence she'd had with Winston Van and other prisoners in Cummins Unit dropped off. She hadn't thought about him since.

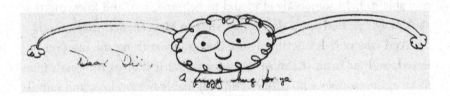

One of the things Joyce and Lucy have in common is that they are both people who every day for many years felt eaten alive with guilt—and probably still do. One thing I know I believe is that neither of them should be: Lucy was an abused, conditioned, and brainwashed cult member earnestly awaiting the end of the world, and Joyce did something that absolutely anyone could have done. But I also know it's impossible for them not to be. Joyce's quest to contact Lucy and her correspondence with her may in an indirect way be a product of that guilt. "Will you ever forgive me?" was the first thing she said to her daughter when Kelly stepped out of the car at the top of Cave Mountain on the day Haley disappeared. And I don't believe that Joyce—not then, not after Haley was found, and not in the decades since—has ever been able to accept what Kelly said to her: "There's nothing to forgive."

Likewise, Lucy needs to believe that Bethany Alana's spirit comforted and guided Haley through her days and nights lost alone in the wilderness because it gives her some small "peace of mind," as Joyce put it. "She had come to the idea that Bethany had actually had a meaningful life if she had existed in some form to help Haley." As Lucy wrote to Joyce in one of her emails, "To know she saved someone else is beyond happiness and I am so thankful she was there for Haley. Being in the Buffalo Wilderness myself, there was no way Haley could have survived her ordeal alone. I suppose one aspect of all this is that Bethany was destined to die to save Haley and Haley had to live to save me in some sort of way."

And Lucy told me, "I don't believe in psychics, I don't believe in mediums, 'cause that's not of God, that's not God at all. People like to rely on things like that, but this was an angel that was sent. And maybe it was for me to heal. I don't know, maybe it was for the both of us. I'm not sure. But it helps to know that her life, it didn't end in vain, that she was able to help somebody else, and to help me, too, and knowing that she's okay. . . . Bethany's alive today, she's in Heaven, and that's good."

And why not? It's definitely not the strangest thing she has ever believed, and far from the most dangerous, and if it gives some salvation to an aging woman who suffered unimaginable horror, loss, and humiliation very early in her life—and then had to carry an onerous burden of guilt, and carry it almost entirely alone, for the rest of her life, I'd say that's a good thing. I'd say it's a good thing even if it's true, as Ray Watkins believes, as did many others at the time, that "she was just as guilty as they were." I think it's a good thing because the most Christian thing I know I believe is the possibility of redemption from sin.

11

F.O.U.

THE FIRST CULT—WITH THE WORD MEANING WHAT IT MEANS to us now—to enter popular consciousness was surely the Manson Family. They committed the Tate-LaBianca murders in August 1969; police put things together and arrested them in December of that year, and the trial, wherein the sensational spectacle—a depraved and utterly batshit story involving rock stars, movie stars, sex, drugs, and a covey of beautiful young women—unraveled under the gaze of TV news cameras in the summer of 1970. I think of the 1970s as a weird golden age of cults and kooky spiritual experimentation, a time when Moonies, Hare Krishnas, Jesus freaks, Rajneeshees, and Scientologists flourished into public visibility, singing and chanting and handing out fliers in airports and shopping malls, an epidemic of fringe religious fevers bookended by the lurid Manson Family murders and the atrocity of Jonestown.

I'm sure great books have been written about whatever poison in the water in the 1970s bred so many loony reptiles of the mind. The surge of rapid and radical cultural change that happened between the end of the Second World War and the early 1970s must have felt disorienting and destabilizing, to say the least. I recently had a conversation with a friend about rewatching *The Godfather* for the first time in a while and noticing how hyperconscious the 1972 film is of being set in the past: the clothes, the cars, the music—the film's mise-en-scène meticulously places it in the late 1940s; it doesn't forget its historical setting for one frame. The gap of time between when it was made and when it takes place is only a little over twenty years. That's the equivalent of a movie made today set in the late 1990s—a thought that sharply brings into focus how stark the difference between then and now must have felt in 1972. All the Homburgs and Packards are saying: those old-world codes of honor, notions of masculinity and femininity, sexual morality and familial duty still hold sway over this culture; it's Don Corleone's principled, grandfatherly refusal to get into the burgeoning drug trade that spurs the plot into motion. The drug-addled and licentious 1970s moviegoers stepped back into as they left the theater were saying: *That* world is gone. The movie itself was a bellwether of cultural change; the Hays Code had ended in 1968, freeing Hollywood to depict sex and graphic violence on-screen for the first time, and filmmakers had begun to exercise their new freedoms. In 1971, the Supreme Court ruled in favor of the defendant in *Cohen v. California* (Paul Cohen was a protestor who wore a jacket with the words "Fuck the draft" scrawled on it in a courtroom), thereby protecting profanity under the First Amendment. The Stonewall riots happened in 1969, and a few years later, in 1973, the American Psychiatric Association removed homosexuality as a diagnosis of mental illness from the *Diagnostic and Statistical Manual of Mental Disorders*. And obviously, there was the bombshell of *Roe v. Wade* in 1972. People remembered a time when religion had served as the social glue holding marriages, families, and communities together, and in the 1970s it felt as though its adhesive strength had recently and rapidly dissolved; society secularized, divorce rates soared, and within a few short years, pornography, profanity, homosexuality, and abortion had all moved from dangerous underground spaces one needed shibboleths and secret handshakes to access into the light of day.

The era in which a sturdy, stable Christianity's role as familial, social, and communal bonding agent dissolved coincided with the Cold War and the nuclear arms race. People were thinking of the end of the world in a way they never had before: as an acutely realistic possibility. In the second half of the twentieth century, the spiritual nourishment that had fed previous generations and given higher meaning to everyday life went away at the same time as the nightmare of nuclear war slipped into the collective human dream. Full of fear and trembling and left to wander the world without a map, lost souls stumbled onto paths that sometimes led in very strange directions.

Not quite four years after members of the Church of God in Christ Through the Holy Spirit, Inc., were convicted of the murder of Bethany Alana Clark, Ray Watkins, then the sheriff of Newton County, would have to deal with *another* violent crime brought about by *another* Christian doomsday cult (sort of) working upon the guidance of a concrete and actionable interpretation of the Book of Revelation. This one began as a comedy, escalated into an outrageous spectacle of vulgar publicity, and ended in tragedy. The story is well worth recounting, as it overlaps with ours in the character of Ray Watkins and the setting of Jasper and well illustrates the mood in the air in the Ozarks in the late 1970s and early '80s, when the Fourth Great Awakening soured into the sleazy heyday of televangelism, as the influence of Jimmy Swaggart and Jerry Falwell swelled along with Reagan's rise and evangelical Christianity yoked itself to the political Right.*

In 1976, a forty-eight-year-old man named Emory Mayo Lamb, originally from West Virginia, moved to the Jasper area with his wife, Shirley, and their teenage daughter, Angela. He bought a five-acre property just outside Jasper and a general store on the southeast corner of the town

---

* If you're interested in reading a more detailed account of this utterly insane story, you can find it in Molly May's 2021 book about it, *Witnesses for the Lamb: The True Story of Hijacking, Murder, and Suicide in the Ozarks*, to which my abridged version is heavily indebted.

square that had been about to close. Emory Lamb—an eccentric bordering on the functional edge of crazy—who favored black leather motorcycle gear and wore an Old Testament patriarch's unruly forked gray beard hanging half a foot from his chin, quickly became a major nucleus of strange gossip in the small community. His shop sold groceries and all the knickknacks and bric-a-brac you'd expect to see on sale in a tiny country general store—as it had before his ownership—with the new addition of baked goods Lamb baked himself at home: bread, cookies, pastries, muffins.

Also, for some reason the new owner of the general store was obsessed with a cryptic acronym of his own coinage, "F.O.U.," sometimes styled "FOU" or "Fou." Next to the Open/Closed sign on the door of the shop, he hung a sign reading simply "FOU." He ordered a bunch of stickers—white circles with the black capital letters "FOU" in them—which he began sticking on walls all over the area: in restaurants, stores, gas stations, the post office, etc. He also ordered a bunch of little wooden coins that read "FOU" and left bowls full of them on the counters of obliging businesses all over Newton County; these FOU tokens were redeemable at Lamb's general store for one free Coke. Emory Lamb also hand-wrote and mimeographed dozens of ziney-looking pamphlets, quoting Bible verses alongside his own harebrained midrash, written in a naive idiolect of heterographic but internally consistent spelling and punctuation rules, which were on sale for a quarter apiece in racks on his store's counter, along with a lot of other Christian bondieuserie like little ceramic angels and whatnot. A Rasputin-bearded, muffin-baking, evangelical biker dude/yeoman-theologian wasn't even necessarily the weirdest character to inhabit the Arkansas Ozarks in the 1970s; he was, in those early days, by all accounts a very warm and friendly guy who seemed harmless enough, and everyone could agree his blueberry muffins were delicious. Also, naturally, everyone started calling him "Fou."

Although he would be coy about it the first few times you asked him, "F.O.U." stood for "Foundation of Ubiquity," a phrase that a mysterious old man had once whispered to him in a mystical vision. (He later realized the mysterious old man was himself from the future, but I'm not going to get into that.)

Fou fished his own Peter from the Sea of Galilee one day around Christmas 1976 when a very lost soul, Keith Haigler, passed through Jasper. Keith, a twenty-two-year-old man from North Carolina, had spent two years in the marines followed by one year adrift, staying with his parents, couch surfing with friends, and living on his dwindling savings from his military pay. In the final weeks of the year, he had decided to drive across the country to California, hoping an idea of what to do with the rest of his life might present itself to him there. On the way he stopped in Jasper, Arkansas, and ducked into Emory Lamb's general store to buy a cup of coffee and a pack of cigarettes. He had a conversation with Lamb, bought one of his zany religious pamphlets, got back on the road and made it to Missouri, where he spent the night at a friend's house. There he read the pamphlet, and the next day, instead of continuing on his way to California, decided to drive back to Jasper to talk with Fou again.

The older man and the younger had a few key interests in common: Both played the guitar, and Keith also harbored a boyish obsession with the biker aesthetic; he wore a leather vest with patriotic patches all over it and a classic black leather Harley-Davidson motorcycle cap, the kind made iconic by Marlon Brando in *The Wild One*, and dreamed of one day buying a motorcycle, although he never actually did or even got a motorcycle license.* Keith was also a religious quester, who read in the Bible on his own but chafed against organized religion; he had been to church, and didn't findfound what he was looking for there—but now he thought he might have found it in Emory Lamb's rather more disorganized religion. Also, he hated his father and found a kind of spiritual allofather in Lamb, who invited him to live in a campervan parked on

---

* I have received my secondhand opinions on the Harley-Davidson Motor Company from my uncle Jay, a true connoisseur of engineering in whom I placed a great deal of trust on the subject; Indians and Triumphs he considered masterpieces, whereas "Harley-Davidson," I remember him saying, "just gets by selling mediocre motorcycles on nostalgia."

his property and by and by permitted Keith to call him "Daddy Fou." During the next few years, they built the F.O.U. Ministry: they converted an old barn on the property into their church, decorating the walls with thrift-shop paintings of Jesus, with a pulpit at the front of the room and pews made of car seats salvaged from junkyards. At the feet of his sensei Keith studied the Bible, and sometimes worked in the general store, and drove around all over the Ozarks, putting up mimeographed posters advertising the ministry. The posters read "Foundation of Ubiquity" in fancy certificate typeface on top with all the other text on them handwritten in Sharpie, mixing Christian and biker semioses ("THE SON OF MAN HAS RISEN / BROTHER'S [*sic*] WE WILL RIDE"), and in time they actually did gather together a small congregation of evangelical bikers. Soon a row of Harleys could be seen parked outside the barn on Emory's property on Sunday mornings.

At some point in his independent Bible study with Daddy Fou, Keith became fixated upon a particular passage in the Book of Revelation, 11:3–12:

AND I WILL give power unto my two witnesses, and they shall prophesy a thousand two hundred and threescore days, clothed in sackcloth. . . .

And when they shall have finished their testimony, the beast that ascendeth out of the bottomless pit shall make war against them, and shall overcome them, and kill them. And their dead bodies shall lie in the street of the great city, which spiritually is called Sodom and Egypt, where also our Lord was crucified. And they of the people and kindreds and tongues and nations shall see their dead bodies three days and an half, and shall not suffer their dead bodies to be put in graves. And they that dwell upon the earth shall rejoice over them, and make merry . . . because these two prophets tormented them that dwelt on the earth.

And after three days and an half the Spirit of life from God entered into them, and they stood upon their feet; and great fear fell upon them which saw them. And they heard a great voice from heaven saying unto them, Come up hither. And they ascended up to heaven in a cloud; and their enemies beheld them.

Keith pondered and pondered this passage, until he arrived at the realization that he himself was one of these two witnesses. Emory Lamb apparently did not try very hard to dissuade him, but he assured him that he himself was not the other witness. At that point, Keith began to kind of slide off on his own theological trajectory. He wrote a pamphlet preaching the divine truth of Fouism, paid thirty dollars to make a thousand copies of it, got into his car and finally continued his cross-country drive to California; he was on a mission trip now, to distribute the pamphlets and preach the good news. The day before he set out, he recorded in his journal the date of the beginning of his one thousand two hundred and threescore days of prophesying: Saturday, January 21, 1979.

In San Francisco he slept in his car at night and by day competed for attention with other guys thrusting documents containing ecstatic proclamations of ecclesiastic gibberish at the passersby of Haight-Ashbury. There, at a skating rink, he met a sun-kissed and dirty-blond California-as-they-come California girl named Kate Clark, who was two years younger than he was and came from a fairly rarefied environment, the sort of laid-back West Coast aristocracy that always makes me think of Joan Didion; Kate's mother was the mayor of the bougie San Mateo County beach town of Pacifica. Kate fell fast and hard for the handsome lunatic in biker duds with a honeydrip southern drawl and apocalyptic visions dancing behind his eyes, and in the *amour fou* (no pun intended) stage of young love he somehow convinced her that *she* was in fact the other of the two witnesses mentioned in the eleventh chapter of the Book of Revelation. They turned around and ran away together, camping and scrounging from dumpsters along the way, at first back east to Keith's family in North Carolina, where they got married at a courthouse; then they went to Jasper, Arkansas, where they were wedded in holy matrimony before God by the spiritual father Daddy Fou, and the new Mrs. Haigler moved in with Keith in the campervan parked on Lamb's property.

By that time, Emory Lamb had closed the general store in order to focus on the Ministry of F.O.U., which had begun to take on the cultlike characteristics of tithing its flock and supplementing its overhead by parasitically farming out the labor of its female members: Lamb's wife and daughter were now both waiting tables at the Ozark Café in Jasper, and soon so was Kate Haigler, and the three women turned all the money they earned there over to the Ministry of F.O.U. Keith continued to drive around Northwest Arkansas, distributing pamphlets and putting up posters. When they were not proselytizing or working, Lamb conscripted Keith and Kate into the urgently important labor of building chest-high pyramids of rocks on his property, constellated in mystical Stonehengesque rings about twenty feet in diameter. (Many of the pyramids are still there, and you can check them out yourself if you're ever in Jasper—just ask the locals for directions to Fou's old place.)

Keith started counting the 1,260 days that the witnesses would prophesy on January 21, 1979. That meant that the day when they would have finished their testimony, when the beast shall ascendeth out of the bottomless pit and make war against them, and overcome them and kill them, was to be July 3, 1982. (After which their dead bodies shall lie in the street for three and a half days, whereupon the spirit of life from God shall enter into them, and they shall stand upon their feet, and great fear shall fall upon those who see them.) These are the same numerological schemes the Church of God in Christ Through the Holy Spirit, Inc., was drawing from: 1,260 is the Jewish lunar calendar of 360 days multiplied by 3.5, half of the mystical number seven; the prophetic seed "a time, times and half a time" planted in the Book of Daniel bears fruit in Revelation.

In June 1982, with the three and a half years of testimony almost up, Keith and Kate journeyed again back to California, this time to Los Angeles, to NBC Studios. From 1979 to 1984, NBC ran a program called *Real People*, a kind of proto–reality TV show whereon the hosts would interview "real people" (as opposed to celebrities) with quirky hobbies or unusual occupations in front of a live studio audience. It was a popular show, and people with goofy, eccentric personalities played well on itamong other notables, Richard Simmons' appearance on the show launched his career as a fitness guru. Keith and Kate Haigler intended to go on the show and tell the world about the coming apocalypse foretold in Revelation, which would begin with their violent deaths in Jasper, Arkansas, on July 3. Whoever was working the front desk of whatever office lobby at NBC Studios Keith and Kate somehow managed to muscle their way into succeeded in turning them away without bothering any higher-ups about it. Oh, well. Keith and Kate turned around and drove back to Arkansas.

At eight thirty on the morning of July 3, 1982, Keith and Kate Haigler boarded Continental Trailways bus 22303 at Union Station in Little Rock, Arkansas, with .22- and .38-caliber handguns concealed in their clothes. The bus was bound for Wichita, Kansas, with stops along the way in Conway, Harrison, Branson, Springfield, and Joplin. At about noon, as they neared the small town of St. Joe on Arkansas State Highway 65, Keith Haigler moved to the front of the bus, put the muzzle of his pistol against the temple of driver Bill Carney—who had his eight-year-old son, Kore, riding on the seat behind him that day—and ordered him to turn off on Highway 123 and drive the bus to Jasper. While Keith held a gun to the bus driver's head, Kate stood up in the aisle, pulled out her pistol, and ordered all of the other seventeen passengers to move to the back of the bus.

Toward the end of the forty-minute diverted ride to Jasper, a seventy-seven-year-old woman on board had a minor heart attack, which threw an unexpected stick between the spokes of their plan. Once they got to Jasper, Keith ordered Carney to park the bus sideways across the bridge along State Route 7 over the Little Buffalo River, a tributary of the Buffalo that runs through Jasper, blocking traffic in both directions. Once the bus was parked across the bridge, Keith ordered James Murray, an able-bodied forty-year-old man on the bus, to carry the elderly woman who'd had a heart attack to a nearby motel, call an ambulance for her, and then return to the bus. He did. Once Murray was back on the bus,

Keith took an envelope from the inner chest pocket of his motorcycle vest, handed it to Carney, and instructed him to go to Newton County Courthouse in the middle of the town square—the building is within sight of the bridge over the Little Buffalo, less than a five-minute walk—and deliver the letter to Sheriff Ray Watkins. Bill asked to take his son with him, and Keith allowed him to do so. Bill took the envelope from Keith, took his son by the hand, and walked with him from the bridge into Jasper's town square. On his way to the courthouse, he glanced inside the Ozark Cafe across the street and saw a uniformed police officer inside. It was Sheriff's Deputy Richard Russman, in the middle of eating lunch with his wife, Newton County's emergency dispatcher. Bill and his son went into the restaurant, explained the situation to Russman—that his bus had been hijacked by two people with guns who were holding the passengers hostage—and gave him the sealed envelope Keith had given him, on the outside of which was scrawled in pencil, "For Sheriff Ray Watkins." Deputy Russman radioed the State Police for backup and ran across the street to the courthouse, where he called Ray, who at that moment was at home a few miles outside town, fixing his bathroom sink.

Ray Watkins had officially served as the sheriff of Newton County for almost four years, but during the six years before that, under Hurchal Fowler's tenure, he had been the only full-time law enforcement officer in Newton County who regularly enforced the law, and the only one with any official training. Hurchal had been a road grader operator before he had run for sheriff; the reason why he'd done so was that he was already the local chairman of the Democratic Party, which held a Tammany Hall–like power grip on Arkansas politics for a long time. The party that Bill Clinton had risen up in was a daisy-chain network of handshakes in smoky back rooms that began in Little Rock and radiated out to rural counties like Newton; the Machiavellian skullduggery was in fact much more nakedly in operation in such places, where the entire government might constitute only a handful of people—fewer knowers of secrets, no whistleblowers—and all the official positions, including judges, prosecutors, and sheriffs, were elected ones. The party had pressured Hurchal Fowler to run for Newton County sheriff back in 1972 because he was a known and trusted entity, a loyal Democrat, and already a party official. The only reason Hurchal had wanted to be sheriff was because the sheriff's office collected the county taxes, as well as all the legal fines and so on, which meant he could make money on the side from the interest the county coffer would collect before he had to turn it over to the state.

"That money all went to the sheriff," Ray Watkins told me. "He had control of it. It all went into a bank account and collected interest on that money. And we collected nearly a million dollars in taxes each year, and we didn't have to pay [it to the state] until the following March or something like that, five or six months later, after they got finished collecting taxes. So you could make pretty good money with just the money you had in the bank."

"So you would collect all the taxes," I said, "let it sit in the bank account and accrue a bunch of interest—and then the sheriff could just pocket that interest?"

"Yes," said Ray, "because there was no legal statutes or anything saying what they had to do with the interest money. The only thing it said was, you'll collect the taxes and then on a certain date, whatever that date was, you would pay in what you collected on the taxes."

Ray had already been serving as a part-time deputy under the previous sheriff, Toot Wagner, and after Hurchal had beat Toot in the 1972 election, he had asked Ray to take the job of full-time officer. "He told me," Ray says, "he said, 'I'll take care of the taxes, and you'll take care of the law enforcement.'" So during the next six years, Ray did most of the actual work of law enforcement in Newton County, while Hurchal focused on delivering the county for the Democrats and skimming the interest money off the taxes. In 1978, when Ray ran uncontested for the job he'd pretty much unofficially already been doing for six years, he also ran as a Democrat, which was typically the main qualification for the position as far as Little Rock was concerned, but he was much less of a party apparatchik than Hurchal had been. Hurchal had been pressured to run for sheriff because he was a Democrat, whereas Ray ran as a Democrat because he wanted to be the sheriff. Ray is still proud of the fact that at the end of his first term in 1982, the Democratic Party, apparently displeased with his insufficient loyalty, ran another candidate against him for sheriff, Jerry Jones, who beat him in the primary, but in the general election in November, Ray won a second term as an independent write-in candidate, beating Jones by twenty-three votes.

I should make it clear that I'm not trying to paint Ray Watkins as a Gary Cooper in *High Noon* sort of figure, the lone man of principle facing down a corrupt system. The sheriff's departments in these rural counties of the Ozarks were notorious for corruption back then, and even the most honest cops couldn't afford to fight against it all the time; it behooved them to work within it to varying degrees, depending on the situation. The suspicious selectivity with which rural sheriffs chose to enforce drug laws was the stuff of legend among the men who wound up behind bars in Arkansas in the 1970s and '80s. The mountainous and lightly populated counties of the Ozarks—Madison, Carroll, Boone, Marion, Searcy, and Newton—were a hotbed of illegal marijuana farming; they had a reputation as the Humboldt of the South, and on college campuses across Dixieland strains of grass from northern Arkansas were nicknamed "Krazo" ("Ozark" spelled backward) and "Razorbud." Much of the police corruption involved classic Mafia-style collusion between organized crime and law enforcement, kickbacks and bribery and so on. Just eight months before the unfolding of that particular afternoon of insanity on the bridge over the Little Buffalo River, there had been a bubble pop of political controversy concerning Haroldean Lepel, a biologist who had been assigned by the Arkansas Game and Fish Commission to manage the large swath of recently acquired government land—the Buffalo National River Wilderness and the Upper Buffalo Wilderness—more and more of which was coming under federal protection as private inholders' grace periods were ending and they were being squeezed out. Lepel was technically a sort of cop, and he wasn't from around those parts; he was an outsider and a somewhat naive man who assumed that part of his job was to call the State Police—i.e., *not* the local sheriff—whenever, in the line of his official duties studying fish populations and things like that, he discovered something indisputably illegal, such as a large marijuana farm—which he discovered fairly often. In August 1980, Lepel led State Police to one of those illegal pot farms near Richland Creek; the following night, he got a threatening phone call from an unidentified man. "The caller said I'd made people mad and that I should have gone about my job and left people alone," he told the *Northwest Arkansas Times.* "He said people were mad enough to kill me and had contracted to have me killed. Then he said I would soon be having some bad luck, and he just wanted me to know where it was coming from." He had been busting pot farms without paying attention to *whose* pot farms they were. Some pot farms are fine to bust—it's the law, in fact—whereas others . . . well, Newton County is a small place where everybody knows everybody. Some people are friends with or related to the sheriff or judges or the circuit prosecutor, and some people may have slipped someone a gift in wink-wink assurance that what a man does with water and sunshine and the dirt on his own private property is none of anybody's damn business. Some of those people even vote in local elections, as do their friends and relations, and in a county with a population of less than five thousand, every vote really, really counts—and if the people in the smaller places that the people in the bigger places know they can work with are voted out and replaced with unknown entities, that could negatively impact things down in Little Rock. Some locals were not happy with Harold Lepel's Goody Two-shoes approach to blindly administering justice. Phone calls were made, and the chain rattled from the bottom to the top and then back down again: in October 1981, Lepel got a call from his boss at the Arkansas Game and Fish Commission notifying him that he would immediately be transferred to Drew County, way down in the southwest corner of the state, where there aren't any marijuana farms because every spare acre of that area is nice wet flat arable land that has been planted in cotton and rice for generations.

Well, there are no heroes and villains in real life—at any rate, no one is a hero all the time or a villain all the time. But it is true that on the afternoon of July 3, 1982, Ray Watkins was a hero to fifteen innocent people who had boarded a Continental Trailways bus from Little Rock to Wichita that morning.

Over the phone, Deputy Richard Russman quickly briefed Sheriff Ray Watkins on the situation, and Ray—who, like Hurchal Fowler before him, did not wear a uniform—pinned his brass star to his short-sleeved plaid shirt, buckled on his gun and holster, and sped down to the Route 7 bridge over the Little Buffalo River, where by now several other police cars had formed blockades at safe distances on either side of the bridge and busy preholiday traffic was stacking up behind them on both sides of the river. No one had yet attempted to communicate with anyone on the bus, which was parked sideways across both lanes in the middle of the bridge. The hijackers/kidnappers had specifically asked for Sheriff Ray Watkins by name, and everyone was waiting for him.

It was early afternoon on a cloudless day at the height of summer, with the sun at its zenith, the light harsh on the baking concrete bridge, the shadows short and sharp, the temperature around 90 degrees Fahrenheit. As Ray walked out onto the bridge alone, he realized that he recognized the two people standing in the open doorway of the bus: "Baby Fou," as Keith Haigler was known around town, and that pretty young beach bunny of a wife he'd brought back from California, Kate. Again, everybody in Newton County knows everybody. Those two colorful wingnuts were hard to miss, and for the past couple of years Kate had been waiting tables at the Ozark Café, the social heart of Jasper. When he came within earshot, Keith—attired per usual in biker cosplay: motorcycle vest, leather Harley cap, jeans and cowboy boots, and (not per usual) holding a .22 pistol—leaned forward against the door frame of the bus and said to Ray, "Afternoon, sir. You want to take that weapon off so we can talk?"

Ray shrugged, took the Colt Python out of the holster at his hip, held it out at arm's length so they could see it, walked back to his car parked at the police barricade, put the gun in the car, shut the door, and walked back out across the bridge to the bus unarmed.

"Look, Ray," Keith said when he returned. "We don't want to hurt anyone. We just want to get our message out."

"Okay," said Ray. "What's your message?"

"It's all in the letter," said Keith.

Ray didn't know what he was talking about. Deputy Russman had forgotten to mention it. There ensued a brief, confusing conversation in which Ray kept telling Keith that he needed to let the passengers off the bus before they could talk, and Keith kept telling Ray to read the letter he'd addressed to him.

Ray walked back to the barricade of cop cars, saying that Keith was talking about some sort of letter he was supposed to read. A cartoon lightbulb dinged above Deputy Russman's head; he apologized for forgetting, fished the folded-in-half envelope addressed to Ray out of his pocket, and handed it to its intended recipient. Ray opened the envelope and unfolded the handwritten letter inside. It read:

> *The world is to know the messiah is here. Contact KY3 News Reporter Jim Caldwell or Jerry Adams and have them come to Jasper for coverage. You have two hours to accomplish this. After two hours, we will shoot one person every half hour until this demand is met. If any attempts are made to come close to the bus, we have the dynamite to blow it apart.*
>
> *We are the witnesses spoken of in Revelation Chapter 11. After we are killed this afternoon, our dead bodies are not to be tampered with, embalmed or any other means of society's funeral rites. The bodies are to be taken to the land of the Messiah, Emory Lamb, whereupon they will lie until July 7, when the spirit of life will enter into them and we will stand on our feet. This demand must be met, or Jasper will be destroyed. Once again, it is not our wish to hurt anyone.*
>
> *Sincerely, with the kindest of thoughts,*
> *Keith FOU Haigler and Kate FOU Haigler*

KY3 News is a local TV news outlet based in Springfield, Missouri, covering northern Arkansas and southern Missouri, and Jim Caldwell and Jerry Adams were two of its most frequent on-the-scene anchors at the time. Ray gave Russman the okay to go ahead and call them, and Russman went back to the courthouse, found the number for KY3 in the Rolodex in the court clerk's office, called the station, and after a few baton passes managed to get ahold of Jim Caldwell at his home in Springfield. Caldwell was enjoying a day off after reporting for ten days straight, but the bizarreness of the situation on the bridge down in Jasper and the fact that the apparent religious nutcase gunman had specifically requested him by name was certainly enough to get him out of the house. He made a few calls, and within the hour he and a cameraman were snipping across the rolling Ozark mountains in a KY3 News helicopter headed for Jasper.

While the helicopter was on its way, Ray kept talking with Keith on the bridge. Throughout most of the afternoon, he was standing right outside the bus, and Keith and Kate were leaning against the doorway, sitting in the driver's seat, or crouched on the steps at the front of the bus. Keith had been living in the area for the past six years and was no recluse. Keith and Ray knew each other well enough to have a friendly conversation, in spite of the circumstances. Ray remembers Keith telling him that he'd voted for him in the primary he had recently lost to the more reliably party-loyal guy the Democrats had run to replace him, Jerry Jones, and telling him that he was sorry Ray had lost. That summer—before he won as a write-in candidate—Ray felt he was almost certainly a lame duck with half a year left on the job; he was then sketching plans to reopen his auto repair business come January.*

Keith and Kate wanted—needed—to be shot to death by the police. They needed it to happen that way to fulfill the prophecy in Revelation 11:7: the beast must ascend out of the bottomless pit and make war against them, and overcome them, and kill them. Ray's main concern

---

* Though I admit the crystal-ball gaziness of this thought, it is even possible that by sucking him into the eye of the shitstorm they created, forcing him into the role of the day's hero, Keith and Kate Haigler won Ray Watkins the election later that year.

then was getting the fifteen remaining passengers/hostages off the bus. The bus driver, Bill Carney, and his eleven-year-old son, after delivering Keith's letter to Deputy Russman, had not returned to the bus, remaining safely behind the police barricade on the south end of the bridge. Besides Keith and Kate, fourteen people were left on the bus. Ray and Keith negotiated a deal: When Caldwell arrived with a cameraman, they would let seven of the hostages off the bus. Once KY3 News finished recording the interview, they would let the other seven off.

The KY3 News helicopter carrying Caldwell and a camera operator landed in a field near Jasper around 2:30 in the afternoon, and a State Police patrol car picked them up and took them to the bridge. Ray walked them out to the bus, explaining that their first priority was freeing the hostages, which was the only reason the police had capitulated to Keith's and Kate's demand to bring the news crew to them—and anything they could do to help get those people off that bus would be greatly appreciated. Ray also warned him that according to the letter, Keith and Kate supposedly had dynamite on board, with which they had said they would blow up the bus and everyone on it as a last resort. Caldwell assured him that they would do all they could do to help free the hostages.

After a little palavering between Keith and Ray, who was standing in front of the bus's open door with Caldwell and the cameraman beside him, Keith and Kate made good on their promise, letting seven people off the bus. When the seven people had walked across the bridge and were safe behind the police barricade, Ray gave them the go-ahead, and the news anchor and cameraman boarded the bus. They recorded an interview with Keith—with Kate occasionally shouting her input from the back of the bus, where she was guarding the remaining hostages—in which he asserted that he and Kate were the witnesses named in Revelation 11, that they had been prophesying for one thousand two hundred and threescore days. Today they had finished their testimony, and they would be killed by the police, after which their bodies were to rest unmolested for three and a half days on the property of the messiah, Emory Mayo Lamb, aka Daddy Fou. All were welcome to come and watch their resurrection, which would happen on July 7. It was only the content of his speech that was crazy; he didn't say it like a crazy person, with lots of dissociative logorrhea and jittery subject jumps. He said it in a fairly calm voice, and with a Mona-Lisa-faint smirk on his face, a cellophane-thin adumbration of irony, as if he himself didn't quite believe what he was saying. It's as though he was saying "Look, I know this sounds crazy, but . . ."

True to his word—and to credit Keith Haigler's character, he was clearly not someone who took any sadistic pleasure in anything he did in the one day of his life he spent as a serious criminal—after Caldwell and the cameraman stepped off the bus, he and Kate released the remaining seven hostages, the last of whom was a young woman who hugged him and kissed him on the cheek on her way out.

Keith and Kate sat in the bus for another hour after that. After KY3 recorded their interview, other reporters and photographers were permitted to walk up to the bus, talk with them through the door, and take pictures of them. Ray still stood nearby, relieved now that all the hostages were safe, but still trying to talk Keith and Kate into giving up their plans and turning themselves in.

Ray remembered Keith at one point asking him "What kind of charges would I be facing if I give up?"

"Probably kidnapping and hijacking."

"How much time would I have to serve?"

"I don't know," Ray told him, truthfully. "The FBI is going to have to talk to you because of your interference with travel on interstate commerce."

Keith paused, thought about this for a moment. "What about an insanity defense?" he asked.

"Maybe," Ray said.

Keith laughed, shook his head. "What am I saying? Insanity defenses are for people who are not responsible for their actions. I've never been saner in my life. I know that there's no way out of this. Either I die, or I go to prison. I don't want to talk about it anymore."

Ray repeatedly and insistently assured Keith and Kate that whatever was about to happen, the police were going to do their best *not* to kill them.

"Well," Keith said, "what if we start shooting randomly into the crowd?"

"Well," Ray said, "if you do that, then yeah, we probably are going to have to shoot you. But I can promise you we're still going to try not to kill you."

Keith and Kate tied the handles of their guns to their wrists with rope so that they could not drop their weapons.

The police considered firing tear gas at them, but there were too many onlookers crowded too close to the bridge. During the long stand-off, State Police Lieutenant Earl Rife had stationed two sharpshooters just north of the bridge. He now told them that Kate and Keith were trying to make the police kill them, and that they had tied their guns to their wrists. If the Haiglers started walking away from the bus, as soon as they had a clear shot, Rife instructed them, one of them was to shoot Keith in his right shoulder and the other was to shoot Kate in her right shoulder.

The media people returned behind the police barricade.

At 3:45, Ray was again standing near the bus door with a couple of State Police officers nearby, making a last-ditch effort to talk them into turning themselves in. Ray remembers the last exchange he had with them.

"Ray," Keith called out from the bus, where he was sitting in the driver's seat. "You're gonna to make sure our bodies get back, right?"

"Keith, there's something else I want you two to think about." (Ray remembered saying that but did not remember what he had planned to say next.)

"There's nothing left to say," Keith said. "I think it's time to do this." He turned and exchanged a few words with Kate. Then he got up, stood in the doorway of the bus with his pistol—the handle tied to his wrist with a length of thin white rope—and motioned for Ray and the two other officers standing near him to move away. "Now y'all go on," he said, "because we're coming off the bus." Ray the two other officers backed away slowly and walked off the bridge.

Keith and Kate Haigler, twenty-six and twenty-four years old, stepped off the bus and started walking across the scalding concrete surface of the bridge over the Little Buffalo River on a bright hot midsummer afternoon, the day before Independence Day, with their handguns tied to their right wrists, toward a line of police cars, with dozens of cops training their weapons on them and a crowd of onlookers behind.

State Police Lieutenant Jim Stobaugh warned them through a PA system rigged through loudspeakers: "You don't have a chance. You will *not* be killed. Please lay down your weapons and surrender."

When they had walked about twenty feet, they both dropped to their knees and continued crawling forward in that position, like penitents entering a cathedral. Ray thinks they probably did this to make it harder to shoot them in the legs.

"This is our last warning," Stobaugh said through the PA: the watching crowd silent, his amplified voice furred with speaker-crackle echoing across the empty stretch of concrete in the hot dead afternoon doldrums. "We advise you to stop. You don't have a chance. We're only going to shoot to hurt you."

Keith and Kate stopped, turned to each other, kissed goodbye, and resumed crawling forward across the bridge on their knees. Neither of them had yet raised their weapon.

The two police sharpshooters fired, and Keith and Kate Haigler both fell instantly. Keith tried to raise his gun, but his right arm—he'd been shot in the shoulder—was paralyzed. He pulled the hammer of the pistol back with his left hand, but couldn't pry the gun out of his own right hand. But the sharpshooter who had shot Kate had shot the wrong shoulder—her left—and Kate, writhing on the concrete with her right arm wildly flailing around, fired a few shots at random—two to the sky and another that ricocheted off the railing of the bridge—before she rolled over, facing Keith. She shot her husband once in the chest, and then she put the muzzle of her gun against her right eye and shot herself in the head. Keith Haigler, who had been shot in the heart, died on the bridge. Kate, despite having shot herself in the head, lived another ten minutes, dying in an ambulance on the way to the hospital in Harrison.

While searching the bus for the dynamite Keith had claimed in the letter to Ray Watkins to have on board, police found a duffel bag full of bundles of one-inch-diameter wooden dowels that had been painted red and bound together with strips of black electrical tape.

Early on in the afternoon's dramatic spectacle, several friends and acquaintances who had known Keith and Kate, and Emory Lamb and his wife and daughter (Shirley Angela Lamb and Kate all waited tables at the Ozark Cafe), and later, police officers, had gone to Lamb's place, found him at home, and pleaded with him to intervene, to come down to the bridge over the Little Buffalo and try to stop what was happening. Lamb had refused to leave his home, saying that he had nothing to do with whatever Keith and Kate were doing; it was a police matter. Afterward, he maintained they hadn't told him anything about their plans for that day.

Keith and Kate Haigler's bodies were not moved to Emory Lamb's property, and they did not at any point resurrect from the dead. Lamb's wife, Shirley, left her husband not long after the incident, taking their daughter, Angela, with her. Emory Lamb continued to live on diminishing resources, he and his property growing increasingly derelict for another thirteen years, until he died of lung cancer in 1995 at the age of sixty-six.

12

You Have Almost Persuaded Me

Lᴜᴄʏ ꜱʜᴇʟᴛᴏɴ (ꜱʜᴇ ʜᴀᴅ ᴛᴀᴋᴇɴ ʜᴇʀ ꜱᴇᴄᴏɴᴅ ʜᴜꜱʙᴀɴᴅ'ꜱ ꜱᴜʀ-name) was dismayed to know that I myself do not believe that there was any immaterial—in the philosophical sense of the word—connection between Haley's imaginary friend and Bethany Alana Clark. I wince to imagine her disappointment in this regard after our long conversations over the phone when she generously opened up to me about unimaginably painful events in her past, during which she broke down in tears more than once. It is true that this belief is vitally important to her, that it closed a wound in her soul that had been open most of her life, but I certainly cannot lie and say that I believe it. She wrote me an email (this isn't all of it, just the last three paragraphs):

> One thing you need to understand Ben is that I was raised to know and believe there was God and Jesus. Through abuse with my husband and through the others, I lost a lot of what I was taught to be good, and they turned it into something totally evil. They used God against me and toward the end, I had been told that I was never going to Heaven along with my daughter and June. That I was cast out. It took me years to get

to where I am at now. There have been many books written, but none as great as the Holy Bible.

  I had to ask God to help me get back to Him. I asked for forgiveness, and I know that God has forgave me. I, in turn had to forgive them also. For if you don't forgive, God certainly won't forgive you. That was not easy and I have been on my knees countless times and cried many tears. I understand that you are sceptic and do not believe as well as others do not that there was a "spirit" or "angel" that helped Haley. As you said why would she lead Haley away from the people? As I stated to Joyce, maybe she was led to safety and those two men were led to find her.

  No Ben, I don't think it is strange her being in Heaven, that is where she is. My question to you is, why write a story, you don't believe? Surely, you must have some sort of faith. The next time you are outside, take a good look around you. You see God everywhere for this is His creation. Sadly, the one place that you won't find Him is in the hearts of skeptical people which are so many today.

I told her it does not matter whether or not I personally believe that Haley was visited by Bethany's spirit. It doesn't even matter whether or not Haley believes this; Haley told me, "There are some things I will never know, and I'm okay with that.") What matters is what Joyce and Lucy believe.

  Why write the story if I don't believe? It's a good question. Why study religion if one is not religious? The most beautiful and fascinating works of art about religious faith are not about having it, but about doubt and struggle with it—and that even includes the Christian gospels; one can read in his last words—why have you forsaken me?—that not even Jesus nailed to the cross in his final mortal moments is perfectly resolute in his belief. As in all things, Christianity's power lies in narrative, and the Christian who believes and has always believed has no story arc. It is the prodigal son, not the faithful one, who needs redemption. Doubt is the essence of faith.

In the summer of 2023, I contacted one of Suzette Freeman's younger brothers, Paul Kleinpeter. Paul and his wife, Kelly, invited me over to their house in Grosse Tête, the same village he and Suzette had grown up in, in the house on the road named after their grandfather, where I spent a few hours talking with them in their living room. Paul was understandably cagey about talking with me at first, as I was there to dredge up a dark and shameful episode in his family's history that they very much do not like talking about and would rather leave buried under the many years of time and silence and relatively normal life that followed. So would the other two of Suzette's brothers with whom I spoke, Jerry and Greg.*

All of Suzette's brothers I spoke with are also deeply religious. Only one of the three, Greg, has stuck with the Cajun Catholicism they were raised in; Jerry and Paul now belong to Evangelical Protestant churches. And the centrality of Christianity to their lives is hard to overstate. One of the first things Paul asked me when we sat down was, "Ben, what is your conviction of God?"

Have you ever experienced a tingling in your gut when a near stranger—a person you have just met but you like so far, or at least have no reason to dislike—tries to convert you to Christianity?† When it happens to me, a feeling emerges within me like a taut wire running from my

---

* I must mention that Suzette's siblings who spoke with me were more accommodating and helpful than they had to be and more than I had expected them to be. They had loved their sister, and they said that the events of 1978 had been deeply traumatic for her and she had paid a heavy spiritual penance for them for a long time—and I believe them. I hope this book does not stain the Kleinpeter family with any opprobrium. They are kind and good people who deserve to be respected and left alone. And while I'm at it, I should point out that if Suzette emerges as the villain of this story, one reason may simply be that she is dead and unable to speak for herself. Another, possibly sympathetic, character might have surfaced had she lived to tell her side of it.

† I say Christianity specifically because that's the only religion anyone's tried to convert me to. The only other major proselytizing religion is Islam, and no one's ever tried that on me.

brain through the center of my body, vibrating like the string of a guitar. I feel my muscles relaxing, my superego retreating to the back of my mind and my emotional attention coming sharply into focus. The person who is trying to convert you to Christianity looks you in the eye and begins to talk with you about things of cosmic importance, about your own death, about the meaning of your life, about eternity. There is none of the nervous, embarrassed deflection to irony, the cushion of jocular small talk that happens when two fellow citizens meet in secular-urban-liberal-land. (Wallace Stevens: "He has managed to shut out the face of the giant from his windows. But the giant is there, nevertheless.") All that bullshit bypassed, we have gone straight to the terror at the center of human existence that we wrap all our days and language and work and art around like papier-mâché wrapped around the void in the shape of the thing that is no longer there. Granted, it might help you get there quicker when you have shown up to ask someone about that one time forty-five years ago when his sister was in a cult that murdered a child. But the startling rawness of the connection comes from knowing that this person *believes* that God so loved the world that he gave his only begotten son, that whosoever believeth in Him should not perish, but have everlasting life. He *believes* that he will live forever, and he is trying to give you the gift of salvation, the gift of everlasting life, and you keep saying "No, thank you" and pushing it back to him. At least I do.

Throughout our conversation that afternoon, I kept trying to steer Paul and Kelly from proselytizing me and back to what they remember happening with Larry and Suzette Freeman in the 1970s. It turned out that Paul doesn't remember it very well, because he was wandering in a dark wood himself at the time and distracted, to say the least. I didn't ask him to get into it in detail, but something happened to him on the Fourth of July 1979: his road-to-Damascus moment when he saw the light; for a period of several years before that day, his life had been at its nadir: he was divorced from his former and future wife, —who sat beside him on the couch as he told me this—with whom he had two young children, and he said he had been living for the Devil—drinkin, slippin, dippin', screwin', and brewin'. I was heavin' up this and heavin' up that. I will tell you, Ben, that my life was a total wreck. I was living in a dark time. All I remember is my dad said, "Hey, we goin' to Arkansas, and I need you to help me drive this truck." So I went there and got my sister with my dad and the U-Haul and got her stuff. They had it all in a barn. We went up a dirt road to the top of the hill and came back down the hill with her belongings, drove back home in the U-Haul. That's the extent of me remembering.

Paul thought that it had been just him and his father who had driven the U-Haul up to Arkansas to pick up Suzette, but about a week later I spoke with Jerry, the oldest brother of the nine siblings—the second born after Suzette—and he told me that he had gone with them, too. Although still nebulous, Jerry's memory of it was a little more detailed than his younger brother's, perhaps because, as Paul said, his brain around that time in his life was pretty fogged with drugs and alcohol. Jerry remembered that Paul had definitely been the one driving the truck. Both of them remembered that Suzette's belongings were being kept in a barn on a farm off a dirt road way up on a mountain, a barn that was still in use as a barn, with hay all over the floor. I think that Hurchal Fowler and Ray Watkins must have moved all the stuff they confiscated from the scene of the crime—everything that had been in the Jeep Wagoneer and the rented moving truck—and stored it in a barn on Hurchal's property right off Cave Mountain Road. Or maybe some neighbor with an empty barn available had leant it to them for storing evidence. Neither Paul nor Jerry remembered where exactly Suzette had been staying since she had been let out of Benton County Jail, but they both remembered their older sister looking sickly and malnourished. "Suzette was really skinny," Jerry said. "She was really in poor health when we found her."

So Jerry, Paul, and their father drove to the top of Cave Mountain, got Suzette's stuff out of whoever's barn the Newton County Sheriff's Office was keeping it in, and drove it and Suzette down to their hometown. At first she stayed in her father's house (her mother had died two years before), the house all her other siblings had grown up in while she had been exiled to her grandparents' house and where Paul, by then divorced from Kelly and staggering from one day to the next in a dark mist of substances, was also living. She stayed there for some months; no one remembers exactly how long. In August, her husband, Larry, joined her there after posting bail in Missouri. That fall, Larry and Suzette rented an apartment in Grosse Tête, and Suzette began working at a department store in Baton Rouge. The couple began attending services at Sunnyside Apostolic Church in Grosse Tête.

"I remember," Jerry said, "some people, because of what happened, they shunned Suzette. They didn't understand how that could happen. Some of the people that she went to high school with. But she stayed around."

Paul Kleinpeter told me many times about Suzette's spiritual rebirth after she returned and began to live life again after the murder, the arrests, the collapse of the Church of God in Christ through the Holy Spirit, Inc., and the trial. He said that she had gotten counseling from the people who had built the house we were at that moment, which was their house now. He and Kelly wouldn't say much else about those people other than that they were very strong Christians and had been dead a long time.

They loved the Lord and said, "Hey, you gotta pick yourself up by the bootstraps. You gotta go back to work." Everybody in the little community probably had some help in getting her through this darkness, through that time. They all gone, they all dead. Dr. Bremman, Russell and Felicia, all of those people are dead. And their kids are our kids' age or a little bit older, but they wouldn't have even told them anything. Hopefully salvation came out of this. I'm thinking maybe the people that counseled my sister, and my sister and my brother-in-law, prayed that "God, you take this darkest vilest time and turn it into good." We have to look inward and say, "Hey, listen, I just messed up bad." Even my sister. Listen, when my sister

Suzette came out of that, all she wanted to tell you is about Jesus and his mercy and his love. "What I was in is so dark, I'm not talking about that"—that's basically what she would say. And I'd rather tell you about the light. I could tell you this, this, this, and this about where I was before. Listen, I used to be like that, but now I'm like this. How he did that was a miracle. I know my sister got it right. Let me tell you, I know my sister and my brother-in-law were locked in with God. Their sole focus was towards Heaven.

Paul Kleinpeter's own sole focus is toward Heaven. At least it is difficult to get him to focus on anything else for very long. He began our conversation with God, returned to God again and again throughout the day, and ended with God. He spoke of his own salvation, his sister's salvation, and my salvation. He tried very hard and earnestly to bring me into the light.

There is at least one thing I now think I had wrong about religion in my angry-young-man days of pugilistic atheism. Back then, I read the anti-crusaders whose books were popular in the mid-2000s— Christopher Hitchens, Sam Harris, Richard Dawkins—but my reading of those books gave me only the cheap, immature pleasure of reinforcing opinions I already held. Before that, the most formative influences on my atheism had been Carl Sagan's *The Demon-Haunted World: Science as a Candle in the Dark* and George Carlin, who defined God as "the invisible man in the sky who needs your money." But I've come to think that the mistake that Sagan made about religion and that Dawkins made, too, and that I made back then, is an overemphasis on religion as a theory of reality, as a tool for understanding and mapping the physical universe. It's not really that important whether or not you "believe," in the most literal sense, in a bluntly concrete invisible-man-in-the-sky God, or in the virgin birth, or the raising of Lazarus, or that Jesus is the son of God and that he returned from the dead and ascended to Heaven and will come again. It doesn't really matter that you can discover and measure and describe reality with microscopes and telescopes and radiocarbon dating and say, "Look—the Bible's wrong!" That kind of atheism misses the point in exactly the same way as a fundamentalist reading of Genesis so literal that fossilized dinosaur bones present a metaphysical problem requiring inelegant theological jury-rigging (for example, that the Devil planted those there to lead us astray). Both Sagan's atheism and that style of fundamentalism fixate far too much on the objective reality that surrounds us, the empty forest in which the tree falls, what Jakob von Uexküll termed the *Umgebung*. I have come to think that this standpoint turns its gaze entirely in the wrong direction: outward. Not a hair's breadth of evolutionary time separates us from the residents of Mesopotamia of four thousand years ago, and religion as an explanation of the physical universe outside ourselves, what's going on in the sky above us, and what the earth under our feet is made of—whether we are the dream of Vishnu or the world rests on the backs of four elephants standing on a giant turtle or the heavenly orbs revolve around the earth or the Titans were vanquished and bound in Tartarus—these painterly ideations were drawn up in the extremely recent past by *Homo sapiens* with exactly the same brains in their bone vaults as you and I have, and I have too much respect for them to believe that any of it was really meant to be read as—or that anyone but suckers ever read them as—anything but poetry. (Of course, there's a sucker born every minute, and art conquers reality in the battlefield of the mind all the time—but that's the mind's fault, not art's.)

The right direction is not outward but inward. Internal, subjective, personal, emotional. Christianity's intense power lies in its openness to forgive sin. Whether "real" or not, an infinite stack of turtles teeters in the inky void just as far away from the realm of human concerns as the rings of Saturn and the moons of Jupiter, and none of it really matters: what matters is the relationship between a human soul and God. The most deeply felt Christian art—or at any rate, the Christian art that makes me feel most deeply—was made by sinners asking for a forgiveness they knew they didn't deserve: for instance, the slave trader turned priest John Newton's hymn "Amazing Grace." I have squandered my patrimony on harlots and riotous living, and returned to my father a disgrace. I have traded in slaves. I have hijacked a bus. I have murdered a three-year-old child. I have let them murder my daughter. Grace will save even a wretch like me.

God saved Paul Kleinpeter from a life wandering in darkness, from harlots and riotous living. God saved his sister from a much deeper darkness. And Paul badly wanted to save me from my darkness. "You're gonna spend eternity somewhere, my friend," he said. "Ben, point this book towards God."

I promised I would do that, and I hope I've kept the promise.

Near the end of my visit to Paul and Kelly Kleinpeter's home in Grosse Tête, after Paul had resigned for the time being his mighty and persistent effort to make me a Christian, he compared our conversation to the episode toward the end of the Book of Acts in which Paul the Apostle, imprisoned in Caesarea, preaches the Gospel passionately to King Agrippa.

"I could talk to you all day," he told me. "I can't convince you. King Agrippa told Paul, he said, 'You almost converted me. You almost made me become a Christian. But let's talk again tomorrow.' Tomorrow never gets here. Tomorrow never gets here."

What Agrippa says to Paul the Apostle (Acts 26:28) Paul Kleinpeter paraphrased pretty closely. (Paul has a lot of scripture down in his memory nearly word for word.) It's a famous verse of the New Testament. It's the third time the word "Christian" appears in the Bible. I later looked it up and found the verse translated very differently in the New International Version than in the King James Version. In the KJV, it's "Then Agrippa said unto Paul, 'Almost thou persuadest me to be a Christian.'" In the NIV, Agrippa says, "Do you think that in such a short time you can persuade me to be a Christian?" That's a completely different sentence. So then I looked it up in the Koine Greek original, and was surprised to find that the KJV—essentially the version Paul Kleinpeter remembered—is, in my opinion, the perfectly accurate translation, not the newer one. In more contemporary English, I would render it "You have almost persuaded me to be a Christian."

John Wesley preached a sermon inspired by that verse, titled "The Almost Christian." It's the second in his *Sermons on Several Occasions*, and it's one of his most famous. The "almost" Christian has "heathen honesty" and the "form of godliness"—that is, he behaves in every way that a Christian would consider right, doing unto others as he would have them do to him—and he does so with sincerity: "Even this poor wretch, in his sober intervals, is able to testify *Oderunt peccare boni, virtutis amore; Oderunt peccare mali, formidine poenae.* [Good men avoid sin from the law of virtue; wicked men avoid sin from a fear of punishment.]" What, then is missing to make him an "altogether Christian"? What is the difference between the "honest heathen" who in all ways, in all his works and deeds from cradle to grave, loves his neighbor and does right by him and never sins against God or man or anyone else, yet "remains still in his damnable estate" and despite his blameless life will burn in Hell for eternity right alongside Herod and Barabbas? One thing only—and Wesley here quotes the most common Christian bumper sticker other than the Jesus fish—John 3:16: "He that believeth in the Son hath everlasting life; and cometh not into condemnation, but is passed from death unto life." That's it. That's all.

John Wesley preached that to the congregation at St. Mary's, Oxford University, on July 25, 1741, and on June 28, 2023, in Grosse Tête, Iberville Parish, Louisiana, Paul Kleinpeter preached much the same to me: "'By grace through faith are you saved, not of yourselves lest any man should boast.' That's a gift from God. And the wage of sin is death but the gift of God is eternal life through Jesus Christ. You know we call upon him where he may be found. Today is the day of salvation. Ben, I think you're seeking for things and you don't even really know what you're seeking for."

And I said, "That is absolutely true."

Years ago, reading John Berger's *Ways of Seeing* sent me on an interesting journey with a certain Rembrandt painting, which I believe I have come to understand more deeply over time. It is a portrait of himself with his wife, Saskia van Uylenburgh, whom he had married the previous year.

Rembrandt was thirty-one years old when he painted it, and Saskia

was twenty-three. Rembrandt was at a high point of both his career and his life. He had just moved to booming, cosmopolitan Amsterdam, where his friend and patron Constantijn Huygens had secured a number of lucrative commissions for him from the court of the Hague. A newlywed, he was deliriously in love with Saskia, his career was in roaring ascendence, and his art was making him famous and wealthy. There is an attitude of triumph in this painting, of the boasting that Paul Kleinpeter might warn about: Rembrandt wears a gilt-handled sword, the mark of a gentleman, and hoists a glass of champagne over his head, as if he is raising a toast or raucously greeting the viewer, who has just walked into the tavern. In the background, a roast peacock rests on a table with a knife beside it ready to carve it, and to tell the viewer that the exotic bird is food and not some strange pet or taxidermy. Rembrandt exhibits his wealth, and sitting on his lap is his most prized possession of all, his young and beautiful new wife, Saskia. His arm is on her back, blocking her from the viewer and the viewer from her, as if saying "Have some champagne on me, have some of this peacock meat, but of all the worldly things my art has won me, this one—Saskia—is for me only."

It is easy to read this painting as a visual feast of genuine joy, and a little less easy to read it as triumphant, materialist boasting, as John Berger does:

> [Rembrandt] painted it in the year of his first marriage. In it he is showing off Saskia his bride. Within six years she will be dead. The painting is cited to sum up the so-called happy period of the artist's life. Yet if one approaches it now without sentimentality, one sees that its happiness is both formal and unfelt. Rembrandt is here using the traditional methods for their traditional purposes. His individual style may be becoming recognizable. But it is no more than the style of a new performer playing a traditional role. The painting as a whole remains an advertisement for the sitter's good fortune, prestige, and wealth. (In this case Rembrandt's own.) And like all such advertisements it is heartless.

Berger then goes on to compare this early work of Rembrandt's with a much later self-portrait, one of his last, painted after he had suffered through the deaths of the first three of the four children he had with Saskia, then Saskia's death of tuberculosis, then his affair with his maid, the much younger Hendrickje Stoffels, the scandal of which occasioned his ostracism from Amsterdam high society (he did not marry Hendrickje because Titus, the only surviving son of his first marriage, would have lost a trust given to him by Saskia's wealthy family that had been arranged in her will), then the loss of his fortune through financial mismanagement, then Hendrickje's death in the plague of 1663, and then at last the death of his only remaining child, Titus. Here is a self-portrait he painted in the last year of his life, just months before he died a forgotten artist and a poor man with an extinct legacy and was buried at small public expense in an unmarked grave in the churchyard of the Westerkerk (twenty years later, his remains were exhumed and destroyed to clear space, as was customary for the dead of the poor).

We see the face of an exhausted old man who has suffered decades of pain: loss, grief, disappointment, failure, abandonment, humiliation, decline, fall. It's the face of a man exhausted with suffering, and ready to die. Gone absolutely is the flashy frippery of his young-man days, when he was riding high.*

That's Berger's assessment, anyway, and I believed it, until I learned

---

* Jane Hirshfield, "Late Self-Portrait by Rembrandt" (2003):
The dog, dead for years, keeps coming back in the dream.
We look at each other there with the old joy.
It was always her gift to bring me into the present—
Which sleeps, changes, awakens, dresses, leaves.
Happiness and unhappiness
differ as a bucket hammered from gold differs from one of pressed tin,
this painting proposes.
Each carries the same water, it says.

that the first painting, that supposedly heartless advertisement for his own wealth and success that he had painted at the age of thirty-one, is titled *The Prodigal Son in the Brothel*. Berger conveniently leaves that out of his analysis. This has complicated my interpretation of it.

A certain man has two sons. And the younger of them says, "Father, please give me my inheritance now"—i.e., before you die. His father gives it to him, and the younger son takes the money and goes off to "a far country," where he quickly wastes it all with riotous living. And when he has spent all, there arises a mighty famine in that land, and he has to get a job as a farmhand feeding pigs—especially dirty and humiliating work for a kosher-keeping Jew. And he's so poor and hungry that when his boss isn't looking, he steals some of the slop meant for the pigs. And he thinks, what I have become that I'm stealing food from *pigs*? My father's servants back home have it better than this! So he goes back home—skinny, penniless, barefoot, in tatters—with the intention of saying "Father, I no longer deserve to be called your son. All I ask is that you hire me on as a common farmhand." But when he is still a ways off, his father recognizes him, and has compassion, runs to him and kisses and embraces him. The son says, "Father, I have sinned against heaven, and in thy sight, and am no more worthy to be called thy son." But his father turns to his servants and shouts, "Put the best robe on him, and put a ring on his finger and shoes on his feet, break open the good wine and kill the fatted calf, and let us eat and be merry, for this my son was dead, and is alive again. He was lost, and now is found." By and by the older son—the obedient, loyal son who never went anywhere—comes home from working his father's fields, sweaty and spent, and is much surprised to find a party going on in the big house. He asks a passing servant what the celebration is about, and the guy tells him that his brother's come home; his father opened the good wine and killed the fatted calf. The older brother's so pissed off about it that he refuses to go into the house, so his father comes out to talk to him. The older brother says to his father, "Here I am, I've been dutifully working for you on this farm all this time, and you never killed the fatted calf in *my* honor! Meanwhile, *that* dipshit asks for his inheritance because he can't wait for you to die, and you actually *give* it to him, and then he takes half your life savings, fucks off with it to a far country and blows it all on harlots. Then he comes home a disgrace, and you throw him a party!" And the father says to his older son, "Son, thou art ever with me, and all that I have is thine. It was meet that we should make merry, and be glad: for this thy brother was dead, and is alive again; and was lost, and is found."

In *The Prodigal Son in the Brothel* Rembrandt depicted the part of the story in which the prodigal son, having taken his moiety of the patrimony before his father dies and absconded with it to the big city far away (city of sin, the urban always representing evil; perhaps it was Rome that Jesus had in mind, but for Rembrandt it was Amsterdam; for me, it was New York City), where he swiftly "waste[s] his substance with riotous living." There's no specification of how exactly he wastes it until after he returns home and the jealous, dutiful older son says to their father that he "hath devoured thy living with harlots." Hence, this scene is set in a brothel, where one may indulge in riotous living: extravagant food, expensive liquor, and, most riotous of all, sex purchased directly with money. Rembrandt has painted himself as a john, and his own wife as a whore.

But unlike the prodigal son in the parable, Rembrandt knows the story, and he knows how the story ends. The prodigal son, irreverent, flush with the money his father gave him, living high on the hog (later, he will be reduced to feeding the hogs, and later still, he will be hungry enough to eat the hogs' feed), is not looking toward the future. But Rembrandt is. Or rather, in the painting, his wife, Saskia, is. On second look, Rembrandt/the prodigal son is not looking at the viewer after all—he bellows a boisterous greeting at someone who has just entered the room somewhere to the left of the viewer. It's Saskia/the harlot who looks directly at the viewer; her expression isn't unhappy, but it certainly isn't thrilled. She, unlike her customer, is sober. She's smirking slightly. I read a little exasperation in her expression. It is the look of a prostitute growing annoyed with the rich, drunk idiot whose lap she's sitting on, still tolerating him, but only until she can take his money, and then she'll be done with him. She is looking forward to parting this fool from his money—soon.

It is worth noting that this is only the right-hand third of the original painting: the rest of it probably depicted an indoor panorama of carousing and debauchery. But for whatever reason Rembrandt felt unsatisfied with that part of the painting, and he cropped it to just this image. This image is literally not the whole picture.

Of course, it is true that Rembrandt was young, rich, successful, and in love when he painted this picture. But giving it the title he did seems to indicate that even when he was at the blind height of his lavish, shallow young man's life, he had a feeling that it would not last.

Rembrandt knew he was a sinner—he knew even when he was in the middle of sinning that he was a sinner—and he knew even then that one day the prodigal son would come crawling home on his knees to beg the Father for a forgiveness he does not deserve.

He had to paint that early painting, so that, many years later, he would paint this one:

It is among the last works—possibly the very last work—Rembrandt painted, and it is titled *The Return of the Prodigal Son*. It is the work of a man getting ready to knock on Heaven's door.

Some stories require one to have lived some life to understand them, and I must confess that the parable of the Prodigal Son—and the parable of Rembrandt growing from an almost to an altogether understanding of the parable of the Prodigal Son—resonates with me so personally that it disturbs me and makes me uncomfortable.

During my trip to Louisiana and Arkansas in the summer of 2023, I listened to an audiobook of C. S. Lewis's *Mere Christianity* as I drove south, because I had heard that it is one of the calmest and friendliest books by a Christian addressed to a secular reader. This passage in particular struck me and stayed on my mind for some time:

> According to Christian teachers, the essential vice, the utmost evil, is Pride. . . . Pride leads to every other vice: it is the complete anti-God state of mind. . . .
>
> In God you come up against something which is in every respect immeasurably superior to yourself. Unless you know God as that—and, therefore, know yourself as nothing in comparison—you do not know God at all. As long as you are proud you cannot know God. A proud man is always looking down on things and people: and, of course, as long as you are looking down, you cannot see something that is above you.

The next day, in Grosse Tête, Louisiana, Paul Kleinpeter asked me if I have sinned.

Paul Kleinpeter: What's your vice? What's your sin? You got sin in a life. Have you ever told a lie?

Benjamin Hale: Everyone has.

[laughter]

PK: Have you ever stole anything?

BH: Not lately.

[laughter]

PK: Have you ever—I can take you down through the whole Ten Commandments, and I bet you've broken them all. I broke them all multiple times. Liars won't go. Thieves. Killers. Did you ever kill anybody?

BH: Nope. I know I can say no to that one.

PK: In your heart?

[laughter]

BH: In my heart I've done a lot of things.

PK: No, but in your heart. You know? "I hate that person. I wish they was dead." Did you shoot him? Just in your heart. Or did you look at your neighbor's wife? Did you covet your neighbor's goods? Do you want to write a book as good as the next fellow did, or the other book you read?

BH: Well, the other day I was listening to C. S. Lewis's *Mere Christianity* on the way over here. I mean, when I drove down here from New York. Somebody told me it was one of their favorite books about Christianity. I was listening to it in the car, and there's a part of the book where he says that pride is actually the worst sin, that all the other sins come from pride in some way. And I thought: That's really interesting, because it made me think I'm definitely . . . I *know* I'm guilty of pride.

PK: You know, I don't see that, though. That's a good confession, but I don't see it in you. I see a very humble man. I see a man that's hungry, and I see a man that's looking, and I see a man that's seeking. Seek and you will find, knock at the door. . . . Listen, I'm telling you, if we knock long enough God's gonna start speaking to you.

I was thinking about C. S. Lewis. I was thinking about John Berger. I was thinking about Rembrandt. I was thinking about myself. I was thinking about pride.

Pride is the utmost evil. Pride leads to every other vice. "Do you want to write a book as good as the next fellow did?" Paul asked me. Yes! Of course I do! I want to write one *better* than the next fellow did. Pride is the wellspring of art. Pride is the reason we create. Yes, the point of creating art is to create beauty. But the artist is motivated by two things: to create beauty and to be the one to have created it. I had a character in an (unpublished) novel reflect on this: "Is it a coincidence that Hitler was a failed painter, and Franco was a failed poet? So was Mao, wasn't he? And didn't Saddam Hussein fancy himself a novelist? And Kim Jong Il a filmmaker? The desire to make art is right next to the desire to subjugate, to rule—to watch crowds of people salute the image of your face, to live forever. The heart of an artist beats wild and childish and prideful in the chest of every dictator."

Pride, C. S. Lewis asserts, is the complete anti-God state of mind, and it is also what drives us to create. Pride drives Lucifer to rise up against God: *Paradise Lost* is one of the greatest works of art about doubt and struggle with faith. As Satan—whose voice, generations have noticed with perplexity, delivers the story's most beautiful poetry—wages his war against Heaven, John Milton the rebel and artist wages war against Milton the Christian. Stanley Fish thinks that this was deliberate on Milton's part; of course Satan speaks beautifully, for evil seduces with beauty; the Holy Grail is not the cup of the king, but the cup of the carpenter. But I much prefer the fulminous romance of William Blake's interpretation in *The Marriage of Heaven and Hell*: "*Note.*—The reason Milton wrote in fetters when he wrote of Angels & God, and at liberty when of Devils & Hell, is because he was a true poet, and of the Devil's party without knowing it." To make art at all is to commit the sin of pride. A work of art is a volley in the artist's war against death, and any attempt to vanquish death other than through the way into Heaven offered by faith is war against God.

Forgive me, for I have sinned. This book you hold in your hands, like any work worth doing, is a work of pride. I have taken other people's lives—other people's tragedies—and turned them into a story: for glory, for money, and most of all out of the desire to create beauty. There are some people in this story, those who did nothing wrong, who don't mind being written about, but there are others who do. I couldn't help feeling shameful and treacherous while meeting the Kleinpeters; they helped me, and they spoke with me candidly and generously, without knowing how badly their sister comes across in this story. Lucy spoke with me only with great hesitance and trepidation, and I have throughout this effort struggled with the feeling that I've betrayed her, too, although I honestly hope that this story exonerates her in the reader's mind. And I hope to redeem the sin with the sin itself in another way, at least in the eyes of Heaven, because there is someone else in this story who also spent most of his life suffering from this tragedy, someone who may or may not deserve redemption, but upon whom I have come to wish forgiveness and grace: Mark Harris.

13

Trust and Obey

THE SAME SUMMER IN ARKANSAS THAT I MET SUZETTE'S BROTH-ers Jerry and Paul Kleinpeter, I learned that Winston Van Harris, after serving fifteen years in prison, had been paroled out of state in 1993 (the Arkansas Department of Corrections wouldn't tell me to which state) and had been out on parole for the next ten years, until he was discharged from the system in 2003. I also learned that he had died of cancer in 2022 at the age of seventy-five. Pursuant to Arkansas Act 539 (Bill 294), passed in 2017 in response to the 2012 US Supreme Court decision *Miller v. Alabama*, which ruled that juveniles convicted of murder cannot be held subject to a mandatory sentence of life imprisonment without the possibility of parole, Mark Harris, after serving forty years of a life sentence, had been released to supervision out of state on July 23, 2018, and the ADC was not authorized to give me any more information than that. That sent me looking for a sixty-two-year-old man with the hopelessly ubiquitous name of Mark Harris (though I was not sure he still went by that name), and all I knew about him was that he did not live in Arkansas.

Toward the end of the summer, through a lot of internet sleuthing, I discovered that Winston Van Harris had changed his name back to some-thing closer to the one he had been born with—Daniel Gobe Smith—

that he had moved to Alpharetta, Georgia, and married a woman named Robin Lynn Holt, who had died in 2020. Since Mark Harris had no other living relatives I knew of and would have had nowhere else to go after his release on parole, I figured it was a good bet that he also lived in or near that town in Georgia. And sure enough, on Whitepages I found a Mark Harris of the right age who had no public records before 2018: a mailing address, an email address, and a phone number. I called the phone number and left a voicemail, and sent him an email, asking if I had the right person, explaining what I was doing, and ended with a request to interview him, if he was indeed the Mark Harris I was looking for. A few days later, he responded with a long email. He had read the article I had written in *Harper's* about both Haley's disappearance and what I had known then about the murder of Bethany Alana Clark, which had recently been published, and he was wounded and extremely angry about it. He ended his email with this:

> *For my part, I hope you decide to abandon your fictional novel project intended to be marketed as non-fiction.*
>
> *And it makes no sense whatsoever for me to participate in a project that will further demonize me and perhaps subject me to further slander and misrepresentation to the public.*
>
> *I have no interest in resuming PTSD-related nightmares, or resuming thoughts of suicide and wishing I had the courage to do that to put an end to experiencing more hatred from people I don't know and don't know me, who will only and ever view me as a heinous murderer.*

It was clear that he had no interest in speaking with me. But I wrote him back to say that I had no interest in demonizing him or painting him as the villain of the story, which is true. I ended my email with this: "I promise that I am coming to you with my hands open and in good faith. I want to get at the truth of the matter, and I would very, very much appreciate your help." Mark wrote back:

> *Thank you for kind response, which I just saw now.*

I am giving your proposal a great deal of thought.

After that, in late August, we had several long phone conversations over WhatsApp, and four months later, during my winter holiday break from teaching, I had a few days free right after New Year's, and I drove from my home in New York's Hudson Valley down to Alpharetta, Georgia,* where I spent an afternoon talking with Mark Harris and his wife, Deborah, in person. Since then, Mark and I have been emailing and texting each other fairly regularly. Back before I started writing this, when I would verbally tell the story that begins with Haley's disappearance on Cave Mountain in April 2001, I would usually end on the unlikely friendship that has developed between Lucy Clark and my aunt Joyce. Now, as a consequence of writing it, I think I can say that Mark Harris has become my friend.

Of all the people who were involved with what happened in 1978, even very peripherally, who are still alive, Mark is the one most on my philosophical wavelength, the one whose worldview and ways of thinking harmonize most closely with my own. Conversations with Suzette's siblings, no matter how they begin, inevitably swing like compass needles toward the magnetic north of God, Christ, the Holy Ghost, and the urgent business of the salvation of my own lost soul from eternal damnation. I found Jerry Patterson to be an incredibly warm, smart, and funny conversationalist, and I like him a lot on a personal level, but the political signs in his front yard made me suspect we would find a lot of uncommon ground should the conversation turn in that direction. Ray Watkins, the octogenarian former deputy sheriff and sheriff of Newton County, who will probably be the guy who rings you up if you buy something at Bob's Do It Best Hardware and Lumber in Jasper, was also generous with his time and kinder and more helpful to me than he had to be when I bothered him at work with questions about things that happened nearly

---

* I have changed the names of some of the people and places connected to Mark Harris.

half a century ago, but Ray has the heart of a Boy Scout and a lawman. "I've never smoked a cigarette," was almost the last thing he said to me, explaining his remarkably excellent health at his very advanced age, "and I've never been drunk in my life." My soul is jaggedly mismatched with that man's, as I had apparently already smoked more cigarettes and been drunk more times during that particular trip to Arkansas than Ray had in his lifetime. Lucy would get away from me, too, sometimes, especially when talk moved in the direction of religion or politics.

About politics, I should say that coming out of the culture war meltdown of the 2010s, which whipsawed with a grand flourish into the total bouleversement of the covid pandemic, I have been dragged by conflicting currents this way and that and now I don't know where I am. Up until a few years ago, I was a good soldier for blue America—a well-educated middle-class *New York Times*-subscribing Democrat who faithfully recycles and votes in every election, even the little ones—but now I am adrift, still hating what I used to hate, but having lost faith in the magi I used to trust. I once furiously threw an ex-boyfriend of my about-to-be wife out of our house on the night before our wedding—on October 1, 2016—after he casually dropped that he planned to vote for Donald Trump. I was bloated with righteous indignation at the time; Caitlin made me apologize to him at the reception the next day, and I did so to make her happy, but I didn't mean it. If I ever see that guy again, I will apologize again for real, and I will mean itthe next time. This book made me spend a lot of time in the reddest parts of red America from 2022 to 2024, a time when blue America had possession of the ball and was fumbling it with long and pitiful maladroitness. I am not a liberal hothouse flower; I have traveled to every state in the country, and I hear America singing, blithe and strong. But in 2022 when I set out, I hadn't left the blue bubble for some time. I remember a fiction workshop I taught at Bard in the spring of that year: the college had decreed masking optional in the middle of that semester, but none dared go barefaced, as a mask had become a loudly visible badge of leftist political allegiance; it happened often that a student emailed me stating her or their refusal to read another student's piece for the workshop because someone else in the class had read it first and warned her or them that it contained triggering material; knitting had oddly become a fad among Bard undergraduates, and there were usually three or four people around the room clicking needles at scarves or shawls as we discussed a work of student fiction; one of the students had an emotional support poodle who usually spent the class napping at their feet next to a portable rubber water dish; the social atmosphere was one of extremely delicate constant censorious moral paranoia, and the triggers were hair. After that suffocating environment, my God was it a relief sometimes to be among the roughs, sounding their barbaric yawp. Around that time cracks were already appearing in the mental dam in my bone-vault that holds up the reservoir of what blue America deems the "correct" views, and its destruction was hastened along by friendly conversations with many relatively sane and reasonable people who are MAGA Republicans and/or evangelical Christians, and even some people who don't necessarily want to piously and obediently inject something into their bodies just because the sage wisdom of the widespread establishment consensus that overwhelmingly predicted Trump's defeat in 2016 told them to. (Don't worry: I'm not an anti-vaxxer, but I have sympathy for them. I can also find sympathy for murderers.) As Haley's father, Steve, said, "Something that keeps me in a ruby-red state when I'm a sapphire-blue dude is, man, the people here are pretty damn awesome. Even though they vote for Donald Trump and Sarah Huckabee Sanders, you know what, the people here are amazing—it was just thousands and thousands of people who gave up what they were doing to look for this kid. Most of them we never met." And as I've spent time with Trumpers and Bible thumpers and anti-vaxxers and mostly found them to be perfectly ordinary and fundamentally decent people who furthermore know how to change a tire without having to look it up on YouTube, I have become increasingly convinced that red America and blue America each indulges in its own set of self-serving delusional mythologies in roughly equal measure. I finished writing this book in June 2024 and sent it to the publisher from my laptop while waiting to board a plane that would take me back to Arkansas to attend my uncle Jay's memorial; the disastrous presidential debate between Joe

Biden and Donald Trump was televised one week later, and now, in May 2025, I am making my last tweaks before it goes to galley. What's happened between then and now is a sickening travesty, and the red and the blue are both responsible for it. I have no mockings or arguments, I witness and wait.

Anyway. I went on something like a spiritual journey while writing this book: reading and rereading the Bible, reading C. S. Lewis, reading John Wesley, reading Martin Luther and John Calvin, reading Reinhold Niebuhr, trying to think seriously about Christianity in a sympathetic way for the first time in my life, even going to church voluntarily (and not for a wedding or a funeral) for the first time ever. I went on a spiritual journey, and Mark Harris was waiting for me there when I came back from it: a man who grew up in a cult and for ordering the murder of a three-year-old girl spent a biblical forty years in prison, where he read a great deal and had a lot of time to think very hard and very, very long about where he has come from and what he has done.

Mark Harris asked to meet me for the first time in public and asked to bring his wife along, both of which I agreed to. I let him pick the place, and he suggested a Panera Bread in a far-flung suburb of Chattanooga, situated in exactly the kind of area Panera Breads always are: clean, flat, economically healthy commercial districts designed for vehicular traffic and naked of local or any other kind of character, strip malls of franchises downmarket of the upper middlebrow (a Chili's, an Applebee's, a Michaels, a HomeGoods, a PetSmart, and a T.J. Maxx all lie within sight of one another); places that look exactly the same whether you are in New Jersey, California, or a suburb of Atlanta; places where middle-class consumers feel comfortable and no one feels at home.

Having briefly gotten lost and arriving five minutes late, I didn't see anyone there who looked like they could be Mark and Barbara Harris, and I worried for a moment he had gotten cold feet and decided not to show, but I was relieved when it turned out that they arrived five minutes later than I was. Mark Harris is tall, over six feet, and thin, with a long, gaunt face, longish gray hair parted down the middle, a mustache of salt-and-pepper stubble that looked as though it had been shaved off a few days before. His wife, Barbara, is a short woman with long gray hair, a few years older than he is. Barbara surprised me with her Canadian accent. The two met through mutual Facebook friends during the darkest days of the covid pandemic in the spring of 2020, and as soon as the border reopened, she drove from British Columbia all the way down to Georgia and married him. The first thing we talked about was the unfinished process of navigating the headachey legal gauntlet to gain her US citizenship.

I bought the three of us lattes; we sat down, and I started recording our conversation on my iPad, wishing I'd remembered to bring a microphone, knowing that all the ambient noise in this room—conversations at other tables, torrents of ice periodically rumbling into the reservoir of the soda fountain, the gurgling hiss of the milk-steaming wand, a woman at a nearby table with an ugly persistent bark of a cough that drowns out everything else about every forty-five seconds—would render the quality of the recording nearly unusable shit, very much unhelped by the low register and near-whisper quietness of Mark's voice, at first. Whenever Barbara or I say something on the recording, it comes through clear as a bell, but Mark's voice is the faintest little beacon of signal, almost lost in a forest of noise. "It's because he's so scared," Barbara told me during her husband's first of four cigarette breaks. Over the course of nearly five hours, his voice grew louder and clearer the more he relaxed. Still, I knew that the transcription service I usually use for interviews would reject the recording as unworkable, so a couple of weeks later I had to do it myself, ear-squinting into my headphones, leaning in the harrier patches on the crutches of context and memory.

Most of the rest of this chapter more or less follows our conversation at the Panera that day, patched together with the transcripts of our phone conversations and emails and texts I exchanged with Mark before and after. This is Mark Harris's story.

———

Mark's mother, Edith Otelia Harris, the daughter of a Methodist minister in Navarro, Texas, was a beautiful woman, Mark said, with dark hair and dark eyes. I have been unable to find a single picture of her. Mark remembers finding a cheesecake picture she had posed for in a photo studio—she must have been in her early twenties, in the late 1940s, around the time she married her first husband, for whom the picture was probably a gift, striking a classic pinup pose in a short pleated skirt and a polka-dotted top with plunging back, ass thrust up at the camera, turning back with a finger on her plump dark lips and an "Oh, you naughty boy!" look on her face—and wondering what she had been like she was young, marveling at how much she had changed. It was disturbing, hard to imagine how the mother he had known could have ever been that sexy midcentury girl in the cheesecake picture.

Mark's first memories rise to the surface at the age of five or six. It was the mid-1960s, his parents were in their late thirties, and they were living in a nice enough suburban neighborhood in Baton Rouge in a one-story ranch house on a street lined on both sides with one-story ranch houses—a lower middle-class neighborhood that looked a lot like a Levittown, the kind of 1950s–'60s neighborhood that postwar America grew up in, where every dad on the block was a World War II vet and the summers smelled of charcoal smoke and DDT mist. Mark's father, Royal, who had an engineering degree from Texas A&M, worked as a systems analyst for the Ethyl Corporation, the guys that made gasoline additives that spread lead around the world. It was a good job, and the small family was doing okay back then. Winston Van Harris, his much older half brother from his mother's first marriage, graduated from high school in 1965, when Mark wasn't quite five years old, and attended Harding College in Searcy, Arkansas, for two years, dropped out, joined the army, and after basic training was stationed in Korea for two years, so he was present during only occasional brief visits during the formative years of Mark's childhood.

Edith Harris was sick, and that is important. Everything revolved around her, and everything revolved around her sickness. She had angina pectoris—chest pain from a weak heart—and frequent migraines, as well as a case of chronic pneumonia that waxed and waned but never seemed to go away entirely. Mark remembers his mother in bed; so many, many hours of the night and day in bed, with sunlight bleeding through shut curtains, moaning in pain. There was an evangelical faith healer type of preacher who had a church in Baton Rouge, and it's highly likely that he may have been somehow connected to Jimmy Swaggart. Mark said that the guy's name was Ray Hubbard; I haven't been able to find any record of him. He was the kind of tent revival preacher who would push on people's foreheads and they would fall back in a swoon, their fall caught by the crowd, and then they would get up a minute later claiming to be cured of whatever had been ailing them. His family attended Ray Hubbard's tent revivals, and one time, the man laid his hand upon Edith's forehead and pushed the love of Jesus into her, and she fell back into the congregants' hands in a swoon, got up, and declared that her chest pain was gone.

For a while, anyway; then it came back. Edith already had religious obsessions that long predated Mark's birth—they were what had brought about the end of her first marriage, before she had met his father—but Mark remembered that episode with the faith healer in the tent, the miraculous and medicine-free curing of her angina pectoris, as setting her off onto a new plane of Christian questing that would lead her and her husband to found their own church. An early fixation of hers was that Christians never should have stopped celebrating the Jewish High Holy Days and that the correct day of the Sabbath was not Sunday but Saturday. This belief is so foundational to Seventh-Day Adventism that the whole denomination is named after it, but it does not appear that Edith was ever curious to experiment with that church.* She became increas-

---

* I find the apparent centrality of this conviction to Seventh-Day Adventism a bit baffling—as if the days of the week "are" Saturday, Sunday, and so on and not useful fictions whose names are arbitrary. Saint Augustine knew that back in 426; there are passages in *City of God* in which he sounds like Clarence Darrow cross-examining William Jennings Bryan in *Inherit the Wind*, reasoning that the first "day" of creation couldn't possibly have been a twenty-four-hour day in a human sense because

ingly obsessed with these sorts of technical issues of Christian doctrine as her physical health steadily declined throughout Mark's childhood. The thing about the High Holy Days and the Sabbath day—and her getting into British Israelism—had to do with a sort of Christian originalism, a desire to clear away two millennia of warping and corruption and get back to the early church, the way Christianity was practiced in the years immediately following the crucifixion, which is a yearning for the Christianity depicted in the Book of Acts, when the power of signs and wonders was transferred from Jesus to his earliest disciples, when Peter and Paul healed lepers and repeatedly escaped from jail with the physical assistance of angels. Edith's descent into such theological nitpickery put her increasingly into conflict with her mother and siblings, all of whom lived in the Dallas area and who were the widow and children, respectively, of a Methodist minister, well versed in and comfortably at home with that fairly normcore Protestant denomination founded by John Wesley. Mark thinks this was when his mother's many illnesses spread from the physical to the mental, and her mental illness—by the dynamic force of her controlling personality—metastasized into those closest to her, namely her husband and her son. Edith's relationship with the family she had grown up in deteriorated into hostility and estrangement.

Mark believes that Edith may have been molested by her father, who died before Mark was born. Mark remembers, at the age of five or six, standing at this mother's bedside—a lot of his childhood was spent standing at his mother's bedside, as she spent so much of it in bed—when she told him something that stuck in his memory and haunted his consciousness for the rest of his life. She told him a memory of when she was a child and she had walked into some room in her parents' house on a Sunday afternoon, where many of her father's congregants often came for lunch after the church services, and she saw her father sitting with

---

how can you measure a day that includes the creation of the sun, which is the very thing by which we define a day?

another little girl in his lap—and the way he was touching her, stroking her bare leg with his finger. . . . He was touching her in a way that was not fatherly. And it made her *jealous*. That was all she said. And Mark for many years raked over the memory of his mother telling him when he was a very young child about something she had seen when she was a very young child and came to suspect that there was something very dark about his mother's relationship with her father. He came to suspect that there was something that had happened between them during her childhood that she wasn't telling him, and whatever it was may have planted the seed that grew into her mental illness as an adult—and it was his mother's insanity that grew into a cult.

Edith may have been drunk when she told him that, or reeling with a hangover. Because one has to bear in mind that his mother said she could not sleep, because every night she had terrifying nightmares, and the only thing that muffled the nightmares was vodka, which she drank in enormous quantities every night until she passed out. A little later, when she came to believe that she was a prophetess, the vodka became a tool to enter the state of divine revelation: She would get very drunk late at night, and in the twilight of consciousness, voices would come to her. She said they would come in whispers seemingly low to the ground, just beneath her right ear. And she would repeat what the voices had said to her and tell her husband to write them down. And he did.

Mark's maternal grandfather died before he was born, and he met his maternal grandmother only a few times in his very early childhood. Edith's relationship with her mother had grown fraught to the point of near estrangement after her second marriage, to Royal, and sometime in the mid-1960s, his grandmother "went insane and had to be placed in some kind of hospital." Mark doesn't know the details because Edith had grown so distant from her mother and siblings, but the family had his grandmother institutionalized, apparently against her will, for the last few years of her life. She died in that hospital in 1970, when Mark was nine years old, and he remembers the same bizarre incident that Edith's brother Paul remembered: the family—Edith, Royal, Mark, and Winston Van, who had returned from Korea and was living in Dallas—

did not attend the funeral but waited outside the cemetery, watching from a distance, and when all the mourners had left, Edith gave them all pebbles, led them to her mother's open grave, and made them each pronounce the curse "Anathema" as they pitched the pebbles onto the casket in the bottom of the hole.

"The intended symbolism," Mark said, "was my grandmother was evil and should have been stoned. That gives a good example of the hatred that she had, and forced on us. People who didn't believe her reading of the Bible would be declared anathema and exiled from the family."

That word, *anathema*, was important to Edith.

"The idea of anathema," Mark said when I asked him to explain it the way Edith understood it, "that word is mentioned in the Bible—you know, no one can turn from me with knowledge, being cast into Hell, and blah blah blah. Supposedly God saying that. It was a tremendous threat to anyone in that group who did not conform. That was the ultimate punishment. No redemption possible. That was my mother's deal. She inculcated in us all in the importance of not being sympathetic or compassionate in any way towards people who reject God, because that was siding with them against God."

When he was twelve years old, Mark's mother told him that she had received a message that he was destined to be a prophet. She was in bed when she told him that, in Tyler, Texas, in the trailer behind Royal's parents' house.

Royal's father had acquired a small fleet of big rigs and started a trucking company; by the late 1960s, the business was gathering momentum, with about a dozen drivers, mostly subcontracting work for C&H Trucklines, based in Dallas, driving goods all over that part of the South: East Texas, Louisiana, Arkansas, Oklahoma. At his suggestion, Royal quit his job at Ethyl, sold the ranch house in Baton Rouge, got a trucker's license, and joined his brother working for their father's company. The family moved into a trailer on Royal's parents' property, in the backyard behind their house; Royal and Edith slept in the trailer, and

Mark slept in a motor home parked next to it. Mark liked the new setup. He remembers the two years they spent in Tyler as relatively happy ones for him, because his father was gone all the time driving the truck, his mother spent most of her time in the trailer sick and drunk in bed, and he had his own separate place in the motor home, where he could be alone.

But during those two years, Edith became increasingly unhappy about the situation she was in, with her husband on the road most of the time. Mark remembers her telling him that "God had sent the keys to the kingdom of Heaven to my father, and God was gonna o take them back—because she was not happy about being abandoned." Meanwhile, fissures appeared in the hull of his grandfather's business. His grandfather was cantankerous, difficult. He got into fights with some of the companies he did business with, and he got into fights with his son. Eventually, whatever the dispute between them was, it got so bad that he refused to pay Royal his salary. The dispute also somehow involved Royal's brother, who sided with their father in it. Royal's father also clashed with his chronically bedridden daughter-in-law in the trailer behind his house; Edith tended to clash with anyone who didn't easily bend to her will, and Royal's father was not a man who bent to anyone's will. The living and business arrangements between Royal and his parents collapsed into spectacular ruin, and Royal leveraged the trailer and the motor home on a bank loan, pulled up stakes, and moved the family back to Baton Rouge, where they moved into a trailer park. After that, they were permanently estranged from Royal's parents and brother.

Royal tried to get his old job at Ethyl back, but the company wouldn't rehire him. The family defaulted on the loan, and the bank took the trailer and the motor home. Although they were somehow able to scrape together enough money to buy another trailer, "From then on," Mark said, "for the rest of our lives, we were very poor."

With the family now socially isolated, Royal struggled to find regular work. That was around the time when he and Edith self-published their book, *The Third Step to Joyful Living, or How to Stop Worrying*, and filed to establish their "church" as a corporation: the Church of God in

Christ through the Holy Spirit, Inc. Around this time, they met Larry Freeman and Suzette Dardenne (née Kleinpeter), who was separated from her first husband but not yet divorced. And it was when Edith began prophesizing about the end of the world.

In 1972, Edith prophesized that in twelve years Germany would start a nuclear war that would level human civilization in a few days and kick off the Great Tribulation, a period of three and a half years of apocalyptic chaos in which people would be fighting World War IV with sticks and stones, scrabbling amid the glowing rubble for resources with the rats and cockroaches, which would end with the blowing of the seven horns and the opening of the seven seals, the second coming of Christ, and the end of the world. (The three and a half years comes from Revelation 11:3, the same passage that would obsess Keith Haigler: "And I will give power unto my two witnesses, and they shall prophesy a thousand two hundred and threescore days, clothed in sackcloth.") Apparently Edith also found some prophetic connection having to do with the fact that Suzette had been born with a German surname, Kleinpeter. The idea that Germany would "start" a nuclear war is not the most improbable part of this prophecy, but it is nevertheless notably ridiculous; in 1972, the United States and the USSR were stockpiling the vast majority of the world's nuclear weapons, and some of them were in the Federal Republic of Germany and the German Democratic Republic, respectively—on American and Soviet military bases.

Mark said that his mother was getting a lot of her apocalyptic prophecies, her thing for British Israelism, and the true Sabbath day and Jewish High Holy Days stuff from the evangelist Herbert W. Armstrong's radio broadcasts, although the family never joined his church, the Worldwide Church of God.

Once Mark's mother threatened him with anathema. When he was a teenager, he drew a lot—and he was obsessed with sex (which, he had absolutely no one to tell him then, is fairly normal for a teenage boy). He was then and is now a skilled draftsman and painter with a steady, confident hand, a talent for drawing graceful lines, and a good eye for composition. And he filled sketchbooks with drawings of nude statues from pictures he found in books—Aphrodite disrobing, the Three Graces, things like that—and from photographs in fashion magazines he could get ahold of, stripping the models of what little they had on and filling in the hidden parts with his imagination. One of the pictures he drew was a sketch of the backside of a woman turning her head to look behind her, over her shoulder—hair pinned up with elegant wisps falling down, the sinuous curve of the neck and shoulders: a classic pose, reminiscent of the *Rokeby Venus*, *The Grande Odalisque*, Man Ray's *Le Violon d'Ingres*— and that cheesecake pinup shoot his own mother had once posed for. "My dad was snooping through my stuff," Mark said, "and found my drawings, and found that drawing. And they decided I was a homosexual." Homosexuality seems an odd accusation to lob against a teenage boy caught fantasizing on paper about naked women. The secrecy of the drawings, and his humiliation upon their discovery, simply had to do with sex—his lightly erotic drawings definitely came from the adolescent tingling of *heterosexual* desire. Perhaps what seemed gay about them to his parents was the highbrow or sissy places where he sought titillation— classical sculpture and fashion magazines—and manifested through the unmanly medium of art. That was when his mother threatened him with anathema. He was fifteen years old. His parents told him that if he persisted in what he was doing, he would have to leave, take nothing with him, and never come back. Homosexuality could not have been further afield from the sexual longings that were really occupying his mind; the subject was, however, another obsession of Edith's. "I wasn't a homosexual," Mark said. "I had never even *thought* of that stuff. But they sort of convinced me that I was a homosexual. And that if I was going to be into this, then I should just go west—blah blah blah. 'You can either choose to stay with us or go away.' Looking back at that, it's almost unbelievable, the crazy shit that occurred. And I never told my brother that they did that to me. He died without me ever telling him. I kind of meant to. To give him an illustration of what I had to go through—how crazy that family was. But I never did. That was one of the worst nights of my life. And they sort of broke me. I became a slave of that cult."

Mark's much older half brother, Winston Van, moved to Baton Rouge in 1972, after the end of his first marriage. Mia Park Harris, his Korean first wife, is an interesting minor character in this story. He devoted all of three sentences to her in his letters to Dina Williams: "Anyway I fell in (what I thought) love and got married. Brought her back to the States and stayed married for the next 3 years. She mainly just wanted her citizenship." Mark remembers a little more about Mia. Winston Van came back to the United States with her in 1969, when Mark was eight years old. That was when the family was still living in the trailer and motor home parked in the backyard of Royal's parents' house in Tyler. Van and Mia initially settled in Dallas, not quite two hours' drive away.

Mark recalled that "Mia divorced him because she had a problem with Edith." Mia saw the tyrannical control Edith had over her family, and she hated her. She often got into nasty conflicts with her mother-in-law, from which her husband was powerless to protect her. After three years of enduring Edith, once she had gained her citizenship, she left her husband. From the tone of his letter, Winston Van seems to have concluded that she was cynically using him to get her foot in the door of US citizenship from the beginning, but Mark isn't totally convinced of that; Mia's surreal nightmare of a mother-in-law would have driven any sane woman away from that family.

Mark remembers a time when he was out with Mia in Tyler and he saw a toy he wanted in a storefront window, "some cheap robot doll," and convinced her to buy it for him. Later, his parents saw him playing with it, and his mother flew into a fury at the unsanctioned secular object in his hands. She snatched it away from him and demanded to know where he'd gotten it. He told her that Mia had bought it for him, which spurred a "huge, huge confrontation about it—about her buying me things that they didn't want me to have." Mark doesn't remember if it was over this incident or some other infraction sometime later that Edith declared Mia "anathema." As Mia stormed out of the trailer, "she hollered out, 'I will see your bones, Edith Harris.' And basically that's one of those mean things that Koreans say, meaning that they are going to outlive the other person." So Mia matched Edith's pronouncement of anathema upon her with some dark folk poetry of her own—"I will see your bones"—and the curse deeply disturbed Edith and stayed on her mind for what would be the last few years of her life. "My mother was so paranoid and concerned about that that she insisted on not having a gravestone—so that Mia couldn't find her body and somehow surreptitiously dig her up, break into a concrete vault, open it up, and *look* at her bones." Sitting in that Panera in Georgia fifty years later, Mark rolled his eyes and threw up his hands. "What the fuck is going on with that? How crazy is that? She was steadily degrading in several ways, including her mental capacity, her ability to think rationally."

Mark believes that his mother essentially committed a sort of slow, passive suicide. Between the angina pectoris and the chronic pneumonia, she was always in ill health and physical pain, abetting the damage the diseases were doing with her nightly ingestion of enormous amounts of vodka, and she was becoming ever more untethered from reality. "I am convinced she willed herself to die," Mark said, "because I believe that she realized, unconsciously, or subconsciously, that it was going to be revealed that these events she foretold would not happen, and rather than face that and be abandoned by everybody, or perhaps be committed to a mental health facility, she really wanted to die."

Edith Harris died of congestive heart failure 1976 at the age of fifty and was buried in a cemetery in Baton Rouge without a gravestone. "I think my brother finally got her a stone," Mark said, "within the last five years or so. Long, long time afterwards. I didn't pay much attention to it. My brother cared about it. I didn't want anything to do with that family anymore."

After Mia divorced Winston Van, he moved to Baton Rouge and for a while dated Suzette, who by then was a member of his parents' church. The relationship between the two must have been fairly brief, because he married his second wife, June, in 1974, the same year he began working as an assistant bookkeeper for Lynch Trucking, a ground freight company based in Baton Rouge (he also worked part-time as a karate instructor).

While still exercising terrifying power over the people who were now the regular congregants of the Church of God in Christ through the Holy Spirit, Inc.—Royal, Van, June, Mark, Suzette, her future husband, Larry Freeman, Johnny Stabler, and another couple whose names Mark can't remember who later left the group—Edith, increasingly mentally unhinged as her physical deterioration accelerated, was drinking herself to death. Suzette married Larry in 1976, and that same year Edith died of a heart attack.

During the last few years of Edith's life, the church established a routine for their meetings. The services were more or less ordinary Evangelical Christian Bible study and prayer meetings, usually held in Royal and Edith's trailer, spiced with the spooky weirdness of glossolalia and its prophetic interpretation. Royal was the pastor of the church, and he would usually open the meetings with some improvised remarks. The congregation would read a passage from the Bible together, and then Royal and Edith would lead a discussion about it. Then sometimes they would sing hymns. Mark remembers "Trust and Obey," written in 1887 by the American Presbyterian minister and prolific writer of Christian hymns, John H. Sammis, being a particular favorite they often returned to:

Trust and obey, for there's no other way
to be happy in Jesus, but to trust and obey.

Then, often, after the pastor's opening remarks, the Bible study and discussion, and the singing of hymns, they would speak in tongues. Glossolalia these days is particularly associated with Pentecostalism, but it has been practiced by various Christian sects going back to the very beginning. It comes from the Book of Acts (Acts 2:1–4, KJV):

> AND WHEN THE day of Pentecost was fully come, they were all
> with one accord in one place. And suddenly there came a sound from
> heaven as of a rushing mighty wind, and it filled all the house where
> they were sitting. And there appeared unto them cloven tongues like
> as of fire, and it sat upon each of them. And they were all filled with
> the Holy Ghost, and began to speak with other tongues, as the Spirit
> gave them utterance.

"Speaking in tongues is mostly babble," Mark says. "You learn to do
it. It's hard to say how. Repeated phrases are important. Anybody with
a rational mind would think it's just a bunch of crap, people deluding
themselves. It's very easy to interpret such things in ways such that you
take what you want from them, that confirm what you want to believe."

After Edith died, "Suzette became much more powerful," Mark said.
His memory confirmed the change in social dynamics within the group
that I had suspected. Although Royal was the pastor and official leader
of the Church of God in Christ through the Holy Spirit, Inc., he was a
gullible and suggestible person, easily manipulated—even into believing
that he was the "leader."

"He always went along with everything that [Edith] prophesized,"
Mark said of his father. "Of course she would insist that he was the head
of the household, just like the Bible says, but in reality she was the one in
control. She was extraordinarily powerful in ways of convincing people
that she had a red phone direct to God." An important element of the
dynamic between Edith and Royal was that she had him convinced that
she had this "red phone direct to God" and he did not. Before she died,
she conferred the direct line not on Royal but on their son, who had,
naturally, inherited the gift of divine communication from her (Royal
was not a carrier of that gene). And Edith trained her son in prophecy,
trained him to hone the gift. Beginning when he was twelve years old,

his mother "taught" him to listen very hard in his right ear for a voice; her encouragement, his wanting to please her, his own psychological priming and imagination worked in concert to create auditory hallucinations. He still doesn't know if he actually heard voices or not; with the weight of all the social pressure being put on him, he can't separate reality and fantasy in his memory. After all, shortly before she died, his mother had somehow convinced him that he was gay when the thought had never occurred to him, and furthermore that it was a black mortal sin of which his soul needed washing clean. She had convinced her son that he could hear the voice of God if he listened hard enough in his right ear and had her husband convinced of it, too. And she died leaving a fifteen-year-old boy who felt enslaved to the cult; the only one among them with a "direct line" to God, with the whole group bound together by him, standing in the shadow of her dominion. The cult was primed for someone to take her place—the social structure was there—and Suzette Freeman nimbly stepped into it.

After Edith died, Suzette "was every bit as fanatical and domineering as my mother had been," Mark said. And not long after Edith's death, Suzette dubbed herself with an official title and role in the church's hierarchy: the "Interpreter." Now Royal was the pastor, Winston Van was the assistant pastor, Mark was the prophet, and Suzette was the interpreter. Mark would listen hard in his right ear for the voice of God, and would tell the others what it said, and Suzette would "confirm" the prophecies through interpretation. Or Mark would go into a trance and speak in tongues—improvised babbling that came from somewhere at the crux of imagination and the actual belief that the Holy Spirit was speaking through him—and Suzette would then "translate" what he was saying into English. Sometimes Suzette would speak in tongues and then translate what she had just said. Either way, she assigned herself a job in the church that stood on a rung technically below the more earthly administrative positions Royal and Van held but partook of the magical, divine power that Edith and Mark had and that held the others in thrall. The position Suzette carved out for herself was really the most powerful one: the intermediary, the point of connection between the invisible world of the spirit and the visible world of matter and flesh.

Interpretation. There is scripture—a motley patchwork of contradic-tory texts, —but the real power rests with the interpreter. The interpreter remakes the story without rewriting it: changes a talking snake into Sa-tan, changes the cryptic phrase "a time, times, and an half" (Daniel 12:7) into John of Patmos's "a thousand two hundred and threescore days" (Revelation 11:3), changes "nation shall rise against nation, and kingdom against kingdom," (Matthew 24:7) into nuclear war. The agency of reli-gion lies not in the text, but in its interpretation.

Susan Sontag in "Against Interpretation":

> The situation is that for some reason a text has become unacceptable; yet it cannot be discarded. Interpretation is a radical strategy for conserving an old text, which is thought too precious to repudiate, by revamping it. The interpreter, without actually erasing or rewriting the text, is altering it. But he can't admit to doing this. He claims to be only making it intelligible, by disclosing its true meaning.

I believe this word, interpretation, lies at the heart of what happens whenever a religion transforms from a socially useful collection of fables and folklore and, most important, the pragmata and physical sensations of ritual that bond a tribe together into something much more danger-ous: something claiming a "higher" or "deeper" second-order layer of meaning. In the particular case of "interpreting" glossolalia, the inter-preter isn't twisting one meaning into another but rather bestowing a first meaning upon meaningless babble—creating something, that is, *ex nihilo.*

The year after Edith's death in 1976, when Suzette stepped in to claim the position of "interpreter" and thus became the primary author of the cult's beliefs from behind the curtain, was when twenty-year-old Lucy Clark, who had a daughter less than a year old, abused and aban-doned by her husband, broke and desperate, walked into an employment agency in Baton Rouge with a soul already whittled weak as a match-stick, looking for temp work—and thereshe met Suzette Freeman and her employee, Van's wife, June. Suzette placed Lucy in a couple of jobs, and also invited her to join her church.

Meanwhile, the Tribulation was coming, and they would need a refuge. Winston Van Harris had attended Harding College in Searcy, Arkansas, for two years before he had dropped out and joined the army. Searcy lies at the edge of the eastern foothills of the Ozarks, and he was somewhat familiar with the area. He had also served honorably as a platoon leader and reconnaissance ranger and had led miliary exercises in Korea and missions in the Demilitarized Zone that, while nowhere near as hazardous as the combat duty many of his fellow enlistees had seen in Vietnam, had given him real survival training and military experience that no doubt would have come in useful if an apocalypse really were on the horizon. So that became his job in the church: drill sergeant, commanding officer. "We spent two years every Saturday listening to him tell us how to survive in a nuclear war," Mark said, rolling his eyes. "How to survive in the wilderness."

Winston Van consulted maps and determined that the north-central Arkansas Ozarks would be a good place to be when nuclear weapons rained down on all major populated areas, well outside the radiation damage radius of thermonuclear warheads if Little Rock, Memphis, or even Fayetteville got hit. The Upper Buffalo Wilderness would also be an ideal place to ride out the three and a half years that would follow, when roving bands of survivors would comb over the devastated earth, squabbling over scarce resources.

So around New Year's Day 1977, the Church of God in Christ through the Holy Spirit, Inc., liquidated all its assets—which didn't amount to very much—except for several vehicles and the trailer, which they towed up to Springdale in Northwest Arkansas, where its members would gather their resources and prepare for the sign to "let them which be in Judaea flee into the mountains" (Matthew 24:16).

For the next sixteen months, the church members lived in Springdale and Rogers. Royal, Mark, Winston Van and June, and their toddler,

Matthew David, lived in the trailer parked at Midway Mobile Home Park in Springdale; Lucy and her young daughter, Bethany, stayed in a camper parked next to the trailer; Larry and Suzette Freeman, Suzette's daughter, Desha, and Johnny Stablier lived in the apartment in Rogers. Lucy worked three jobs—one at the Tyson poultry plant, another at a Long John Silver's, and a third as a waitress at a diner. Winston Van also worked at the Tyson plant. Mark had dropped out of school (not much point in graduating from high school when the world is about to end) and worked part-time in the mornings making deliveries for Daylight Donuts. Royal and Suzette did not work, and if Larry Freeman and Johnny Stablier had jobs, no one I spoke with could remember. Everyone who worked turned all their earnings over to the church.

As to what brought matters to a head after the year and a few months the cult spent in Northwest Arkansas preparing for the Great Tribulation, several people's memories somewhat conflict. In Jerry Patterson's telling, the moment that spurred everything else into motion was that Mark or Suzette or both had prophesized about some sort of treasure buried in a grave on some mountain in Tennessee and that Suzette had sent Larry and Johnny to go out there and look for it. When they returned from the mission empty-handed, Suzette decided that the reason they had failed to find the buried treasure was because three-year-old Bethany Alana Clark was contaminated with the Devil. But Mark does not remember the buried treasure episode; it could be that Jerry misremembered, or that Mark wasn't around for it or doesn't remember it because it didn't involve him directly. He does not remember what exactly provoked the incident wherein someone held the three-year-old Bethany's hand over a fire in a coffee can until the skin cracked and blistered. "My memory of the incident is fuzzy," he said, "but essentially it was Suzette's idea of 'scaring Bethany straight.' I am not sure, but I think it was Larry who held the child's hand over the fire. Suzette yelled at Larry to do that."

The crisis that brought about their undoing happened a few days later. Mark remembers that it started when

Bethany complained to her mother that her vagina hurt. You know, a three-year-old is not gonna be able to verbalize that very well, but that's what was communicated ultimately. She indicated that this had something to do with June Harris. Lucy confronted June. And at one point there was something about soap. I forget what exactly she said, but it had something to do with soap, and I remember Lucy got very mad and got up and she screamed, "You put soap in her?" and then she slapped the woman. And then June starts talking about how she was worshipping Satan and how she masturbated with the candelabra that we used for ceremonies to celebrate the beginning of the Saturday Sabbath on Friday. Crazy stuff like that. And I actually do not know whether that woman was simply that crazy or if she was just making things up that would ultimately get her thrown out of the group because she was tired of putting up with us and wanted to be declared anathema. Because it was totally absurd. Masturbating with the candelabra—that stuck out. She was declared anathema, and she drove back to Baton Rouge or something or other, and then she filed charges of child abuse because of what Suzette did to Bethany, about burning her hand.

If Mark's memory of what exactly happened in what order here isn't terribly clear, it may be because he was sick; he was running a high fever and couldn't keep any food down. When the Benton County sheriff's officers arrived at the trailer to get June's son, Mark was lying in bed with a bucket beside him on the floor to catch vomit, fading in and out of consciousness, his mind bobbing in a swamp of dreams. He was in that state for the next few days. Everyone else was sickly, too, and malnourished. "None of us were eating correctly," Mark said. "We couldn't afford to keep our diets up."

After the police took Matthew David, Suzette told everyone that the time they had left before the beginning of the Tribulation had been "shortened." "I remember Suzette telling us it was time to go to the wilderness. It's kind of obvious now why she was wanting to get away from there. Because she knew she was probably going to jail."

Something about the cops knocking on their door had caused the schedule of the end of days to be moved up the calendar a bit—as Suzette heard from God—and now it was time to let them which be in Judaea flee into the mountains.

While Mark lay delirious in bed, fever dreaming and periodically turning over to vomit, Suzette dispatched Larry and Johnny—her go-to foot soldiers for out-of-state missions—to Columbia, Missouri, to kidnap Larry's two children from his previous marriage from his ex-wife's house; meanwhile, Royal and Winston Van took Lucy and Bethany to a motel and had them check into a room under a fake name; then they rented a U-Haul truck—which, as human civilization would be wiped off the face of the earth in a few days, they were not planning on returning. By the same reasoning, much of the artillery, ammunition, food, survival gear, and other supplies they acquired around this time they purchased with hot checks. Mark doesn't remember exactly when they acquired all the weaponry (all told, twenty-two firearms and more than two thousand rounds of ammunition). Lucy thinks they probably bought most of the guns during those chaotic few days between Suzette declaring June anathema and kicking her out and the group fleeing into the wilderness after the police's visit to the trailer.

Larry and Johnny had been dispatched to Missouri, Lucy and Bethany were in the motel room, and the U-Haul and the Jeep Wagoneer with the camper-trailer in tow were packed and ready to go. While Royal, Suzette, Desha, and Mark waited in the Jeep, Winston Van splashed gasoline all over the inside of the trailer, dropped a lit match onto the floor, stepped out, locked the door behind him, and climbed behind the wheel of the U-Haul. As flames began to roar inside the trailer, the two-vehicle caravan drove from Midway Trailer Park in Springdale to the motel, where they picked up Lucy and Bethany, who rode in the cab of the U-Haul with Winston Van, and they took off into the Ozarks.

Winston Van had decided upon a place called Bowers Hollow, a ravine on the south face of Cave Mountain through which a creek forms from runoff and snowmelt in the spring and trickles down into the Buffalo River. It is indeed a very remote place that's pretty hard to get to. They probably got there—or close to there, anyway—by taking US-412 due east of Springdale, turning south on AR-23 in Huntsville, then going east on AR-16 until they got to Cave Mountain Road, climbed the western slope of the mountain on the narrow dirt road's many winding gut-sloshing switchbacks, turned right on County Road 405 (there are only two smaller roads that turn off of Cave Mountain Road; one, about another three miles up the mountain, is the private road where Doc Chester and Tim Ernst would go in together to purchase a property in twelve years, and CR 405 is the other; some of the locals still call it Kaypark Road), and then left on Forest Service Road 1410—which does eventually lead through the Upper Buffalo Wilderness all the way out to AR-21, but I do not recommend getting there this way.

Reader, I know that road. It was probably a little more often traveled and better maintained back then, when there may have still been a few holdouts living on it who hadn't yet been strong-armed off their land by the government. Today the road is two tracks of wheel ruts with a hip-high strip of brush growing between them. On my first trip to the area, looking for the spot where they had camped, I got stuck on the road in a rented Jeep Wrangler I had hubristically thought could handle it. And it might have, had it not been so wet—it was late afternoon, rain had been pounding down all day, and the lowest troughs of the road had become bogs of sucking mud. It was stupid to try driving on it that day. I got the Jeep stuck in one of those mud bogs in the last hour of daylight. The car's front wheels were stuck as fast as Br'er Rabbit's foot in the Tar Baby. I panicked, decided that the only way out was to get it towed, grabbed my backpack and started hiking in the other direction, back up the road. I made it about thirty feet before considering: (1) how many miles I would have to walk to get to someplace with any cell reception, (2) how long it would take to find a towing company that would come all the way out here to beyond-buttfuck nowhere, (3) if and when I found one, how many hours it would take them to get here, (4) how willing they would be to risk their own truck getting stuck in the mud, (5) how many dollars they would charge me if they were able to tow it with no further problems presenting themselves, and (6) the look on the face of whoever would be driving it, and I decided I hadn't yet tried hard enough to get the car unstuck. So I went back to the Jeep, flung my backpack down on the grass to the side of the road, and spent the next hour and a half twisting the wheel, pumping the gas, pumping the brakes, toggling back and forth between first gear and reverse, putting it in neutral and getting out to push and rock it as much as I could, repeat, repeat, repeat: and after about a nine-hundred-point turn, with my boots and jeans encrusted with mud up to the knees, I managed at last to get that motherfucker out of the mud and roaring back up the mountain the way I'd come, pumping my fist and shouting hallelujahs all the way back to my hotel room in Jasper, where I realized I didn't have my backpack with me. In the backpack was the iPad I'd brought to record interviews with. The next day was comparatively dry, and I went back to get it in the morning, in an abundance of caution parking well above the sinkhole I'd been stuck in the night before, went on foot back down to the spot, and there was the backpack, lying in the grass beside that pond of mud. A book and a notebook in it were ruined, but the iPad was unharmed. On my short hike back up to the car, a couple of hunters in camo passed me in a lightweight UTV, the only kind of vehicle in which it is at all wise to travel that road. I didn't know it then but would later realize that the spot where I'd gotten stuck was probably within about a hundred meters of the place where members of the Church of God in Christ through the Holy Spirit, Inc., struck their camp in late April 1978, and I am honestly astounded they managed to get a twenty-four-foot U-Haul moving truck all the way down there, even allowing that the road was probably at least a little more often traveled on back then.

But they did indeed somehow squeeze that enormous U-Haul up Cave Mountain Road and all the way down that Forest Service road to an area near tiny Kaypark Cemetery—a fence made of sticks and sunken wires corralling about thirty tombstones, mostly weathered illegible, marking the graves of people who died in the nineteenth century, poking up at odd angles here and there like jagged rotten teeth and so obscured by overgrown brush that one could easily fail to notice the cemetery at all—and another stone's throw down the road, the trailhead for the Kaypark Trail, which leads a ways up the side of the mountain and back down into Bowers Hollow, where Van had decided they were going to hide out from the apocalypse.

Unsurprisingly, probably near the same place on that road where I would get a much more rough-terrain-worthy vehicle stuck forty-five years later, their U-Haul got stuck. All of those others who would soon become involved with this story who are still alive today—Jerry Patterson, Ray Watkins, and Katherine Nance—distinctly and independently of one another remembered the U-Haul getting stuck as the impetus for murdering Bethany: that the church members believed that Bethany's being possessed by the Devil was what had somehow caused the truck to get stuck, and believed that killing her, like Jesus sending the legion of demons into the herd of swine and drowning them in the Sea of Galilee, would make the Devil quit interfering with their plans. Mark does not remember that. Jerry, Ray, and Katherine also all independently remembered that it was Fred Bell and his friend Ed Burton who found them camped in the woods while turkey hunting on the morning of Monday, April 24, and Mark also does not remember that—but again, he was still deliriously ill with a fever and spent most of those couple of days lying on a foldout cot in the camper-trailer, fading in and out of consciousness when he wasn't vomiting, and it's probable that he wasn't awake for a lot of it.

Benjamin Hale: So you were trying to get into Bowers Hollow, but the truck got stuck, and you camped in the woods near where the truck was on the road that night?

Mark Harris: Mm-hmm.

BH: And then was Bethany killed in the morning of the next day?

MH: Yeah, I think so. It was one night.

BH: Can you tell me what you remember from that night?

MH: Well, I told you I'd been throwing up all day and was terribly ill. And about three in the morning I woke up, groggily, and got this message about burying the child and stuff like that. I just said what I heard. Suzette confirmed it that morning.

BH: And what do you mean, what you heard? Did you hear a voice?

MH: Yeah. That's the idea, is that you listen very hard from your right ear for a voice. That's what you're supposed to do, and God supposedly uses that as a way to do prophecy.

BH: That's what your mother had taught you?

MH: Yeah. Now, that is a psychological fantasy or something, that when it's forced to happen, it works like that. Or that is some kind of an opening to a spirit-channeling situation, where you're just open to anybody or whatever. It just seemed to be working finally. It took a long time to be able to do that.

BH: And so you said this to . . . were you in the camper-trailer?

MH: Yeah.

BH: Yeah, and was Suzette there?

MH: Yeah, she was there.

BH: And who else was there?

MH: My dad and brother.

BH: So the four of you were in the camper trailer?

MH: Mm-hmm.

BH: Yeah. And Lucy and Bethany and Dasha were in a tent. Is that right?

MH: I don't know. I don't remember.

BH: Okay. And then what do you mean when you say Suzette confirmed it?

MH: She used her supposed gift of tongues and interpretation.

BH: And it was what she had heard you say when you got up kind of groggily at three in the morning and said that?

MH: I did not get up. I was laying in bed.

BH: You just said it when you were laying in bed.

MH: Yeah. It was three in the morning.

BH: Yeah. And so she heard you when you said that, lying in bed at three in the morning?

MH: Yeah.

BH: And what happened when you all got up the next morning?

MH: Well, we needed to find out if that was for real. And I heard that same thing again and said it. Later I reported to my dad that the nature of the voice had changed. It was lower, where it seemed to be coming from. And Suzette confirmed what I said.

BH: Can you describe how exactly she confirmed it? What did she do?

MH: She would open herself to speaking in tongues and then have these ideas about what it meant, supposedly, guided.

BH: She would say things. Was it kind of babbling?

MH: Kinda like speaking in a different language.

BH: And so she spoke in tongues and then decided that the thing that she had babbled in the tongues was to kill Bethany?

MH: Yeah.

BH: And what happened then?

MH: See, it's not a deciding thing, it's supposed to be . . . supposedly, it's a guidance thing, about what that meant. But all those spiritual gifts from those ancient times seem very suspect in our modern world, especially prophecy with hearing. I read somewhere that hearing voices and things like that is connected to schizophrenia frequently, things like that. Auditory hallucinations are particularly dangerous. In spiritual churches and things having to do with spiritual subjects, those kind of things are particularly vulnerable to unconscious or subconscious influences. And as they are like that, they should be considered as highly suspect, of anything that comes from that type of route.

BH: And so after this, this was the morning of, was it . . . it was Sunday morning, the twenty-fourth. Or the twenty-third, pardon me, of April. Is that right?

MH: Yeah, as long as I remember.

BH: Yeah. And then what happened? In your memory, just from your perspective?

MH: Well, my dad talks with Lucy before the group, and told her, "This is your child. We don't care what God may have said. If you decide, it's up to you about what to do. We know there's nuclear war and all, but this is your responsibility, it's your child. And if you decide you're not gonna do this, then we will respect your choice, and no one's gonna be upset with you or . . . nothing."

BH: Yeah. Go on.

MH: And Lucy chose to have the child killed.

BH: Can you say that again?

MH: He laid the entire responsibility on her. "It's up to you." And Lucy chose to have the child killed.

BH: Right. Yeah. And so Royal told her that the . . . did he say that if they're not going to kill Bethany, then they have to leave?

MH: No, didn't say anything like that.

BH: He said . . . he told her that the interpretation was that she had to be killed. And he asked Lucy what to do, and Lucy said "Go ahead."

MH: Mm-hmm. And if she had decided not to do that, she was assured there wouldn't be any penalties, you wouldn't be exiled or anything like that for not deciding to kill a child. But there's no reason to do that to a mother.

BH: Right. And then what happened?

MH: Daniel and Royal took the child in the woods, near wherever the place was. I can't go back, I wasn't there. I didn't go back to the area, I didn't have anything to do with it after they did that.

BH: And so they took her away. And how long were they gone?

MH: About an hour, maybe two or something. I don't know.

BH: Yeah. And you said you heard the shots?

MH: Yeah, there were four. Everybody heard four shots.

BH: And the people who were there with you, Suzette, Lucy, and Suzette's daughter, Desha. Is that right?

MH: Yes, sir.

BH: And then what happened?

MH: Well, they came back, and my brother seemed particularly shook up. My dad was just kind of, I don't know, maybe he was in shock or something. And we proceeded to try to get into the area we needed to be in supposedly.

BH: And you said you got a little farther into the woods that day.

MH: Yeah.

BH: And you said you cut down a tree.

MH: Yeah. To move the U-Haul.

BH: Yeah. And were you able to move the U-Haul farther into the woods?

MH: Yeah, I think so.

BH: Okay. And what happened then?

MH: We went to sleep that night, and got up the next morning and were doing prayers, and then we got arrested.

The reader will notice that part of Mark's account of these events directly contradicts Lucy's, which concerns Lucy's complicity in the murder. After talking with Mark, I just could not call up Lucy again like a responsible little journalist cross-checking his sources and say, "Well, Mark says you did in fact directly cosign on the decision to have your daughter murdered—any comment before we go to press?" Especially if it turns out that Mark's version is true—because even if it is, she still deserves forgiveness. I prefer to let both versions stand in opposition on the page without trying to reconcile them. There are some things you will never know, and I'm okay with that.

Royal Harris and Winston Van Harris murdered Bethany Alana Clark sometime in the morning of Sunday, April 23, 1978. Royal and Van—fifty-three and thirty-one years old, respectively—took Bethany by the hand and led her away into the woods to a spot about fifty feet away from where they had camped for the night. They would have been carrying with them a five-gallon plastic paint bucket, a black plastic garbage bag, and a shovel—or perhaps they had already carried these things beforehand to the place where they planned to kill and bury the three-year-old girl. Mark distinctly remembered hearing four shots; as the coroner reported that she had been shot eight times and the ballistics report found that she had been shot with two different weapons, I think it's possible that Royal and Van, both armed with .22-caliber pistols, fired their guns simultaneously four times.*

Then they stuffed Bethany's body in the bag, which they stuffed in the bucket, dug a hole in the ground several feet deep, put the bucket in it, covered it, spread the dirt around, and dragged several rotten logs over the spot. The process took one to two hours.

The group spent the rest of the day trying to get the U-Haul off the road and into the woods, which they were able to do after cutting down a tree with a chain saw. They spent the next night camped in the same place, and then, early the next morning, they had a brief conversation with Fred Bell and Ed Burton as the two passed through while hunting turkeys. I think Mark was still asleep in the camper-trailer for that. Perhaps an hour or two later, around nine in the morning, all of them—Royal, Van, Mark, Suzette, Desha, and Lucy—were sitting in the camper-trailer, reciting Philippians 4: "I know both how to be abased, and I know how to abound: every where and in all things I am instructed both to be full and to be hungry, both to abound and to suffer need. I can do all things through Christ which strengtheneth me."

That was when Newton County Sheriff's Deputy Ray Watkins knocked on the door of the camper-trailer.

---

* Mark Harris believes that the coroner either mistook four shots that all went through her body—four entry wounds and four exit wounds—for eight different gunshot wounds, or someone somewhere down the line lied in order to make the crime sound more heinous. (I ask myself: If I were a juror, how much differently would it make me feel to learn that a three-year-old child's death had resulted from *four* rather than *eight* gunshots? Not very.) "Van told me one time about his shooting the victim," Mark wrote to me. "He said she screamed, so he shot her three more times. I don't remember where we were when he told me this, whether in jail awaiting trial or when I visited him and Royal a few times in the early years of imprisonment. I suspect the latter. Royal took the blame for the actual shooting during the trial. But Royal did not shoot her, and likely could NOT have. No one else in that group could have brought themselves to do that except Van, who was trained as a Recon Ranger in the Army. And to the best of my knowledge, only one gun was out of the vehicles, that .22 pistol used in the crime."

Ray remembers Mark Harris refusing to come out of the camper for a long time after the others had come out and submitted to arrest. The Newton County Sheriff's Office had one only pair of handcuffs, which Hurchal Fowler's son, Eddy, remembers they put on Winston Van Harris, as he was the healthiest and strongest of the five and the jumpiest, the most talkative, the one who most made them nervous. Ray remembers Mark Harris repeatedly seeming to reach for his gun and repeatedly yelling at him to stop it and smacking him on the chest. Mark Harris does not remember this.

Neither Ray Watkins nor Eddy Fowler remembered Suzette's nine-year-old daughter, Desha, but she had to have been there.

Mark Harris does remember that as they were marched out of the woods by Hurchal Fowler, Eddy Fowler, Ray Watkins, Fred Bell, and Ed Burton, Suzette looked up, and again and again, she wailed into the sky, "It's over. It's over. It's over."

In the synoptic Gospels, the last words of Christ on the cross are quoted in Aramaic and then translated into Greek: *"Eloi, Eloi, lama sabacthani?,"* which is translated as "My God, my God, why hast Thou forsaken me?" But in the Gospel of John, Christ's last words are "It is finished."

It is over. It is finished.

But it wasn't over. It wasn't finished. Certainly not for Suzette Freeman, anyway. After they were taken to Newton County Jail and then to Benton County Jail, Suzette called David Matthews, the family law attorney who had represented her six months prior in the custody battle with her ex-husband over Desha. The following day, Matthews negotiated a plea deal with the Benton County prosecutor, giving Suzette immunity from prosecution in exchange for her agreeing to testify as a witness for the state in the others' coming trial; once granted immunity, she told the prosecutor, her lawyer, and a State Police detective about Bethany's murder—which they did not know about, because even though later on the previous day Hurchal Fowler had returned to the campsite, discovered Bethany's body, and called the state coroner in Little Rock to come get it, no one in the Newton County Sheriff's Office or the Arkansas State Coroner's Office had thought to notify the police in Benton County that they had found a murder victim. Suzette was released from Benton County Jail on May 1; her father and two of her brothers drove up from Louisiana to get her. She was free for the rest of her life.

Mark Harris spent the days after the arrest "crying in a jail cell, chewing on cigarette butts, and things like that." The Benton County police took him into an interrogation room to question him, but he refused to talk, as did Royal, Winston Van, and Lucy.

Before the trial began in September, Suzette Freeman wrote an eighty-four-page witness statement in which, Mark said, "she got our names right, but most of the rest of it was lies. 'It's their fault, they did this, they did that, I was an innocent bystander.' Blah blah blah. Yeah, she did really good on escaping the penalties of her true culpability."

Suzette's witness statement, along with all of the court transcripts that weren't archived with the Arkansas Supreme Court because of Winston Van's appeals in 1983 and 1986, has vanished. The only documents having to do with the case archived at the Newton County Courthouse in Jasper are the one-page official briefs noting that the various court proceedings took place. I discovered this on my own, but Mark already knew it because a friend of his (Mark can't leave the state of Georgia) did him the favor of driving to Jasper to look for them; she was surprised to find nothing in the archives, and was given no explanation. Mark believes that someone at the Newton County District Court deliberately destroyed the case records "because they were protecting themselves from lawsuits and other things, because they ramrodded this through with a disqualified jury." Jerry Patterson, when I met with him, was incredulous that the case file isn't there. "But there *is* a case file in that courthouse," he said. "It has to be. I mean, that's the deal, man." I went back to the courthouse in Jasper and looked again once more, just to be sure. There is no case file: no records of the lengthy jury selection process, no court transcripts, no witness statements. There's nothing there except for the documents noting that the proceedings happened.

In the four months and two weeks Mark spent in the Benton and Boone County Jails awaiting the trial, his weight dropped from 180 to 140 pounds. "I was in a juvenile area, and they fed us like one or two biscuit things in the morning and one small hamburger at night." The night before the trial was to begin, Royal, Winston Van, and Mark were transferred to a cell in the Newton County Jail—the first time the three of them had been in a room together since the day they were arrested—and a guard caught them trying to escape. Mark doesn't remember how Winston Van got ahold of the hacksaw blade; he managed to saw through one of the bars on the window of their cell on the upper story of the jail before the person working in the jail that night heard the noise and came to check on them. The following morning, with the small court-room packed to capacity, TV crews bivouacked on the courthouse lawn outside, the crowd murmuring about the outrageous news of the previous night's escape attempt, and the court-appointed defense attorneys at their wits' end, before the trial began, Royal and Mark decided to switch their pleas to nolo contendere. "There was no way that we could face a crowd like that," Mark said. "And we had the idea of protecting the basic church doctrines from further ridicule and association with that crime." Pleading no contest was Mark's idea. "We decided together, but I think I influenced him." The prosecution offered each of them a sentence of fifty-five years in prison in exchange for a guilty plea—which Winston Van, later that morning, after listening to advice from his attorney and his biological father, Gobe Smith, Jr., decided to take. In the long term, that would prove to be a good decision; he would ultimately serve only fifteen years in prison. Upon their pleading no contest, Judge Kenneth Smith sentenced both Royal and Mark to life in prison without the possibility of parole.

"Why did you plead no contest instead of guilty?" I asked Mark in the Panera Bread in suburban Georgia.

"Because if you plead guilty, in our minds—me and my dad—you're saying that there's no way God could have said anything, right? So pleading no contest is the only way to avoid that." Mark sat back, sighed, rubbed the corners of his eyes. "Look. We were crazy. And stupid. But we were sincere in our motivations to protect the cult."

Mark and Royal Harris were sent to the Arkansas Department of Corrections' Cummins Unit, a maximum-security prison where they were placed together in protective custody almost immediately. Soon afterward, the state transferred Mark to the Tucker Unit. "Which is very fortunate, that I was away from him," Mark says. "It allowed me to try to recover from all that shit."

Forty years would pass in the social death of incarcerated life. After the first year, Suzette appeared to Mark in a dream. "She was telling me to keep going. She was encouraging me not to kill myself. Because I prayed to die for the first three years I was in prison." (Jerry suspected that there had been a sexual relationship between Suzette and Mark; when I asked him about it, Mark strenuously denied it. However, he confirmed what Jerry Kleinpeter told me, that Suzette and Winston Van dated—and yes, had a sexual relationship—for a short time before Winston Van married June and Suzette married Larry.) He thought about suicide constantly during those first three years, but he never did attempt it. Eventually, after enough time separated from his father, for the first time in his life, Mark began to think with a new clarity and independence. His mind began to change.

His parents had alienated their small family from their extended relations long before the crime happened, and the only people he had ever been close to, except for Suzette, were also in prison. He was alone, with no one on the outside to contact. Winston Van Harris, paroled out of state to Georgia in 1993, made no attempt to contact his still incarcerated younger half brother for the next decade. He changed his name to Daniel Gobe Smith and started another life. Daniel had met the woman who would become his third wife, and Mark thinks his brother did not disclose to her the full truth about his past for a long time, if he ever did. "He wanted to forget about me," Mark said. "He left me completely alone after he got out of prison. I didn't hear from him for ten years."

"He was probably afraid he would have to tell details he'd kept hidden," Barbara added. "He didn't want his wife or anybody to know anything."

Twenty years into Mark's sentence, his father died. "Some religious volunteers felt bad for me," Mark said. "They put together some money so I could go to the funeral. They got me a suit to wear." The warden granted Mark a temporary furlough. The funeral for Royal Harris was a small graveside gathering of about a dozen people. "I spoke briefly," Mark said, "about the tragedy of his life. And then he was buried. That was in Star City, I think."

Twenty-eight years into his sentence, at the age of forty-five, Mark, who had never so much as kissed a girl before he had entered the system at seventeen, got married while in prison. This, it turns out, is another sad story. In 2006, Mark, a longtime model prisoner, had been in the Wrightsville Unit minimum-security prison for six years; there the inmates were allowed access to pay phones, and Wrightsville is close enough to Little Rock that he was able to get onto a Little Rock dating chat line, where he met a woman. "And we fell in love," Mark said. "And we got married soon after that."

"They could never consummate it," Mark's second and current wife, Barbara, chimed in. "It wasn't allowed."

"The preacher that married us was the prison chaplain," Mark said. "And it was very kind of him to do that, because they didn't usually do it. But after that she moved in with this guy that she had been with previously. This was within a month. And I told my chaplain about it, and he said, 'You can do better.' She also did not tell me she had significant mental health issues. Dissociative personality disorder. She was molested as a child. A lot of different stuff."

His new wife's letters, phone calls, and visits to the prison steeply dropped in frequency soon after they were married, and as time went on, they ceased altogether. "And I found out later that she had been using me as a tax write-off," Mark said.

"What?" I said. *"How?"*

"She was claiming me as a dependent. The IRS figured it out, and they told her she couldn't do that anymore. That's when our relationship degraded. And finally she divorced me."

Since 2000, tobacco has been prohibited from Arkansas prisons, but for some years afterward, that difficult-to-enforce policy was not followed very strictly. That changed suddenly for some reason in the mid-2000s, when corrections officers were told to start cracking down on inmates with tobacco. While Mark was still married to the woman in Little Rock, a CO at Wrightsville caught him rolling cigarettes, and as punishment he was sent back to the maximum-security Tucker Unit. He had a bunch of possessions he'd been allowed to keep at Wrightsville—"a photo album, a guitar, a lot of hobby craft stuff, painting supplies, things like that"—that he was forced to give up. He had them sent to his wife. After divorcing him, "she threw all my stuff away."

Mark worked many different jobs in his four decades in the Arkansas Department of Corrections. He worked in the prison library for three years before he was transferred to mental health services, where he worked for twelve years. He started as a clerk, typing up psychiatrists' medication orders. Later he learned to read the Minnesota Multiphasic Personality Inventory and administered the tests to fellow inmates and scored them. He underwent hundreds of hours of therapy with his boss at mental health services, studied psychology, and took college courses at night (he took many courses over the years but has no formal record of how many credit hours he would have earned, because inmates serving life sentences were not allowed to take classes for credit). Eventually he became a peer counselor and led a variety of therapy groups. Later, he taught reading and painting classes. After his long employment in mental health services, he was transferred to another prison, where he began working for the chaplaincy services. "Which was interesting," he said. "I was able to interact with a lot of different religious faiths and be a part of the Kairos program and things like that."

Kairos is a word I'm well familiar with from studying classics; it's an important word in Ancient Greek, and it essentially means a critical moment of opportunity. The word occurs frequently in the New Testament, as in Mark 1:15: "The time [*kairos*] is fulfilled, and the kingdom of God is at hand: repent ye, and believe the gospel." Founded in 1976, the Kairos Prison Ministry is an interdenominational Christian organization. According to its website, "The mission of the Kairos Prison Ministry is to share the transforming love and forgiveness of Jesus Christ to impact the hearts and lives of incarcerated men, women and youth, as well as their families, to become loving and productive citizens of their communities."

"It's a ministry dedicated to inmates where they're shown Christian love and basically indoctrinated to become a Christian," Mark said.

"Even in prison?" Barbara said, turning to her husband. "All those Bible thumpers?"

"Especially in prison," said Mark.

"It's a captive audience," I said.

Mark nodded in agreement. "That's a big deal within the prison system. The Christians want to proselytize people. And inmates are the perfect target. They need love, they need acceptance. So you can use that population to more or less bolster your membership in the Christian faith. You can pretty much sense my skepticism about that whole situation."

Throughout his four decades in prison, Mark read—constantly and widely. He was particularly interested in comparative religions, philosophy, science, and especially psychology. The works of William James and Carl Jung affected him deeply. He acquired a small library over the years, ten boxes full of books that now line shelves in his apartment. On one of our Zoom calls, I could see his bookshelves on the wall behind him, and I asked him what was on them. "I have a huge number of books about science," he said. "And mathematics. I have some religious stuff. A couple of Bibles, an interlinear Bible. The *Oxford English Dictionary*. Let me see. I've got several books on languages—Greek, Latin, Sanskrit.

Some books on mythology, photography . . . a lot of books on art. Art history, history of architecture. *The New York Times Guide to Knowledge*, *The Treasury of the Encyclopaedia Britannica*, the *Underground Education*. Books on all kinds of different subjects that made me a whole lot more aware of how bad people can be, and what to watch out for."

Through all of his many, many years of reading and thinking, Mark gradually became, if not an atheist exactly, perhaps an agnostic—but whatever he is, he is deeply mistrustful of formal religion. "I can't say that suddenly I woke up one morning and had this attitude. It's a long process of development, of study, of reading hundreds of books from different sources. There were so many questions I faced during those forty years. The conclusions I came to weren't very supportive of my connection with faith."

"You wrote in your email to me the other week that you are no longer religious," I asked Mark in another conversation. "Can you remember the evolution of your thinking about religion over the course of all this time?"

"I studied occultism for a long time. Kabbalah, and things like that, and was able to get insight into the various risks and errors that Christian doctrinal acceptance is prone to. And because of that exposure to Kabbalah and things like that, Jewish mysticism, models of reality that they came up with during the Babylonian exile, I became more firm in my belief that while there may be a God the absolute, he's certainly not the God that any of the religions that human beings have. All those are attempted approaches to something that we cannot really comprehend. God the absolute is universal, the unity of all things. Even worshipping that—whatever you call it, *consciousness*—seems kind of odd in a way. Instead of being the best people we can be, and doing our best to help others and to experience compassion for other people."

"Did you," I asked, "eventually come to the idea that human religions are—how to put it—misdirection?"

"They are attempts to interact with—all that is—that relate to human beings. They are attempts to curry favor and dissuade misfortune through the belief in various deities, or a monotheistic God, or whatever.

And to somehow be able to get assistance in controlling one's life, to have pleasant things happen, rather than bad things."

"Am I right in saying that you don't believe in any of it?"

"Religious doctrines and dogmatic assertions tend to interfere with human cognition and what we see around us. They're inherently danger-ous in that way."

Mark believes that if he had accepted Jerry Patterson's deal to plead guilty in exchange for a sentence of fifty-five years in prison, as his brother did, then, like his brother, he probably would have been paroled after a frac-tion of that time. And if he had maintained his plea of not guilty and gone to trial, the jury might have been persuaded to take into account his age, his horrifying upbringing, and his brainwashed state, and there's a possibility that he would have been given a much lighter sentence, as was the case with Lucy. Mark Harris, the autodidact, after many years following his mother's death, after many years separated from the people who had brainwashed him and themselves at the same time, after many years of therapy, education, self-directed reading, intellectual explora-tion, deeply serious thought and reflection, came to see all of this more clearly, and still had to sit there in prison as the consequence of the de-cision he had made when he had been the seventeen-year-old "prophet."

He tried, in any way that he could, to find a way out. *The way out.* In Franz Kafka's story "A Report to an Academy," Rotpeter, the captive ape who has assimilated into human society, describes the feeling of being confined in a cage with no way out:

Over and above it all only the one feeling: no way out.

I fear that perhaps you do not quite understand what I mean by "way out." I use the expression in its fullest and most popular sense. I deliberately do not use the word "freedom." I do not mean the spacious feeling of freedom on all sides. As an ape, perhaps, I knew that, and I have met men who yearn for it. But for my part I desired such freedom neither then nor now. In passing: may I say that all

too often men are betrayed by the word freedom. And as freedom
is counted among the most sublime feelings, so the corresponding
disillusionment can be also sublime. . . .

No, freedom was not what I wanted. Only a way out. . . .

Today I can see it clearly; without the most profound inward calm
I could never have found my way out.*

Mark had thought that his first wife, whom he loved and who he believed loved him, might help him find a way out, before he learned that
she had no incentive to help him get out because the only reason she'd
married him was to claim him as a dependent on her taxes. His brother,
the only contact he had on the outside, abandoned him for ten years after
he was paroled, and even after Mark managed to get in touch with him,
Daniel was a sporadic and unreliable correspondent and not much help.
For forty years, Mark Harris had no way out.

In 2012, the Supreme Court ruled in *Miller v. Alabama* that mandatory sentences of life in prison without the possibility of parole are
unconstitutional for juvenile offenders; it was later strengthened by
Montgomery v. Louisiana in 2016. Following the decision, many states
passed new laws to bring their justice systems into compliance with the
new ruling. Arkansas passed Act 539 in 2017, and after it went into ef-
fect, Arkansas inmates serving life sentences for crimes committed when
they had been minors became eligible for parole. The difficulty was
getting their cases heard by the parole board. Whatever the Supreme
Court's decision, giving clemency to violent offenders, Mark believes,
was bad political optics for the governor.

So they got around that. What the Department of Corrections did

---

* Kafka wrote the story at a time when he was becoming interesting in Zionism
and thinking seriously about emigrating to Palestine; some scholars have read it as
an allegory for diaspora Jews in Europe. "The way out" is a literal translation of the
Greek title of the second book of the Torah, Exodus—which I am confident Kafka
was acutely conscious of.

was they cherry-picked people that had only served twenty years or less to go before the parole board. That is, those cases they could reasonably reject for parole. And the rest of us, who had served thirty, forty years, were ignored. We were told, in my case, that I had to be added to the list by some kind of legal process, right? And my brother was supposedly trying to do that, but it wasn't happening. So at any rate, I wrote to the governor, Asa Hutchinson. I told the governor in my letter that I believed they were cherry-picking who they were allowing to go up for parole. And I sent that letter on a Friday. I sent it registered certified mail so it couldn't get lost. And Monday morning, I get a call from the parole officer. I'm going up next month! And when I went up for parole, I was the first person they called. And they were very nice to me. And the head of the parole board was looking at my file, and he said, "So you've done twenty years?" "No, sir. I've done forty." And he was looking down at the file. He says, "That's interesting—it says here you've done twenty." So obviously somebody had mistyped the number so that I would look less likely to be considerable. But they were very agreeable. Anyway, I made parole.

In July 2018, at the age of fifty-seven, after serving forty years in prison, Mark was paroled out of state to Georgia. His brother, Daniel Gobe Smith, took him in. He was then taking care of his wife, Robin Lynn Holt, who had stage 7 senile dementia. "That was a thirty-six-hour day for him," Mark says. "He had somebody coming in to help take care of her during the day and such. Finally she had to go to a senile dementia facility because she kept falling. She lived out the rest of her life in that facility, and he was unable to visit her there for some time, until the very end of it, because of the covid epidemic. Except through glass." She died in November 2020. Not long after his wife died, Daniel was diagnosed with lung cancer—stage 4 when it was detected—and Mark spent the next year and a few months taking care of him, until he had to go into hospice care. He died a few days later, in January 2022.

When he got out of prison, Mark was still bitter about his brother's having abandoned him for so many years and then about his fairly minimal and ineffectual help after they were back in touch again—but he had nowhere else to go. I asked Mark what it had been like living with his brother in his first years out on parole.

"He was an alcoholic," Mark said. "He would drink at night."

"And a Bible thumper," Barbara added. She likes that phrase.

"Yeah, he was still into that track," Mark said. "Couldn't get him out of it. He was still into that cult belief stuff, basically. Still 'doomsday prepping,' for whenever that happens. It's just really sad. My dad carried that until he died. My brother carried that until he died. I'm the only one who escaped from that craziness."

Later, Mark was reminded of another anecdote: "He told me that he would always respect homosexuals because when he was in prison, the administration refused to feed him when he was in isolation. And the prison homosexuals—who apparently all worked in the kitchen—were sneaking him food. So it's an irony that all these outsiders to his faith had shown him so much love. And it's sort of a testimony that love is so much bigger than religious doctrine."

What a year 2018 was to see the outside world for the first time as an adult, with red and blue America both spasming with paroxysms of madness and much of the country literally on fire—followed in short order by the covid pandemic, when the whole world became a prison, when Daniel, asshole though he may have been (and, well, a murderer), had to watch his wife die from behind glass, not allowed to touch her. Around the time his brother lay dying, deep in the lockdown in the fall of 2020—while I was teaching a "hybrid" class, trying to talk about a Flannery O'Connor story through a KN95 to six remote-learning Bard freshman Zooming in from their childhood bedrooms and seven in person in surgical masks sitting at desks spaced six feet apart in the middle of the basketball court—Mark met Barbara Shaw, a Canadian woman eight years older than him, through mutual friends on Facebook.

"He is the kindest, sweetest person I've ever met," Barbara told me. "The most giving, the most thoughtful. That's why I fell for him."

Barbara has had a full life. Originally from Edmonton, she lived in Victoria, British Columbia, for many years; she's worked many jobs—hypnotherapist, website designer ("I'm like a jill of all trades")—and she has three children and had been married three times before she met Mark. "My first marriage, he was on the abusive side. I left with two little kids. Then my second husband, he died of an epileptic seizure. And then I found out my first husband, the nasty one, died of a heart attack when he was forty. When I was with Doug, my third husband, I thought, Well, he's younger than me, he's probably not going to die on me. Nope! He got ALS. ALS, of all things! And so I had to watch him die in increments. It was terrible. So I nursed him until he died. He had social anxiety disorder, so he couldn't really go anywhere. He wanted to stay with me the whole time. It was really hard. But I did it until the day he died." Shortly after her third husband died, she met Mark. "We just talked every day, and then we started video chatting. And he really helped me through the grief process. But it wasn't just how kind and sweet he was to me, it was watching how he talked to other people in groups we were in on Facebook. Constantly thoughtful, decent and kind. I thought, Gee, he's kinder than I am, you know? He's like a role model for kindness." Barbara has been retired for several years, with a pension from the Canadian government. At the time she began talking and video chatting over the internet with Mark, who was himself nursing his older brother unto death, she and her recently deceased husband had for some years been living in Kewlona, British Columbia, where her youngest daughter lives with her husband and daughter. "I had to think long and hard to marry him and not be with them," she says. "And I know they miss me, but . . . we really love each other. It's just so easy."

When I met Mark and Barbara at that Panera Bread, Mark apologized for being groggy. He was sleep deprived, as he'd had to work until one in the morning the night before and then had trouble sleeping due to the anxiety of meeting me. He had told me in the course of a phone conversation that he worked at a candy factory. I asked him if he worked a night shift. No, he said; it was only a few days after New Year's, and the factory had closed for two weeks for the holidays. But this is America, after all, and the South to boot; the factory did not give its workers those two weeks off but furloughed them without pay, which meant that Mark had to pick up gig work in the meantime, and was making deliveries for DoorDash to make ends meet until the factory reopened. I asked him what he does at the candy factory.

"I carry boxes," he said. "I package stuff into boxes. I made Mensa when I was in prison. I've got one month short of a degree in social work. And I work in a factory doing manual labor." He shrugged, and went on, "I am married and living about as happy a life as I possibly can be, although it is much later than I had hoped. And my entire youthful life was spent in prison. So my desire for a doctorate or maybe a master's in social work even are pretty much out the window, because I can't afford to go to school. I'm just trying to survive."

As I was driving back home, he texted me photos of some of his paintings, as well as this afterthought:

Another thing I may have mentioned before is the danger of the Christian doctrine of Sola Scriptura, where the Bible alone is studied by ignorant and uneducated Christians with varying levels of intelligence, education, and possible mental disorders or obsessive agendas, without the benefit of exposure to the historical traditions of the developing Church through the centuries, and the stressed importance of human cognitive reasoning.

This is avoided in the Anglican Church and the Episcopal Church by the emphasis on the three things, envisioned as a three-legged stool supporting the Church's doctrines and beliefs: Scripture (of the Christian Bible, including the Apocrypha); Tradition (of the Church, including the Church's understanding and interpretation of Scripture); and Cognition or Cognitive Reasoning (of each individual member of the Church). This last emphasis is particularly stressed in

Episcopal Seminary Schools.

I believe this, along with dissatisfaction felt by people about many forms and practices of the organized and matured Christian faiths, was one of the major contributing factors to the rise of bizarre Christian cults in the 70s and 80s, and may continue to be a significant danger in our society at present.

Of the various Christian denominations he studied with the Kairos Prison Ministry, it was the Episcopal Church that most deeply affected Mark's religious thinking. The prison chaplain he worked under at one point was an Episcopal priest, and Mark had been close with him. He was impressed with the Episcopal Church's humility and moderation, as well as the stress it places upon the importance of reason.

"The emphasis on reason allows for a greater freedom of thought and interpretational viewpoint of individuals within the faith," Mark wrote to me when I asked him about it. "Since the primary focus of the Episcopal Church is of the Liturgy of the Church, the structure of the worship services, instead of what the individual worshipper BELIEVES (so stressed in many of the Protestant faiths, such as Baptists, Pentecostals, etc.), there is much less conflict among the membership." In that I heard an echo of what the practicing but not-terribly-fervent Christian Jerry Patterson had said about religion: It can be a wonderful thing as long as you don't actually believe it. The practice of religion matters more than belief in it.

Perhaps the Episcopal Church affected Mark's thinking more than it intended to, as he would eventually think himself out of the Christian faith entirely, exiting with a vague and agnostic definition of God as maybe, if it exists, a sort of pantheistic universal consciousness that certainly could not ever involve itself in his affairs or anyone else's—a belief in a deist, Cartesian kind of God there is absolutely no point in praying to, which for all practical earthly purposes is not functionally different from atheism.

Sola scriptura was one of Martin Luther's doctrinal cornerstones, and it is a crucial load-bearing pillar in the ecclesiastic architecture of many

Protestant denominations, especially the ones descended directly from Luther and Calvin, such as Presbyterianism. (The Episcopal and Methodist Churches emphasize the less extreme *prima scriptura*, holding that scripture is not necessarily the only thing a Christian needs but should come first.) *Sola scriptura* is one of the first three *solae*, the key beliefs that differentiated the Protestant Reformation from the theological doctrine of the Roman Catholic Church: *sola scriptura*, *sola fide*, and *sola gratia*. By scripture alone, by faith alone, by grace alone. Or: scripture over tradition, faith over works, and grace over merit.

To take the second two first: Faith over works means that all you need to enter the kingdom of Heaven is faith in Christ. One of John Wesley's illustrations of this is Luke 23:39–43, when one of the "malefactors" (in the KJV) crucified alongside Jesus says, "Jesus, Lord, remember me when thou comest into they kingdom. And Jesus said unto him, Verily I say unto thee, Today shalt thou be with me in paradise." That anonymous malefactor presumably led a life of sin that resulted in his being tied up there and left to die on Golgotha, and he hadn't enough time left alive to counterbalance it with any good works. What you actually *do* with your life doesn't matter; all that matters is faith in Christ. (I enthusiastically recommend James Hogg's 1824 novel, *The Private Memoirs and Confessions of a Justified Sinner* for a disturbing and phantasmagoric work of art that revolves around the principality of this concept to Calvinism.) Grace over merit is a similar concept. God bestows grace upon you because he wants you to have it, not because you have done anything to earn it. "'Twas grace that taught my heart to fear," John Newton wrote of the moment on March 21, 1748 (it was a very important date to him, and he remembered it, just as Paul Kleinpeter remembers July 4, 1979, as the day Grace appeared and turned him from his riotous living), when the slave trader, aboard a tempest-tossed ship off the northern coast of Ireland, prayed for his life and God reached down and saved a wretch like him—"and grace my fears relieved." The concepts of faith over works and grace over merit are what make Protestant Christianity particularly attractive to criminals, alcoholics, and other such people who have badly fucked up their own and other people's lives: Grace allows you to be born again; it forgives the unforgivable. As the father says of the prodigal son returned, you have to be lost before you can be found.

But *sola scriptura* comes first. It is the principle that the Bible is the sole infallible source of authority for Christian faith and practice. From Luther's perspective, it makes sense; the Reformers saw themselves as rebelling against a Church that had grown from a dozen Jewish bumpkins preaching in the desert boondocks of the Roman Empire to eventually supplanting that empire and moving into its hollowed-out structure like a hermit crab, with a pope instead of an emperor and a well-organized and militaristically hierarchal pyramid of ecclesiastical authority trickling down from him in widening tiers and resting upon the foundation of the illiteracy of most of its parishioners. A major influence on my angry young man's atheism was William H. Gass; in the essay "Spectacles" he describes the medieval Church with characteristically nimble brutality of wit:

> Throughout the medieval period, the Church had carefully confined intellectual study to authorized and holy texts, and even among those of the public who might be able to read, only a select few were allowed so much as a peek at the Word of God. Instruction in matters of the faith was performed by pictures; consequently, painters—visual artists of all kinds—were commissioned to illuminate pages and adorn walls, to carve figures and design windows that would depict and applaud the Christian message. The masses were illiterate and spoke a vulgar tongue. Their culture was crude and had been created close to those sharp edges of want and necessity that were likely to sever the lines of life at any luckless moment. God's Word might beat in the heart of things, but ordinary language was no more than the body's bad breath. Kept chaste and forced into clerical service, thus from a surfeit of both denial and privilege, the Latin language died.

Last weekend Caitlin and I visited the Cloisters at the northernmost tip of Manhattan—the arcades of four French Gothic monasteries that were disassembled, shipped to New York, and reassembled into a very beautiful museum of medieval art—and I was reminded of the overwhelming dominance Christian imagery held over every hour of the day of medieval life. (Religion wasn't *a part of* life, it *was* life.) The clergy hoarded and kept guard over the written word and interpreted it for the masses, told them what it said, and then told them what it meant, keeping them dazzled into obedience with images, statues, ornaments, and conducting their rituals in a magical language the hoi polloi didn't understand. (One theory of the etymology of "hocus pocus" supposes that it's a garbled corruption of the opening words of the liturgy of the Eucharist in Latin, *"Hoc est corpus meum,"*—"This is my body"—which the priest says as he transubstantiates bread into the body of Christ.)

One of the noblest deeds of the Protestant Reformation was its emphasis on the importance of literacy. It was Johannes Gutenberg who, like John the Baptist, stood in the river and pointed to Luther when he invented the printing press in the fifteenth century. The most famous book he printed with it was the Bible, an affordable product mass-produced for the masses to learn to read and read for themselves, and soon to translate into secular and living languages.

Sola scriptura follows in the educate-thyself spirit of the Reformation: to take the power away from the obfuscating clergy urging trust in their secondhand account of the text, to take scripture out of the dark ages and turn on the reading light. If a text is truly holy, it needs no human political intercession, no third parties between the reader and it. A Christian doesn't need anything between him and scripture in order to be a Christian.

The foundational principle of *sola scriptura*, and therefore the importance of literacy to the Protestant Reformation, carved for the Christian soul a path that forks in two directions. If you choose one road, Protestantism is simply the first step toward a secular society. One who travels down this road begins with the Bible, but even though he learned to read in order to read it, he is now able to read a great many other texts as well—science, philosophy, literature, whatever else—and winds up an atheist or an agnostic or a secular person who doesn't worry about the God question too much, or a mainline Protestant Christian of moderate, reasonable, quiet and personal faith who can live without constant moral and existential crisis in the everyday modern world of science, humanism, democracy, enlightenment values, and the separation of church and state, who does not interpret scripture literally or fundamentally. One who travels down the other road turns away from all the saints and icons and costumes and ritual and narrative and art and all the rest of the ancillary (so he believes, though it is in fact essential) material razzle-dazzle of Catholicism toward iconoclasm, austerity, refusal of ornament, scorn of tradition, toward the "purity" of the text and what it "means"—and at the end of this road lie fundamentalism, fanaticism, insanity. Because if you truly believe that scripture is all you need and you truly believe the scripture, you will inevitably arrive at a Christianity that looks less like, say, the United Methodist Church and more like the one practiced by the Church of God in Christ through the Holy Spirit, Inc., with its glossolalia, its prophecy, its belief in an interventionist God and the usefulness of praying to that God for specific outcomes, and its absolutely foundational beliefs in the existence of the Devil and the imminence of the end of the world.

I mistrust and reject any arguments for the usefulness, moral or otherwise, of literature. "All art," as Oscar Wilde writes in the preface to the expanded edition of *The Picture of Dorian Gray*, "is quite useless." I am a proud and constant warrior for *l'art pour l'art*, and Oscar Wilde's knee breeches are blazoned on my shield. Any entreaties for art's power to instruct or improve cheapen it, ask it to be propaganda. But it's undeniable that sometimes a work of literature—usually an aesthetically hideous one such as *Uncle Tom's Cabin*—brings about positive change in the universe.

Toward the end of one of our conversations, Mark Harris asked me if this project might somehow lead to his being released from parole. I don't know the answer to that. Maybe, but probably not. The woman I spoke on the phone with at the Arkansas Department of Corrections while trying to locate him told me that he would assuredly be on parole for the rest of his life. Mark is now essentially free in most of the ways that count in immediate, day-to-day life. As he said, he is as happy as he possibly can be, although he is five years on the labor force and very poor, scrabbling to supplement his income with gig-economy work when not packing boxes at a candy factory at an age when most people are readying for retirement—and he has to check in regularly with his parole officer, and can't leave the state of Georgia. Not being allowed to leave Georgia is a hell of a lot better than not being allowed to leave prison, but if this book somehow ever exerts any pressure on the world outside its pages, I hope that it might flip the switch of some legal Rube Goldberg machine that will in the end result in his parole being lifted. Mark has already traveled across the universe in books and in his mind much farther than many people ever do, but I, at forty, have seen London and Rome and Athens and surfed in Hawaii and hiked to the craters of volcanoes in Costa Rica and stood on the Cliffs of Moher in Ireland—to name a few of my favorite places on Earth where my body has physically been—while Mark, at sixty-two, has seen Tyler, Texas, trailer parks in Baton Rouge and Springdale, Cave Mountain in the Ozarks, the insides of many jail and prison cells, the cemetery in Star City, the place where his father is buried in Arkansas, and now, Georgia.

The slave trader John Newton did not merit grace, but was given it. I am not sure I believe in grace, but I believe that Mark Harris deserves to be given the chance to see the world outside Georgia, perhaps if only to partake in the marvel of being alive at a time when it is possible to see the clouds from above as well as from below, which he never has, as he has never been on an airplane. I know that suffering is not measurable or comparable, but I believe this man has suffered more than he has sinned. I believe he deserves a way out.

14

Christ of the Ozarks

ONE OF THE EARLIEST KNOWN DEPICTIONS OF THE CRUCIFIX-
ion—it may even be the earliest—is called the Alexamenos graffito.
Scratched into the plaster wall of an interior room in a house near the
Palatine Hill in Rome, believed to date from somewhere between the
late first century and the late third, it shows a young man—the most
fastidiously rendered element of the picture—venerating a crucified human figure with the head of a donkey; the Greek sentence (with either
an obscure local variant or a phonetic spelling error in the second word)
"ALEXAMENOS SEBETE THEON" bashed out below the image in
sloppy, violent strokes: "ALEXAMENOS WORSHIPS HIS GOD."

The graffito is probably mocking some guy named Alexamenos who
was an early Christian living in Rome. The Romans associated donkeys
with Jews and Christians—a lowly association Christians subverted and
embraced and wove into the narrative, as Jesus rides a donkey into Jerusalem at the beginning of the end of the story in all four canonical
gospels, fulfilling Zechariah 9:9: "Rejoice greatly, O daughter of Zion;
shout, O daughter of Jerusalem: behold, thy King cometh unto thee: he
is just, and having salvation; lowly, and riding upon an ass, and upon
a colt the foal of an ass." The image of an ass-headed theriocephalos
was a grotesque of buffoonery in antiquity and beyond; Nick Bottom for

most of *A Midsummer Night's Dream* is the other most notable example (I once played that role in a production of *Midsummer*—it's a fun part, requiring the actor to both don the donkey head mask and later dress in drag). The graffito probably implies something like, "*We* worship gods and goddesses worth worshipping, like Jupiter, Apollo, Venus—deities depicted as idealized human specimens radiating dignity, strength, and beauty—but get a load of that loser Alexamenos, worshipping some scrawny Jewish peasant, a criminal executed in the most painful and humiliating way." This crude work of vandalism was almost certainly done at a time when crucifixion was a method of execution still regularly conferred upon the worst criminals (Constantine, the first Christian emperor, abolished it in the fourth century), and whoever drew it was someone for whom tortured human bodies nailed to crosses and left to die was a sight of everyday life. It was drawn from within a pagan culture that hadn't yet undergone what Nietzsche would call the transvaluation of values, in which people still exalted strength, wealth, and beauty: outward and visible power. They still lived in a world of Good and Bad, and had not yet entered the more counterintuitive Judeo-Christian paradigm of Good and Evil.

The ubiquity of the image of the crucified Jesus has numbed it into a neutral banality, but if one bores through that and really focuses one's attention on it, it again becomes terrifying and bizarre. The Buddha, at rest, beams with wisdom and serenity, and Islam refuses to grant its faithful the childish gift of an image—Mohammed is an abstract void who cannot be depicted at all—but what religious figure other than Jesus is most often depicted as the object of the extremes of human sadism and cruelty? Other than the Christian saints—beheaded, stoned, flayed, pincushioned with arrows, etc.—I don't know of any.

The Alexamenos graffito sharply illustrates how recently and dramatically Christianity has reshaped the psychology of Western culture. It's a change Machiavelli didn't like: "Our religion, moreover, places the supreme happiness in humility, lowliness, and a contempt for worldly objects, whilst the other, on the contrary, places the supreme good in grandeur of soul, strength of body, and all such other qualities as render men formidable; and if our religion claims of us fortitude of the soul, it is more to enable us to suffer than to achieve great deeds."

I recently heard someone call the image of Jesus on the cross "the ultimate example of topping from the bottom": that's what Machiavelli thought of it, and in my proudest, "most anti-God mindset" days, I agreed. Sometimes I still do.

Matthew 27:39-42:

> And they that passed by reviled him, wagging their heads, And saying, Thou that destroyest the temple, and buildest it in three days, save thyself. If thou be the Son of God, come down from the cross. Likewise also the chief priests mocking him, with the scribes and elders, said, He saved others; himself he cannot save. If he be the King of Israel, let him now come down from the cross, and we will believe him.

With my aloof, skeptical heart, I'm afraid I probably would have been one of those bystanders, mocking, pointing out the demonstrably obvious absurdity, needing proof to believe. Those passersby on the very day Jesus was crucified, before he was even dead yet, the chief priests, the scribes and elders, who said, You who supposedly cured lepers with your touch, multiplied loaves and fishes, turned water to wine and raised the dead, if you're really magic, if you're really the son of God, save yourself, come down from that cross—*then* we'll believe you: they were the first in a long line of doubters that would include the author of the Alexamenos graffito, Machiavelli, Voltaire, Richard Dawkins, Christopher Hitchens, George Carlin, and, in my nastier moods, me. (And with our blithe jeering and mocking we keep on refueling Christianity's energy—it *needs* us: why else would the Gospel of Matthew have included that anecdote?) And all of us, all down the line, arrogantly, blunderingly miss the fucking point.

What is the point? That's much harder to say. One can't really say it. Or write it, or think it. One can only feel it.

In 1978, the year members of the Church of God in Christ Through the Holy Spirit, Inc., murdered Bethany Alana Clark and buried her on Cave Mountain, my parents were living in Fayetteville. My father was an undergraduate studying physics at the University of Arkansas, and my mother, who had recently graduated from the same with a degree in history, was teaching high school in Siloam Springs, a small town about forty minutes away near the Oklahoma border. My parents had just met, and at the time, my mother was drifting away from a raucous circle of friends who knew one another from the university's MFA program in creative writing.

The novelist and short story writer William Harrison and the poet James Whitehead founded the program in 1965. Soon thereafter, they hired the poet Miller Williams, and those three guys formed its core faculty and led it for about thirty years. Now Miller Williams is probably better known as the father of the country/folk/rockstar Lucinda Williams, who is around my parents' age and briefly attended the University of Arkansas at the same time they did. "Lucinda used to be my daughter," Miller said to me once. "Now I'm her father." He said that in the longest conversation I ever had with him, when we had lunch together during a month in 2012 I spent in Fayetteville taking care of Jay and Joyce's chickens while they were in Australia photographing a solar eclipse. After lunch, we went back to Miller's house for a while, only a few blocks from Jay and Joyce's, where I saw a framed painting on the wall of his living room—an amateurish but by no means bad watercolor portrait of a much younger Miller Williams. I think mostly because he was a bit embarrassed by it and wanted to explain why he had a portrait of himself on the wall of his own house, he said, "Johnny Cash painted that." (Johnny Cash is the most immortal Arkansan, and the most Arkansan immortal.) The signature in the bottom corner was childishly readable. I had not known that Johnny Cash was an amateur watercolorist or that he sometimes painted portraits of his friends and gave them as birthday presents—which was what that picture was.

"How did you become friends with Johnny Cash?" I asked. Miller had Alzheimer's; he was lucid that day, but he knew his memory was vanishing. He shrugged and shook his head.

"I don't remember," he said.

Miller Williams died a few years later in 2015. Right before he died, Lucinda Williams set one of her father's poems, "Compassion," to music, and it's on her 2014 album, *Down Where the Spirit Meets the Bone*; the title is a quote from the poem. There's another Lucinda Williams song, one of her best, "Pineola," which begins "When Daddy told me what happened/I couldn't believe what he just said." It's about the death of the poet Frank Stanford, who had been a student of her father's and a regular visitor at his house in the 1970s. Stanford was living in Fayetteville when he committed suicide at the age of twenty-nine on June 3, 1978, a month after Newton County Sheriff Hurchal Fowler and Deputy Ray Watkins arrested Suzette Freeman, Lucy Clark, and Royal, Mark, and Winston Van Harris in the Upper Buffalo Wilderness. Frank's wife, Ginny Crouch, and the poet C.D. Wright, with whom he had been having an affair, were in another room of the house when he did it, and those who knew them and the situation have told me that it might not have been the only factor in his suicide, but that love triangle blowing up into the open was what spurred it. He shot himself three times in the heart with a .22.

In 2009, I was living in Iowa City with one of my best friends then and now, the poet Kevin Holden. That year, Kevin and a few other poet friends drove down to Fayetteville for a long weekend to attend a conference celebrating the work of Frank Stanford, which included an all-night marathon reading of Stanford's magnum opus, the 15,283-line epic poem *The Battlefield Where the Moon Says I Love You*, which he had spent many years working on and published in 1977. As we were talking about it after Kevin returned from that trip, I was somewhat surprised to learn that Stanford had achieved a kind of mythic cult-hero status

From left to right: Sandra Wood, John Wood, Frank Stanford, Allen Ginsberg, Peter Orlovsky, Lynnice Butler, Jack Butler

among a certain milieu of poets, and Kevin was somewhat astounded to learn that my mother had known Frank Stanford.

In the late 1960s and '70s there was a cadre of writer friends in Fayetteville—people who were in the MFA program, taught in it, or had recently left or graduated from it—which included C.D. Wright and Ellen Gilchrist, and orbited around the gregarious, charismatic, brilliant, movie-star handsome and demoniac Frank Stanford. Everyone involved with that scene was very frequently very drunk. The most serious boyfriend my mother had before she met my father was the poet Leon Stokesbury, who was part of that circle, and that's how my mother spent a lot of her time in Fayetteville in the 1970s hanging out with poets. It's true my mother knew Frank Stanford, and by the time she broke up with Leon, she hated his guts.

In early May of 1969—a few years before my mother met these people—Allen Ginsberg, who a month before had given an interview in *Playboy* in which he frankly and openly discussed his homosexuality, along with his longtime partner Peter Orlovsky, visited Fayetteville for a few days. One of the things they wanted to see was *Christ of the Ozarks*, which had been erected a few years before in 1966. John Wood, another poet in this circle, an MFA student at the time, describes this thing pretty well in an article he wrote about Ginsberg and Orlovksy's visit to Arkansas in the September 1, 2012 *American Poetry Review*:

> I do remember that the next day Allen, Peter, Jim, Frank, Jack and Lynnice Butler, and Sandy and I all went to Eureka Springs to see The Christ of the Ozarks, a tasteless monstrosity built by Gerald L. K. Smith, the anti-Semite. A brochure given out at the statue remarked how it could support two Volkswagen buses from each arm and withstand certain high mile an hour winds. . . . I remember that Allen made a comment to whomever we paid the entry fee that he had a beard just like Jesus had.

The American isolationist and anti-Semitic demagogue Gerald L. K. Smith had had that massive concrete statue installed on top of that hill near Eureka Springs as the first step towards the religious theme park he intended to build. Smith, a supremely ugly character, is worth a few words. Originally from Wisconsin, he was ordained as a Disciples of Christ minister at the age of eighteen, moved to Louisiana, and rose to national prominence during the Great Depression as the national organizer of the populist firebrand Huey P. Long's Share Our Wealth movement. Jews were Smith's main bugbear from the beginning; even before he hooked up with Long, he had been influenced by *The International Jew*, published in four volumes starting in 1920 by Henry Ford's Dearborn Publishing Company. After Long's assassination in 1935, Smith failed to take control of his faction in Louisiana, soured on the political Left, and switched sides as he began to focus on anti-communism. For the next quarter century after that, he dwelt as a fascistic, anti-Semitic troll under the bridge of mainstream American politics, founding the America First Party in 1943 and running for president three times in 1944, 1948, and 1956 (receiving 1,781 votes the first time, then 48, then

8). Toward the end of his life, he bought a house in Eureka Springs, Arkansas, and began to fantasize about a religious theme park that would include a life-size recreation of ancient Jerusalem and a massive statue of Jesus on the peak of Magnetic Mountain. He raised a million dollars toward the cause and hired Emmet Sullivan, a sculptor who had worked under Gutzon Borglum on Mount Rushmore, to design the monument and oversee its construction. The rest of the religious theme park was not completed in Smith's lifetime, but he did live to see *Christ of the Ozarks* standing on that high hill just outside Eureka Springs.

I've heard that it was inspired by *Christ the Redeemer* in Rio de Janeiro, which the statue sort of resembles—the same cross-not-depicted-but-suggesting-crucifixion pose, except that the one in Arkansas is blockier and far less elegant, a bit more like a cigar store wooden Indian, the face strangely absent of any expression. Locals have nicknamed it "Gumby Jesus" and "Our Milk Carton with Arms." From the back it looks kind of like a giant Pez dispenser.

The sprawling Evangelical theme park Smith envisioned did later materialize itself around *Christ of the Ozarks* after those poets' ironic visit to it, and today the park includes the 1:1-scale model Jerusalem circa AD 33, which serves as the set of the lavish Passion Play the park puts on every year. The Messianic Colossus now stands as the last stop on the road and the park's centerpiece.

Jeff Nash, the husband of Joyce's friend Dina—to whom Winston Van Harris wrote all those rambling love letters from prison—told me a funny anecdote about watching the Passion Play at the Holy Land in Eureka Springs: At the play's finale, when the resurrected Jesus ascends into Heaven, the actor who plays him is harnessed into a complicated rig of cables that whisks him above the heads of the audience and into the woods; as Christ ascends, several stagehands positioned at various points in the amphitheater release flapping flurries of white doves from cages—and that time, just as they did, an opportunistic hawk watching from a tree at the top of the hill swooped down and grabbed his free lunch to a mixture of gasps and reluctant muffled laughter from the audience. The Lord shall provide.

There are now several hotels right outside the park to accommodate the thousands of pilgrims who flock to the site every year to visit the religious theme park, see the statue, and attend the Passion Play. I don't know if the people who work at or visit the Holy Land in Eureka Springs today spend much time thinking about its origin as the final fever dream of an anti-Semitic hate-monger. My guess is no. There's definitely no mention of it anywhere on the premises. I would guess that most of the tourists are simply (not my favorite kind of, but nevertheless) devout Christians.

On Sunday, April 28, 2024, my cousin Haley Zega and I went hiking on the Hawksbill Crag Trail on Cave Mountain. We planned to try to retrace the footsteps she had taken as a six-year-old twenty-three years earlier.

I wanted to undertake this expedition as close to the same day of the year as possible, when the foliage on the trees would be about the same, the same wildflowers in bloom—birdsfoot violets, wild sweet williams, pink azaleas, and early buttercups—and a similar volume of water in the Buffalo River and the little mountain creek that spills over the ledge of Haley Falls. We ambitiously aimed to approximate her entire journey as closely as possible: Begin at the waterfall, head east on the trail along the edge of the bluff past Hawksbill Crag until the trail vanishes into the forest floor, find a place on the mountainside where the slope becomes gentle enough to allow us to carefully descend through about half a mile of raw wilderness all the way down to the banks of the Buffalo River, then follow the river north another mile and a half to the mouth of Dug Hollow, about the spot where Lytle James and William Jeff Villines found her. And then, of course, we would have to climb back up. It's not a long hike—only about five miles round-trip—but it runs over very difficult terrain, particularly the scrambling-down-the-mountain part (getting back up would be more tiring but less treacherous).

I had flown in on Friday in the hope of undertaking the trek on Saturday, but all day Saturday a violent and uninterrupted rainstorm pounded the Arkansas Ozarks: the kind of flower-bringing April shower that looks like Golden Age Hollywood rain, stagehands dumping buckets from the rafters, and sounds like an avalanche of loose gravel battering the roof of your car and even at the highest-tempo setting the wipers can't push the water away fast enough to see through the windshield. Unfortunately, the weather wasn't much better the next day; the sky was a uniform milky gray and the atmosphere humidified with a constant drizzly mist punctuated by brief desultory bursts of downpour. Not ideal for hiking, but it was the only day we could do it; I had to teach a class on Monday, and I would be flying home on a redeye that night.

Although it was a weekend, the inclement weather kept more sensible outdoorspeople away, and Haley and I had the trail to ourselves. Haley turned thirty a few days ago as of my writing this sentence. She graduated from Pace University with a BA in Acting–International Performance Ensemble in 2017, and spent the next few years paying the dues most artists starting the game without generational wealth, astounding luck, or famous parents have to: waiting tables, auditioning like hell, landing small roles in off-off-Broadway productions, eking by being ambitious, young, and broke in New York City. The pandemic put a stop to that. In March 2020, her father drove up north, packed her things up, and took her back to Fayetteville, where she could wait out the lockdown in the more comfortable conditions of home. She's been there since, acting in local theater and trying to save enough to move back to New York. I was a theater kid, too; I dabbled in acting before focusing on writing, although I never pursued it as seriously as she has. It's something we have in common, and we spent the drive from Fayetteville to Cave Mountain that morning talking about Konstantin Stanislavski, Stella Adler, and Sanford Meisner. And we talked about Jay—my uncle, her grandfather—who was suffering badly from cancer and advanced dementia and who we all knew was fast approaching the end of his great and storied and fascinating life. He would die exactly one month later, and I would fly out to Arkansas again in June for his memorial service.

Haley and I have other things in common that have nothing to do with the rest of this story. I was eleven when Haley was born, and she was the first baby I remember holding. (I was four when my brother James was born, and I have photographic evidence but no memory of my holding him.) I have always felt a certain special connection with her, more than with the other members of my extended family. Everyone on my father's side of the family is intelligent, interesting, and good-hearted in a fundamental way. None of them, to my knowledge, deranged themselves with social media into froth-gargling, spiral-eyed Q-Anoners in the past ten years and counting of our mounting cultural shame and vileness. Most of them lead functional and dignified middle-class lives. Some have served in the military; many regularly engage in some sort of public service. They own hair salons and veterinary clinics; a lot of them are scientists and engineers. They read books and newspapers, they are unafraid of exotic cuisines, they have passports and sometimes vacation abroad, where they take their children to museums and cathedrals and ancient ruins. They are good people. But Haley and I share a spark of something a little weirder and darker. I call it a glory drive. It's both a gift and a curse. It's what spurred me to try to be a writer and spurred her to try to be an actor. Most people who want to be artists have it, and it's a bit different from what drives people who want to be famous athletes or politicians, or get really rich. If you have it, you can see it emanating from the soul of someone else who has it like an aura that remains invisible to normal people with healthier relationships to reality, work, and life. If you have it, you can see it fuming off the words written by a man who died forty-six years ago: Frank Stanford *definitely* had it, in spades. So does Lucinda Williams. It involves a passionate, life-consuming love of art, and I will readily admit there are also a few pinches of poison admixed into this personality type: a certain childishness and narcissism. In conversations with Haley I am often delighted and unsurprised to find that we have independently discovered and love the same books, movies, music. Among my extended family, Haley is my closest personal friend. The last few years of working on this book, which have required frequent communication with them, have also made my friendships with Joyce and Kelly stronger than before, but Haley and I are much closer in age and grew up in more similar worlds. She is a smart, funny, engaging person to talk to, and I think we would have become friends if we hadn't been related and had known each other some other way.

After an hour and a half's drive from Fayetteville, we parked on Cave Mountain Road at the trailhead of the Hawksbill Crag Trail at about eleven in the morning. The previous day's torrential precipitation had made the ground a sodden sponge cake of squelching mud that sucked hard at our hiking boots, which we rinsed off several times that day while crossing streams, and Whitaker Creek, which disappears at higher elevations in the driest months, thundered with spring runoff and gushed picturesquely over the waterfall named after my cousin: Haley said that the creek was the fullest she'd ever seen it.

I finally learned the way down the ledge onto the lower shelf, where you can get a good look at the waterfall: Haley showed me how to shimmy down the rock face, jam a foot into a tight crevice created by a thin, flexible tree growing out of its side, hold on to the tree, and hop down the last few feet. (Getting back up the same way is a little more troublesome.) We sat awhile on the fateful rock upon which Joyce last saw her on April 29, 2001, before continuing on the trail along the edge of the bluff. The water-fattened flora glowed almost neon green on that cool, gray day, dotted with the yellows, pinks, and purples of buttercups, larkspur, and dogtooth violets. We hiked past the crag, followed the trail until it faded away, and kept on going—cautiously, as we knew we were now trespassing on private land—all the way to Cloudland, Tim Ernst's old house on the edge of the cliff, with operatic views of the Buffalo River valley from its back decks. Whoever owns that house now does not appear to spend much time there (it's probably someone's vacation retreat), and what used to be a flat swath of grass beside it, where Haley remembers attending Tim and Pam Ernst's wedding a few months after her rescue, is now overgrown with waist-high weeds and nettles, which we bushwhacked through to a tiny wooden gazebo where we took shelter from the fresh burst of heavy rain that had just begun to fall, ate the sandwiches we'd brought for lunch, and together decided that it would be extremely unpleasant and maybe dangerously stupid to try to climb all the way down the mountain from there in the current conditions: the mud soft and loose, the leaf-matted ground slick as slime, and no sign of the downpour abating. So we headed back the way we'd come, and when we were back in the Jeep Wrangler I'd rented at the airport, I drove us the few washboard-rumbling minutes over to Kaypark Road, prudently parked a good ways up the slope from the boggy dip in the road where I'd gotten stuck two years earlier, and we hiked through the mist down to Kaypark Cemetery and the trail that leads to Bowers Hollow, the approximate spot where Royal and Winston Van Harris shot Bethany Alana Clark and buried her in a five-gallon plastic bucket.

The skies finally began to clear late in the afternoon as we were driving home, and when we got to the interchange at Huntsville, I asked Haley if she'd like to take a detour up to Eureka Springs to see *Christ of the Ozarks*. Despite having grown up in Northwest Arkansas and lived there most of her life, she had never seen it up close. She was game.

Eureka Springs is a quirky, pretty town—after Fayetteville, my favorite one in Arkansas—with an interesting history: a nineteenth-century spa town whither tuberculosis patients used to pilgrimage to bathe in the supposedly healing waters of the mountain spring it's named for, with a downtown business district of ornate Victorian buildings crazily jumbled together on hills so steep that the sidewalks graduate at places into stone staircases. A lot of counterculture back-to-the-land types, hippies, and lesbian separatists moved there in the 1960s and remade it into the enclave of weirdness and fun it still is today; Frank Stanford spent some time living there, as did C. D. Wright and Forrest Gander soon after they married. The town still has a vacationy vibe, but not ritzy (like, say, Aspen or Martha's Vineyard); everything is a bit charmingly rundown and rustic, not-updated-since-the-1970s–looking. A lot of conferences and conventions and so on are held there, such as the water diviners' convention that was happening at the Crescent Hotel the weekend Haley went missing, and many hotels and motels encircle the town, getting cheaper and dingier the farther outward they radiate from its center. We drove past them and through the town on our way to Magnetic Mountain a mile to its east, where Gerald L. K. Smith erected his giant concrete Jesus, which since his death has been expanded to into his envisioned theme park including various religious tourist draws, such as a museum with an original 1611 King James Bible on display, and the Disneylandish fake ancient Jerusalem at the bottom of a 4,100-seat amphitheater.

When Haley and I—tired, muddy, and damp from our drizzly hike in the woods—pulled up to the booth on the way in, the woman in it asked us for a donation. It's not an official entrance fee—you can pay whatever you want—but yeah, it's basically an entrance fee. We didn't have any cash with us, which meant we had to park in front of the gift shop just beyond the booth, where we could go inside and pay with a credit card. There, amid shelves stocked with religious tchotchkes probably not unlike the wares Daddy F.O.U. had for sale at his general store in Jasper, we had to interact face-to-face with several other warm, earnest, and friendly people while pretending we were Christians who had come here in good faith and not mocking, ironic anti-tourists, as those poets had been back in 1969. They asked us where we were from and made other such casual chitchat. I got the sense that they don't see a lot of young people coming to this place on their own. They clearly thought we were a couple, which made us even more uncomfortable. We smiled and answered their questions perfunctorily but politely, trying not to let on what a hurry we were in to get the hell out of there and back out to the Holy Land, where we could be by ourselves and not feel so much like smug, disingenuous rats. The experience mostly made me feel like an asshole—even considering the theme park's ugly anti-Semitic backstory.

I am not a Christian. I am not religious. I think that organized monotheistic religion as we know it today emerged out of a chain of unlikely events that started happening to the human species around ten thousand years ago with the development of agriculture and that has mostly been disastrous for our planet and our general mental health and . . . etc., etc., etc.

Sigmund Freud published *Civilization and Its Discontents* right after *The Future of an Illusion*, which is less of a Hitchensesque bellicose bromide against religion and more of a polite (and perhaps for that reason even more condescending) diagnostic exploration of what might happen to Western society now that surely no serious person seriously still believes in God (this was in 1927), and he begins the book by discussing how his mind had been changed somewhat on the subject by a letter he received from a friend—the French poet Romain Rolland, though Freud doesn't name him in the book—a person whose intelligence he deeply respected, who told him he had "not properly appreciated the true source of religious sentiments," which he said was a particular subjective feeling he was never without; "a sensation of 'eternity,' a feeling as of something limitless, unbounded—as it were, 'oceanic.'" In the next paragraph, he writes: "The views expressed by the friend whom I so much honour, . . . caused me no small difficulty. I cannot discover this 'oceanic' feeling in myself. . . . From my own experience I could not convince myself of the primary nature of such a feeling. But this gives me no right to deny that it does in fact occur in other people."

Those sentences have stuck in my memory since I first read them as the most admirably humble and compassionate attempt I know by a non-believer to empathize with—or at least seriously understand—a believer. I don't think I've ever felt that oceanic feeling, either. But perhaps there is something in the world, memory lines of energy buried in the earth, down where the spirit meets the bone, that the water witches can feel with their dowsing-rods, which our fancy gizmos cloud us from seeing.

Haley and I arrived at *Christ of the Ozarks* late in the day, during what photographers call the golden hour, and verily, I say unto you: The most sublime conditions in which to stand on top of a mountain and gaze out across the Ozarks are late in the afternoon just after the clearing of a heavy two-day vernal rainstorm. It looks as if God has pulled the clouds apart like cotton candy, roseate and ringed with golden light, the day's last sunbeams slanting down like Jacob's ladder, a warm, brazen glow giving everything crisp edges, everything we could see across the wet, forested hills flashing and sparkling, and—arching across the sky to seal a covenant with the one tribe He has saved on the deck of the ark teetering on the peak of Ararat—a rainbow. I don't know if it was God we felt standing at the feet of that enormous, ugly statue of Jesus Christ with his arms winged open to a heavenly view of the beautiful and troubled place our family comes from, but we felt something.

ACKNOWLEDGMENTS

THANKS MOST OF ALL TO THE THREE GENERATIONS OF WOMEN at the center of the story, without whose help I could not have written this book: Joyce Hale, Kelly Hale Syer, and Haley Zega.

I am immeasurably grateful to Lucy Clark and Mark Harris.

Tremendous thanks to Noah Eaker, whose keen editing has greatly improved this book, and many, many thanks to my agent, Brian De-Fiore. Thank you to Christopher Beha for publishing and helping to shape the earliest version of this story in *Harper's*.

I am particularly grateful to Tim Ernst for all of his indispensable help with this project.

I would also like to especially thank Jack Butler, Arthur Evans, Eddy Fowler, Forrest Gander, Barbara Harris, Jane Hirshfield, Vixen James, Paul, Kelly, Greg and Jerry Kleinpeter, David Matthews, Molly May, Chris McNew, James McWilliams, Katherine and Joe Nance, Jeff and Dina Nash, Colleen Nick, Jerry Patterson, Steve Stern, George Stowe-Rains, Ray Watkins, Carol and Daffyd Wood, and Steve Zega.

Thanks also to the other people who helped me accomplish this project in some way, however small: Ralph Adamo, Kyle E. Burton, Donnie Davis, Randall Dixon, Eli Frankel, Joanie Harp, J. D. Harper, Kevin Holden, Gary Isbell, Crow Johnson, Judd Johnson, Ann Lauterbach, Robert McCorkindale, Randy Nicholson, Andres Restrepo, Rex Robbins, Scott Syer, William Jeff Villines, Gordon Webb, and Lucinda Williams.

Caitlin Millard: thank you for everything.

ABOUT THE AUTHOR

BENJAMIN HALE is the author of the novel *The Evolution of Bruno Littlemore* and the collection *The Fat Artist and Other Stories*. His writing has appeared in *Harper's Magazine*, *Paris Review*, *The New York Times*, *The Washington Post*, *Conjunctions*, and has been anthologized in *Best American Science and Nature Writing*. He is a senior editor at *Conjunctions*, teaches at Bard College and Columbia University, and lives in a small town in New York's Hudson Valley.